W9-BHJ-661

THE ARMOUR

Other National Historical Society Publications:

THE IMAGE OF WAR: 1861-1865

TOUCHED BY FIRE: A PHOTOGRAPHIC PORTRAIT OF THE CIVIL WAR

WAR OF THE REBELLION: OFFICIAL RECORDS
  OF THE UNION AND CONFEDERATE ARMIES

OFFICIAL RECORDS OF THE UNION AND CONFEDERATE NAVIES
  IN THE WAR OF THE REBELLION

HISTORICAL TIMES ILLUSTRATED ENCYCLOPEDIA OF THE CIVIL WAR

CONFEDERATE VETERAN

THE WEST POINT MILITARY HISTORY SERIES

IMPACT: THE ARMY AIR FORCES' CONFIDENTIAL HISTORY
  OF WORLD WAR II

HISTORY OF UNITED STATES NAVAL OPERATIONS IN WORLD WAR II
  by Samuel Eliot Morison

HISTORY OF THE ARMED FORCES IN WORLD WAR II
  by Janusz Piekalkiewicz

A TRAVELLER'S GUIDE TO GREAT BRITAIN SERIES

MAKING OF BRITAIN SERIES

THE ARCHITECTURAL TREASURES OF EARLY AMERICA

For information about National Historical Society Publications, write:
The National Historical Society, 2245 Kohn Road, Box 8200,
Harrisburg, Pa 17105

THE ELITE
The World's Crack Fighting Men

THE ARMOUR

Ashley Brown, Editor

Jonathan Reed, Editor

Editorial Board

Brigadier-General James L. Collins, Jr. (Retd.)
Former Chief of Military History, US Department of the Army

Ian V. Hogg
Authority on smallarms and modern weapons systems

Dr. John Pimlott
Senior Lecturer in the Department of War Studies,
Royal Military Academy, Sandhurst, England

Brigadier-General Edwin H. Simmons (Retd.)
US Marine Corps

Lisa Mullins, Managing Editor, NHS edition

A Publication of
THE NATIONAL HISTORICAL SOCIETY

Published in Great Britain in 1986 by Orbis Publishing

Special contents of this edition copyright © 1989 by the
National Historical Society

Library of Congress Cataloging-in-Publication Data
The Armour / Ashley Brown, editor, Jonathan Reed, editor.
    p.   cm.—(The Elite : the world's crack fighting men ; v. 9)
  ISBN 0-918678-47-1
    1. Tanks warfare—History—20th century.   2. Armored troops—
History—20th century.   I. Brown, Ashley.   II. Reed, Jonathan.
III. National Historical Society.   IV. Series: Elite (Harrisburg,
Pa.) ; v. 9.
UG446.5.A683   1989
358′.18—dc20   89-12495
                                                      CIP

CONTENTS

INTRODUCTION

It is an old concept in warfare. Shielding, whether of wood, or bronze, or iron and steel, can both protect a warrior in defense and make him more potent on the attack. But then early in this century something new was added—mobility. And when men, weapons, steel, and gasoline were all added together, they created armour.

From its first combat appearance in World War I, down to its role in the present balance of conventional land forces, armour and its auxiliaries have time after time provided the measurement of advantage on the world's battlefields. Generations ago the saying may have been that the almighty was on the side with the biggest battalions; since 1942 that allegiance has lain on the side with the most and best tanks.

Their story goes back to antiquity in some forms. Leonardo invented a sort of "tank" back in the fifteenth century. But by all modern standards, the story of armour really begins with the fight at Villers-Bretonneux in April 1918. There a mere three British Mark IV tanks halted a German advance spearheaded by A7V tanks, the first engagement in history between armour. Often called "landships" at the time, the lumbering behemoths quickly evolved into the terrible machines of World War II.

The tanks themselves, the men who served in them, and the support and affiliated units that accompanied them, were truly members of the ELITE, as were those special groups like the Royal Horse Artillery that were assigned the mission of combatting enemy armour. The stories of their heroism are legion. J. Battery of the RHA battling against Afrika Korps, fighting right down to its last gun in November 1941 . . . the French 2d Armoured Division racing to be the first to enter Strasbourg . . . the 5th SS-Panzer Division's daring breakout from Red Army encirclement in February 1944 . . . the incomparable Rommel and his 7th Panzer Division striking boldly through Allied lines in France in 1940. Whatever their stories, and wherever they fought, the men in the iron machines made bold history.

And armour is still there today. The Royal Armoured Corps stands ready to meet any enemy in Europe. The 4th U.S. Cavalry, aboard their Armoured Cavalry Assault Vehicles, went into action in Viet Nam time after time. In Israel's Yom Kippur War of 1973, their 7th Armoured Brigade, though vastly outnumbered, fought a desperate battle against the Syrian Army and drove them back, opening the way for an Israeli offensive.

In the Falklands, in Lebanon, wherever major armies meet or have met, the armour has been there for three-quarters of a century, well winning the rightful claim that the men and their machines have to be numbered among THE ELITE.

J BATTERY (SIDI REZEGH) ROYAL HORSE ARTILLERY

Formed in 1805, as the Madras Horse Artillery Troop, the unit served in the Mysore and Mahratta wars in India, and saw action during an expedition against Dutch colonists in Java in 1811.

In 1861 the Troop was absorbed into the Royal Artillery and was redesignated A Battery, 3rd Horse Brigade, Royal Artillery. It assumed its present title of J Battery, Royal Horse Artillery, in 1889.

J Battery took part in General Sir Archibald Wavell's Operation Compass, 1940-41, and thereafter fought with the 7th Armoured Division in Libya, Italy and northern France. After D-day, J Battery saw action at Caen, Falaise and during the Rhine Crossing.

It ended the war covering the approaches to Hamburg. On 21 November 1941, during operations to relieve Tobruk, the battery earned its honour title, which was officially awarded in 1954. Since the war, the battery continued to serve with the 3rd Regiment in Germany, the Middle East, Kenya and Hong Kong, returning to Devizes in 1975.

In 1977, when responsibility for long range anti-tank guided weapons passed from the Royal Armoured Corps (RAC) to the Royal Artillery (RA), the battery was re-equipped with Swingfire and moved to Paderborn as an independent anti-tank battery in support of the 4th Armoured Division. The return of Swingfire to the RAC in 1984 saw the battery once again under the command of the 3rd Regiment, Royal Horse Artillery, equipped with eight 105mm Abbott self-propelled guns.

Right: A Panzer Mark IV. Rommel's skill in co-ordinating heavy tanks with infantry, artillery and Luftwaffe support, forced the 7th Armoured Division to use every available weapon at its disposal, including 25-pounders (far right) and a Bofors AA gun to counter his attack on Sidi Rezegh.

In November 1941, as the might of the Afrika Korps was brought to bear on Sidi Rezegh, J Battery, RHA, fought to its last gun

IN THE WORDS of Brigadier A.F. Hely, commander of the 60th Field Regiment, Royal Artillery, Sidi Rezegh was 'the toughest battle of the (North African) campaign and one that will always stand out in the memory of those who took part in it as the bloodiest and most heroic encounter of the war.'

The British Eighth Army was formed in the autumn months of 1941, under the command of Lieutenant-General Sir Alan Cunningham. In November of that year it comprised the XIIIth and XXXth Corps; the former was composed of the New Zealand Division, the 4th Indian Division, less one brigade, and the 1st Army Tank Brigade. In XXX Corps were the 7th Armoured Division, commanded by Major-General W.H.E. Gott, the 4th Armoured Brigade, the 1st South African Division less one brigade, and the 22nd Guards (Motor) Brigade. The 2nd South African Division was held in reserve, while in Tobruk, ready to break out when the signal came, were the 70th Division, the 32nd Army Tank Brigade and the Polish 1st Carpathian Infantry Brigade Group.

With this force at his disposal, General Sir Claude Auchinleck, commander-in-chief of British and Commonwealth forces in the Middle East, hoped to drive the Germans out of Cyrenaica (eastern Libya). On the left flank, the armoured XXX Corps would

thrust from Maddalena towards Gabr Saleh and engage the enemy armour. From the southeast, XIII Corps would overrun the frontier positions at Sollum and then advance west to aid XXX Corps. Once the Afrika Korps had been toppled, XXX Corps would press on to Sidi Rezegh to join up with the Tobruk garrison, which, on the signal, would break out from their beleaguered positions to meet up with the British forces advancing from the south.

The operation, codenamed Crusader, began on the night of 17 November 1941 when the Eighth Army crossed into Libya in complete radio silence. The early stages of the battle were fought out between XXX Corps and the German and Italian armoured forces in the vicinity of Sidi Rezegh, southeast of Tobruk, on a desert track known as the Trigh Capuzzo. The Sidi Rezegh escarpment was occupied on 19 November and the British armour fanned out into three groups.

The following day, Major-General Gott and Brigadier Davy, commander of the 7th Armoured Brigade, decided to move the brigade and support group onto the escarpment and hold a defensive position. Providing the mobile anti-tank force for the 7th

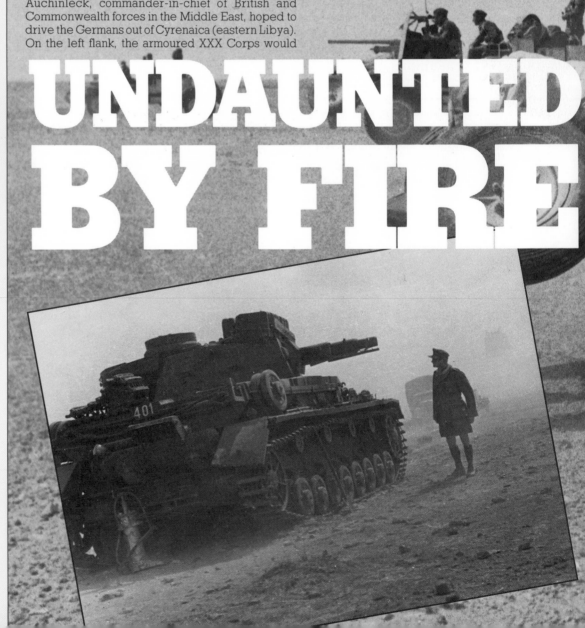

UNDAUNTED BY FIRE

Armoured Brigade was the 3rd Regiment, Royal Horse Artillery, commanded by Lieutenant-Colonel C.P.B. Wilson. This consisted of three batteries of 2-pounder anti-tank guns, which were mounted on portées. The guns had a maximum range of 1200yds, but, during the battle that was to follow, their elevated position made them extremely vulnerable to both direct and indirect fire. Defending a raised plateau with the enemy to the south and north, the batteries took up position under sporadic bombardment from the German artillery and the Luftwaffe. J Battery, commanded by Major Bernard Pinney, faced east, with A Troop, under Second-Lieutenant George Ward Gunn, looking southeast. B Troop was

Raised on portées (main picture), guncrews range sights before firing their 2-pounder anti-tank guns during a practice shoot in the western desert. Below: Outgunned but undaunted, the gallant Major Bernard Pinney. Below (centre): The three-man crew of a 2-pounder fire from the ground position.

9

DESERT WAR

Field Marshal Rommel arrived in Tripoli on 21 February 1941, along with the first elements of the Afrika Korps. Following the defeat of the Italian Army at Beda Fomm, two weeks earlier, a substantial portion of the British force, under Major-General Richard O'Connor, had been withdrawn to Greece. Accordingly, in March, the 'Desert Fox' launched his counter-offensive. Within two weeks Rommel had forced the British out of eastern Libya, except for the Tobruk garrison.

It was quickly apparent that the Germans outclassed the British in virtually every area, apart from gallantry and desert experience. Rommel had developed what is now known as 'All Arms Tactics'. In task force combinations of tanks, guns, infantry and Luftwaffe, the Afrika Korps was detecting and exploiting opportunities without hesitation. In June 1941, the British tanks outnumbered the Germans by 200 to 170, yet they were very much the underdogs. Throughout the summer, General Sir Archibald Wavell, Commander-in-Chief, Middle East, had attempted to break through the German lines in Operations Brevity and Battleaxe. It was Rommel's success during Battleaxe which created the myth of his invincibility. In July 1941 General Sir Claude Auchinleck replaced Wavell, and the new commander-in-chief began to build up British forces in preparation for Operation Crusader. Meanwhile, Rommel was planning an attack on Tobruk using the Afrika Korps and the Italian XXI Corps. His intended offensive was to be pre-empted, however, by the British effort to drive his forces from eastern Libya.

positioned in the centre and C Troop looked north-east.

Crusader had caught the Germans totally by surprise. A Luftwaffe recce had failed to locate Allied troop concentrations and ammunition dumps, while torrential rain had grounded all aircraft on the night of the offensive. However, by late evening on 20 November, Field Marshal Rommel had organised his forces in preparation for a counter-attack. The Panzergruppe commander intended to use both his 15th and 21st Panzer Divisions, under Lieutenant-General Ludwig Cruewell, in a lightning sortie against the Sidi Rezegh positions. Cruewell's Afrika Korps was equipped with Panzer Mark IIIs and IVs, armed with 50mm and 75mm guns, and able to engage at distances up to 1000yds. In addition, these tanks were shielded by 60mm-thick armour. The nature of such opposition made a kill by the British anti-tank 2-pounder gun very difficult. Lieutenant-General Cruewell signalled his two divisions: 'A punctual start to the operations of 21 November will

be decisive.' The battle was about to begin.

After enduring the cold desert night, the men at Sidi Rezegh woke early to hear the distant rumblings of tank and gun fire in the plain below. Brigadier Hely described the morning:

'The slow first light of 21 November 1941 broke on the usual desert scene at Sidi Rezegh. Leaguers were dispersing. From every quarter came the noise of transport starting up, guns rumbled slowly and cautiously into battle positions; chilled and silent men with sleep-heavy eyes moved mechanically into their appointed places. Everywhere, full use was being made of the valuable 30 minutes of half-light, when visibility was too poor for the enemy to pick out a target. Support Group of the 7th Armoured was preparing for battle.'

As Major Pinney toured his troop positions, the 2-pounder guns on their portées were ready – the ammunition was prepared and the arcs of fire confirmed. A Troop, commanded by Second-Lieutenant Ward Gunn, was tasked to provide anti-tank fire for

the support company, from the 2nd Battalion, The Rifle Brigade, on the southeast of the escarpment.

At dawn, the onslaught began. Enemy artillery, having recced the area the previous day, smothered the British positions with a concentrated bombardment, while Luftwaffe Stukas attempted to take out the main defences.

At 0830 hours the 7th Hussars were attacked on both sides by the 15th and 21st Panzer Divisions. Despite stout resistance, many of the Hussars' tanks were set ablaze and the commanding officer, Lieutenant-Colonel Byars, was killed. The regiment had suffered heavy casualties and, with all communication lines knocked out, it withdrew to the northeast. The 2nd Royal Tank Regiment, on the enemy's left flank, were unable to provide assistance as they were pinned down by an anti-tank screen.

Following this furious exchange, the German panzer divisions moved to Abiar en Nbeidat, three miles east, where they were resupplied with fuel and ammunition. It was during this refuelling that a number of tanks from the 15th Panzer Division moved forward to recce the Sidi Rezegh positions. A member of the 2nd Rifle Brigade's support company later wrote of this moment:

'Sixteen tanks...moving slowly...about 800yds away into the valley to the northeast. The 2-

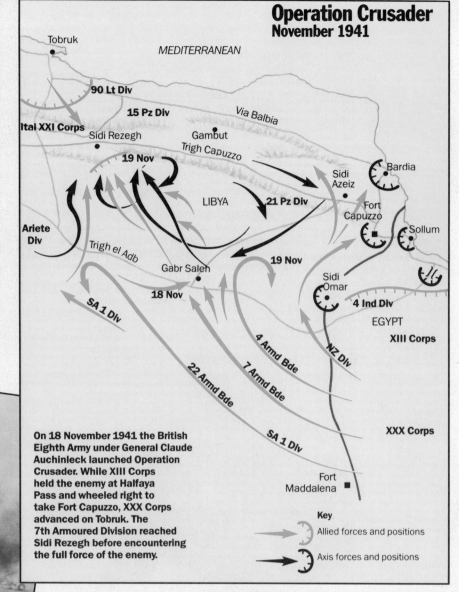

Operation Crusader
November 1941

On 18 November 1941 the British Eighth Army under General Claude Auchinleck launched Operation Crusader. While XIII Corps held the enemy at Halfaya Pass and wheeled right to take Fort Capuzzo, XXX Corps advanced on Tobruk. The 7th Armoured Division reached Sidi Rezegh before encountering the full force of the enemy.

Key
→ Allied forces and positions
→ Axis forces and positions

Left: Accorded pride of place in the officers mess of the 3rd Royal Horse Artillery, is this picture, by artist David Shepherd, of Second-Lieutenant Ward Gunn (far left) bravely manning the 2-pounder despite intense enemy fire. His medals of honour (inset) include (left and second left) the Victoria Cross and the Military Cross. Below left: In the aftermath of battle, two disabled tanks of the 15th Panzer Division lie deserted.

pounders on the ridge to the north under command of Ward Gunn opened fire on them. The 25-pounders of the 60th Field Regiment engaged them over open sights. Four of them went up in flames. The remainder halted, dodged about and, finding that they could make no headway against our fire, but having had a good look at our positions, withdrew just out of sight. They had returned our fire and the two anti-tank guns had been knocked out. It was quite clear that the enemy's retirement was only temporary.'

After a short lull, both panzer divisions, comprising over 150 tanks, advanced on Sidi Rezegh. As the panzers came into view, every available weapons system, suitable and unsuitable, was brought to bear on them. A Bofors anti-aircraft gun, commanded by Lieutenant McSwiney, the 25-pounders of the 4th Regiment, RHA, and the 60th Field Regiment and the four 2-pounders under Ward Gunn prepared to resist the enemy onslaught.

Within minutes, the two 8cwt 'pick-ups' at the headquarters of the 2nd Rifle Brigade were set alight. They had made easy targets, with wireless masts giving away their location and status, and thin armour affording precious little protection against the enemy bombardment. The 7th Armoured Brigade immediately sent in its mobile reserve of five Crusader tanks in order to bolster the sector. Outnumbered 30 to one, they were soon picked off and set ablaze.

Machine-gun and tank fire became more intense as the enemy concentrated their efforts against the Bofors and 2-pounder guns. This was quickly supplemented by the German infantry's mortars and artillery and Stuka bombardments. Raised on the backs of vehicles and protected by only a thin shield of armour, the British gunners were extremely vulnerable and soon began to take casualties. Inevitably, a 2-pounder was destroyed and the Bofors set ablaze. As Major Robin Hastings recalled, in the history of the Rifle Brigade: 'The men of the Rifle Brigade watched these three (two-pounder) guns firing away at the enemy, watched the crews, completely composed, completely undaunted, picked off one by one.'

Although the German tanks were drawing closer,

Six months after Sidi Rezegh, on 27 May 1942, the Afrika Korps launched a fresh offensive designed to outflank the British Eighth Army. The two brigades of the 7th Armoured Division were routed by Lieutenant-General Ludwig Cruewell's 15th and 21st Panzer Divisions. On 29 May, however, an enemy plane flying across the battlefield was shot down by anti-aircraft fire and forced to crash-land. From the wreckage emerged Lieutenant General Cruewell himself. Below: After his capture, the disconsolate panzer commander was taken to headquarters by armoured car. Although Field Marshal Rommel continued with his attack, recapturing Tobruk in June, he was increasingly plagued by supply problems. By November 1942, his strategic plans were in ruins and the tide of war in the Desert had turned.

now only 1000yds away, Second-Lieutenant Ward Gunn continued to travel around the position, moving ammunition and encouraging the crews. Eventually only one gun remained, but this was subjected to intense enemy fire and the crew were either killed or wounded. Furthermore, the portée was ablaze. Sergeant Gray, the gun's No. 1, decided that the fire was too intense to put out by himself and, to prevent the flames spreading to the ammunition behind the crew seat, Gray attempted to drive the gun to safety.

Seeing this, Major Pinney drove his vehicle over to the gun position and started to tackle the fire. Second-Lieutenant Ward Gunn also raced across, through a deluge of fire, to assist his battery commander. The flames were slowly put out, but the intensity of enemy fire increased.

Bodies were dragged from the portée and the gun was brought into action. Ward Gunn jumped into the layer's seat, while Gray acted as loader. The panzers were now less than 700yds away, their 7.9mm machine guns raking A Troop's position. Despite this, Ward Gunn coolly laid the gun on the tanks and, within a few minutes, destroyed two panzers and damaged a number of others. Ward Gunn loosed off between 40 and 50 rounds at the enemy before the gallant second-lieutenant was shot through the forehead, dying instantly. Sergeant Gray was hit in the arm and fell back across the ammunition. Undeterred, Major Pinney pushed Ward Gunn's body to one side and jumped into the layer's seat himself. He continued to fire the gun until, eventually, the portée was hit by a 50mm shell, causing the front wheel to catch fire. Sergeant Gray was again hit by machine-gun fire and flames began to envelope the cab and ammunition boxes.

The fighting had been so ferocious that the panzers had started to run out of ammunition

At this stage, in Pinney's own words: 'I then felt justified in leaving.' Jumping down from the portée, he helped Gray and another wounded gunner into the vehicle he had used to join them earlier. Incredibly, Major Pinney then drove to B Troop, which was also being heavily shelled, to assess the situation and help wherever possible.

The fighting had been so ferocious that the panzers had started to run out of ammunition and were eventually forced to fall back to a position near Abiar en Nbeidat. Although it had suffered immense casualties, the 7th Armoured Brigade had been successful in thwarting Rommel's plans. Major Bernard Pinney and Second-Lieutenant Ward Gunn were recommended for the Victoria Cross, and the award was given to Ward Gunn posthumously. On 22 November, Pinney was killed during the preliminary shelling prior to another German attack.

Eventually, Rommel's forces were pushed back into Tripolitania (western Libya), and, although the men of J Battery were not aware of it at the time, their heroic defence of Sidi Rezegh had played an important part in the success of Operation Crusader.

THE AUTHOR CWT is a serving officer in the Royal Horse Artillery and has served with J Battery in its modern role in the British Army.

F 19745

MAN AND MACHINE

The armoured units of the Waffen SS devised tactics perfectly suited to the battles of attrition on the Eastern Front during World War II

THE WAR on the Eastern Front (1941-45) was the greatest conflict in history, one in which millions of men fought and died in a titanic struggle between the two totalitarian states of Hitler's Germany and Stalin's Soviet Union. The vast open spaces of the Russian steppe meant that tanks, the pivots of mobile warfare, played a decisive role, and both sides placed great importance on their armoured formations which became the elite of the battlefield.

Armour was the cutting-edge of the attack and the means to exploit a breakthrough, while on the defensive it could be employed as a mobile reserve to plug gaps in the line and, once in combat, act as a strongpoint, destroying the impetus of the enemy assault. Although the Soviet Army emerged as the victor because it was able to overwhelm the German armed forces, the panzer divisions remained the finest exponents of armoured warfare throughout World War II. And within the German armoured forces the role of the Waffen SS grew in importance as the war progressed.

The Waffen SS had played only a minimal role in the great German victories of 1939-40, and even as Hitler launched his onslaught on the Soviet Union in the summer of 1941 they were still an insignificant force. Himmler and the other SS leaders were determined, however, to increase the importance of the Waffen SS within the German armed forces, and the war against the Soviet Union gave them a golden opportunity to realise their ambitions.

The three senior formations within the Waffen SS –

Above: The PzKpfw V Panther, one of the most formidable tanks of World War II. Behind the distinctive curved mantlet of the powerful 7.5cm gun the well-sloped turret (a feature copied from the Soviet T-34) has been given supplementary armour in the form of spare track links.
Inset: The Panzerkampfabzeichen (Tank Battle Badge) was introduced in 1939 and awarded to panzer units that had engaged the enemy. To differentiate their roles, tank crews received a silver badge (as above), panzer grenadiers a bronze one. After July 1943 more elaborate badges were awarded to tank crews for having fought 25 and 50 battles (silver and black) and 75 and 100 battles (silver and gilt). Panzer grenadiers received these later awards in bronze or bronze with a gilt wreath.

Leibstandarte SS Adolf Hitler, Das Reich and Totenkopf – were not formed as panzer units, but instead were merely motorised troops. Once in Russia, however, the need for armoured forces became ever more necessary and in the summer and autumn of 1942 they were pulled out of line and transferred to France. There they were reformed and upgraded to become panzer grenadier divisions.

A fourth Waffen SS division, Wiking, had remained in Russia but likewise was re-equipped and re-designated as a panzer grenadier division. The Wiking Division contained a large proportion of volunteers from Scandinavian countries, and was similar in standard to the original three Waffen SS divisions.

The armoured cutting edge was provided by the tank battalion

By early 1943 the Waffen SS thus had four panzer grenadier divisions at its disposal and they were rapidly thrown into the developing conflict on the Eastern Front. The panzer grenadier division had evolved within the German armed forces as a motorised infantry formation to supplement the true panzer division but distinction between the two types became increasingly blurred during the course of the war, especially within the SS as their panzer grenadier divisions' allotment of armoured fighting vehicles (AFVs) grew larger. The well-equipped armoured units of the Waffen SS divisions gave them the same firepower as an Army panzer division.

The most important single element of a 15,000-strong panzer grenadier division was the motorised panzer grenadier brigade consisting of two or sometimes three regiments, each of three battalions. The

TANK ACES

The war on the Eastern Front saw the rise to fame of several 'tank aces' – tank commanders who demonstrated a special ability to destroy enemy armour. The Waffen SS carefully nurtured the tank aces within its ranks, and some amassed large scores in short periods of time: during the Battle of Kursk in July 1943 Untersharführer (Corporal) Franz Standegger destroyed 20 tanks – with the assistance of Leibstandarte panzer grenadiers – when repelling one major Soviet counter-attack.

Right up to the end, Waffen SS personnel proved able to carry on successful local actions, and Untersturmführer (2nd Lieutenant) Karl Bromann, a Tiger tank commander with SS 103 Heavy Tank Battalion, took out 55 tanks, 44 guns and 16 lorries between 2 February and 18 March 1945.

The qualities of a tank ace consisted of an ability to 'read' the immediate tactical situation, a sixth sense for the likely movements of enemy vehicles, the coolness under attack to hold fire until the very last moment, and, perhaps most important, a superbly trained and experienced crew that almost anticipated its commander's orders.

All these elements were present in the successes of Obersturmführer (Lieutenant) Michael Wittman, who was credited with a total of 119 Soviet tanks. Wittman was lucky in having a superb gunner in Balthasar Woll (above) who had a near unique ability to fire accurately while on the move.

SdKfz 251

Crew 2 + 10
Weight 9 tons
Performance Max road speed 55km/h; range 320km
Armour 7-12mm
Armament Two 7.92mm machine guns (in APC role)

Wespe

Crew 5
Weight 12 tons
Performance Max road speed 40km/h; range 140km
Armour 10-20mm
Armament One 10.5cm howitzer; one 7.92mm machine gun

Although the SdKfz 251 was designed as an armoured personnel carrier it was a versatile multi-role vehicle which could be adapted, for example, as a general weapons platform, rocket launcher or bridge-layer. As an APC it could transport its 10 panzer grenadiers right into the midst of the battle, providing them with both mobility and protection.

Introduced in 1942 the Wespe (Wasp) was a light self-propelled howitzer whose gun was mounted on a PzKpfw II chassis. Although space was cramped for the five-men crew the Wespe was a reliable gun platform and an essential component of the panzer divisions' mobile artillery.

Below: The crewmen of a PzKpfw VI Tiger I of the Waffen SS at Kursk take advantage of a safe moment in the conflict to slake their thirsts. The shell of their 8.8cm L/56 high velocity gun could penetrate 112mm of armour plate at 450m, making the tank particularly dangerous in an ambush position. In mobile warfare the Tiger fared less well, however, as its weight (56 tonnes) meant that it was slow (top speed 38km/h) and had a short operational range (100km). There were high Tiger casualties in the fluid battle at Kursk. The turret had a full traverse and was powered by the main engine: if the engine was stopped the turret had to be traversed by hand.

battalion had an establishment strength of around 850 men organised into three rifle companies and one support company, liberally equipped with mortars and heavy machine guns. The armoured cutting edge of the division was provided by the tank battalion (organised into three companies), the size of which varied considerably, depending on campaign losses and the rate of re-supply, but when operating at full strength the battalion could deploy as many as 96 tanks.

The Waffen SS divisions relied upon two cornerstones: high mobility and concentrated firepower

Additional armoured firepower was to be found in the reconnaissance battalion and artillery units. Within the German armed forces the reconnaissance battalion was a powerful force of 1000 men, fully motorised and equipped with armoured cars and a number of self-propelled guns. Equipped to fight for information, the reconnaissance battalion was often in the forefront of encounter battles, finding the weak points in the enemy line. Besides its conventional mix of 10.5cm and 15cm towed guns, the artillery regiment had its own self-propelled artillery which could fight alongside the tanks in a fire-support role. In addition, the anti-tank battalion fielded three companies, one of conventional towed artillery supplemented by two companies of assault guns. Thus, despite its origin as an infantry formation, the Waffen SS panzer grenadier division was, in fact, a formidable armoured force.

Weapons and equipment were constantly improved during the course of the war and, as the SS had a powerful patron in Himmler, it was usually able to get its pick of the available new equipment. The AFVs used by the Waffen SS consisted of four broad classes, used according to function. The tank was clearly the most important AFV; fully tracked and

armed with a powerful main gun in a fully mobile turret it was a highly effective offensive weapon. During the first part of 1943 the Waffen SS was equipped with PzKpfw IIIs and IVs, plus a number of heavy Tiger tanks, the latter being organised into semi-independent tank companies (and battalions).

The self-propelled assault gun was similar to the tank in being armed with a high-velocity gun but was lighter in weight and lacked a turret. Faster and

StuG III

Crew 4
Weight 24 tons
Performance Max road speed 40km/h; range 160km
Armour 30-90mm
Armament One 7.5cm L/48 gun; one 7.92mm machine gun

Utilising the chassis from the PzKpfw III the StuG III was a self-propelled gun which saw continuous service on the Eastern Front; its low silhouette and relatively good armour protection and armament made it an ideal tank destroyer.

PzKpfw III (Ausf J)

Crew 5
Weight 21 tons
Performance Max road speed 40km/h; range 175m
Armour 15-50mm
Armament One 5cm L/60 gun; two 7.92mm machine guns

The main battle tank of the early years of the war, the PzKpfw III proved itself efficient and reliable, but when faced with Soviet T-34 and KV tanks it was clearly outclassed. By 1943 it had been withdrawn as a front-line AFV in the Panzer divisions.

Panzer assault
German armoured tactics on the Eastern Front

Throughout the war on the Eastern Front German armoured divisions were able to use tanks, self-propelled artillery and motorised infantry in well co-ordinated mobile attacks. The concentrated use of firepower led to German tactical successes until the end of the war.

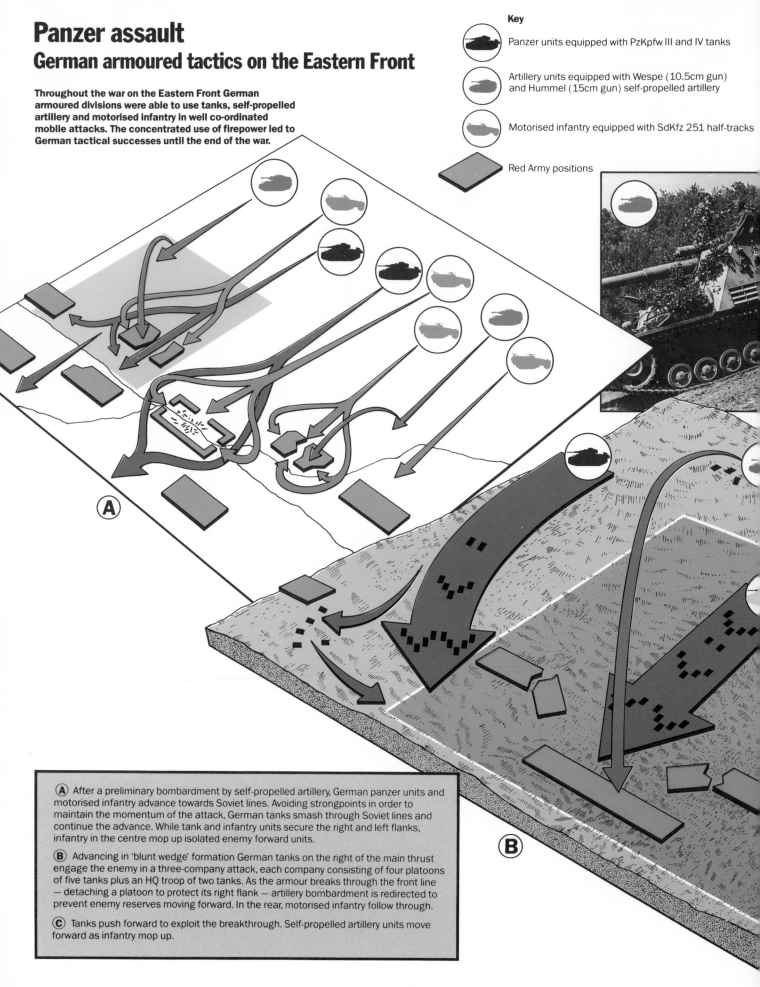

Key

Panzer units equipped with PzKpfw III and IV tanks

Artillery units equipped with Wespe (10.5cm gun) and Hummel (15cm gun) self-propelled artillery

Motorised infantry equipped with SdKfz 251 half-tracks

Red Army positions

(A) After a preliminary bombardment by self-propelled artillery, German panzer units and motorised infantry advance towards Soviet lines. Avoiding strongpoints in order to maintain the momentum of the attack, German tanks smash through Soviet lines and continue the advance. While tank and infantry units secure the right and left flanks, infantry in the centre mop up isolated enemy forward units.

(B) Advancing in 'blunt wedge' formation German tanks on the right of the main thrust engage the enemy in a three-company attack, each company consisting of four platoons of five tanks plus an HQ troop of two tanks. As the armour breaks through the front line — detaching a platoon to protect its right flank — artillery bombardment is redirected to prevent enemy reserves moving forward. In the rear, motorised infantry follow through.

(C) Tanks push forward to exploit the breakthrough. Self-propelled artillery units move forward as infantry mop up.

cheaper to manufacture than the tank, the self-propelled gun lacked its versatility in offensive operations but was an excellent defensive weapon. Self-propelled artillery consisted of a gun firing low velocity high-explosive rounds mounted on a tank chassis. The function of self-propelled artillery was to deliver concentrated firepower in support of the tanks and self-propelled guns which lacked its high-explosive indirect-fire capability.

The last class of AFV was light armour, which consisted primarily of armoured cars – wheeled vehicles mounting a variety of light weapons – and, most importantly, armoured personnel carriers, lightly armoured half-tracked vehicles which transported the infantry and their weapons to and on the battlefield. The armoured personnel carrier enabled the panzer grenadiers to be both mobile and protected.

The tactics employed by the Waffen SS divisions were those of the German Army and relied upon two cornerstones: high mobility and concentrated firepower. These were achieved by the full integration of all the separate elements within the division.

In the offensive the tank battalion would act as the forward element, spearheading the attack and punching through the enemy line. Paradoxically the tanks were to refuse combat as much as possible, avoiding enemy strongpoints by either by-passing them or bringing up support arms to destroy them. Once a breakthrough had been effected the tank's main duty was to race forward to exploit the situation, disrupting enemy movements and throwing its commanders into a state of complete disorientation.

Anticipating the breakthrough by softening-up a chosen position in the enemy line was the first

PzKpfw IV (Ausf G)

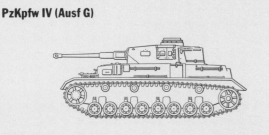

Crew 5
Weight 25 tons
Performance Max road speed 40km/h; range 200km
Armour 10-50mm, plus bolt-on armour
Armament One 7.5cm L/48 gun; two 7.92mm machine guns

Progressing through a series of marks which extended its service life to the end of the war, the PzKpfw IV was a mainstay of the Waffen SS panzer divisions during World War II. Originally intended to be a fire support AFV the PzKpfw IV expanded this role to that of a main battle tank when a high-velocity gun was installed.

PzKpfw V Panther (Ausf G)

Crew 5
Weight 45 tons
Performance Max road speed 45km/h; range 200km
Armour 20-120mm
Armament One 7.5cm L/70 gun; two 7.92mm machine guns

In the Ausf G the teething problems that had plagued early Panthers had largely been resolved. Its well-sloped and thick frontal armour and high-velocity main gun made the Panther one of the most feared AFVs on the Eastern front.

PzKpfw VI Tiger I

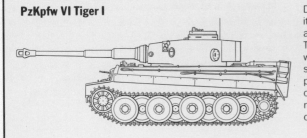

Crew 5
Weight 56 tons
Performance Max road speed 38km/h; range 140km
Armour 26-110mm
Armament One 8.8cm L/56 gun; two 7.92mm machine guns

Despite its weight and its overloaded engine and transmission the Tiger was highly effective when used in battalion-sized formations; its potent fire-power could overcome all but the most skilfully-handled opposition.

responsibility of the artillery. Subsequently the artillery had to move forward in support of the tanks and infantry, reducing enemy strongpoints and disrupting counter-attacks. The infantry would follow closely behind the tanks to take physical possession of the ground gained by the tanks, to destroy and occupy enemy strongpoints and to hold the line against counter-attacks.

If engaged in a hotly contested struggle, the ability of the Germans to fight an all-arms battle was crucial. Each arm had its own special strengths and weaknesses and success on the battlefield depended upon them being used together in a coordinated manner. Thus, for example, tanks were vulnerable to well-sited Soviet anti-tank guns but they in turn were vulnerable to air-burst bombardment from artillery. Consequently, a self-propelled artillery unit would be positioned a short distance behind the advancing tanks and would lay down a short barrage of fire to cover a combined dash by the tanks – and supporting infantry in armoured halftracks – who would then be able to overrun the Soviet position.

While in the latter part of the war German operations were strategically defensive in nature, the armoured units of the Waffen SS were still employed in an offensive manner, their role being to act as a mobile fire brigade to plug gaps in the German line and launch local counter-attacks.

Plans were made for two enormous armoured pincer movements to reduce the Kursk salient

In February 1943 the Waffen SS armoured divisions were given their chance to prove themselves as elite formations. Leibstandarte; Das Reich and Totenkopf were grouped together as I SS Panzer Corps under Obergruppenführer (General) Paul Hausser and were deployed in the Kharkov sector. Alongside the Army's elite Grossdeutschland Division, the SS Panzer Corps was instrumental in holding the German line and acting as the vanguard of the counter-stroke which led to the destruction of the Soviet Sixth Army and the retaking of Kharkov.

After the victory of Kharkov the German position was secure, and, as the spring thaw brought armoured operations to a muddy halt, preparations began for the summer offensive. Plans were made for two enormous armoured pincer movements to reduce the Kursk salient. The offensive got underway on 5 July and the SS Panzer Corps formed part of the southern column of attack. Unfortunately for the Germans, the Red Army was well prepared and in a series of gigantic tank battles blunted the German advance. On 12 July the SS Panzer Corps fought it out with the Soviet Fifth Guards Tank Army, resulting in a swirling tank melee which saw each side lose 300 tanks, with neither side giving way. Hitler, appalled by the rising scale of casualties, lost his nerve, however, and halted the entire offensive. The Russians promptly responded with their own summer offensive which marked the beginning of the great Soviet advance. The strategic initiative lay with the Red Army from Kursk onwards, and the Germans were forced onto the defensive.

Over the next two years the Waffen SS was to play an often critical role in preserving the integrity of the German front line. It had grown in size and importance as a consequence of the victory at Kharkov, as Hitler henceforth viewed Himmler's requests for expansion more favourably. In October 1943 seven

Top left: The crew of a 5cm Pak 38 manhandle their antitank weapon uphill into position. Behind them is a Kubelwagen (utility vehicle). Above: Fully-armed panzer grenadiers move forward, clinging to their armoured vehicle. The soldier second from the right carries a captured Soviet PPSh-1941 sub-machine gun with curved box magazine. Left: The Hummel self-propelled gun was a 15cm field howitzer pedestal-mounted on a working platform. Since operating space was restricted, ammunition was normally carried by a second Hummel without armament. Bottom: The SdKfz 232 was powered by an air-cooled engine. Its armament consisted of a 20mm automatic cannon and a 7.92mm machine gun.

Above: SS panzer grenadiers clamber aboard their PzKpfw III and IV tanks in readiness for a counter-attack during the battles for the Ukraine in 1943. Left: Stug III self-propelled guns force their way through the thick mud of the steppe after a thaw.

full Waffen SS panzer divisions came into being. They consisted of the original Leibstandarte, Das Reich, Totenkopf and Wiking divisions, plus the 9th Hohenstaufen, 10th Frundsberg and 12th Hitlerjugend Divisions. In addition, three independent heavy tank battalions were formed, equipped with Tiger tanks.

After the Allied landings on the Normandy coast on 6 June 1944, the Leibstandarte, Das Reich, Hohenstaufen and Frundsberg were hastily sent to France where they joined the Hitlerjugend Division in the ultimately fruitless attempt to destroy the Allied beach-head. Only Totenkopf and a badly mauled Wiking remained on the Eastern Front. Hitler's predilection for shipping his Waffen SS divisions around Europe was less than sound at a strategic level, denying crack units to both fronts at vital times.

In January 1945 the SS panzer divisions – now the Sixth SS Panzer Army – were once again deployed on the Eastern Front in a hopeless last-ditch attempt to retake Budapest and hold onto Germany's remaining sources of oil supply. But although the Waffen SS divisions fought to the end, their position was hopeless.

By May 1945 defeat was a physical reality as the Allied armies of the East and West overran what was left of the Thousand-Year Reich. The remnants of the battered SS panzer divisions destroyed their arms and equipment and marched into captivity.

THE AUTHOR Edward Trowbridge is a military writer specialising in the tactics of modern warfare and weapons technology. He has written extensively on German operations on the Eastern Front, and has contributed to publications on the Vietnam War.

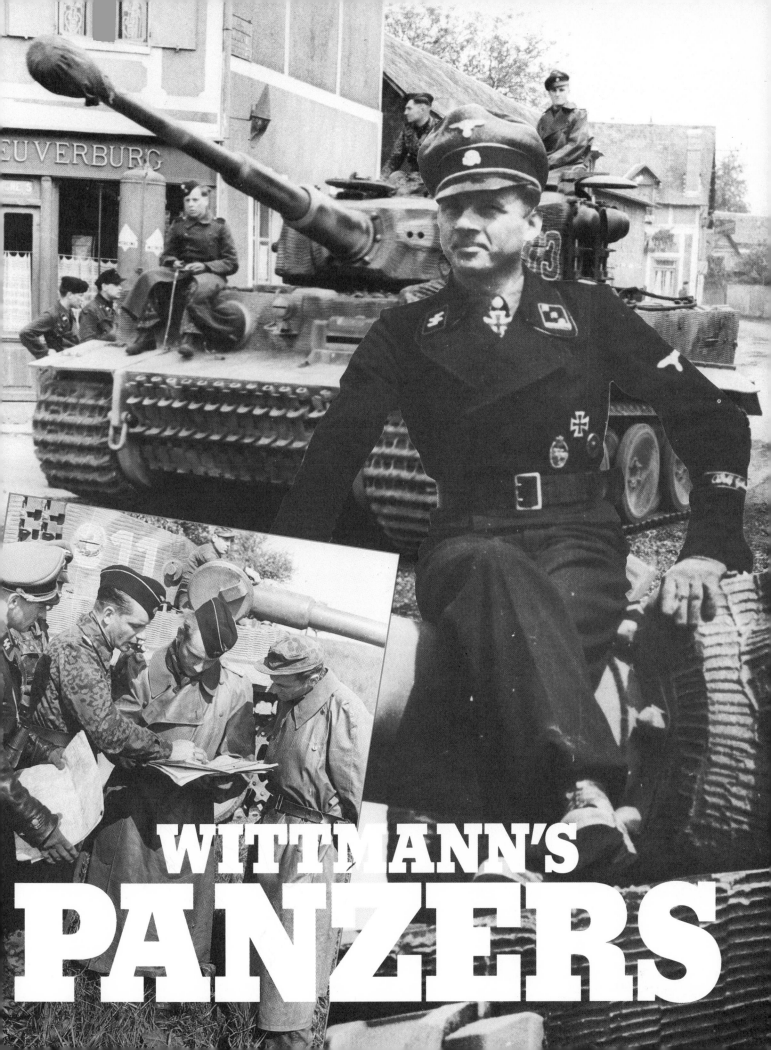

WITTMANN'S
PANZERS

When the 57-tonne PzKpfw VI Tiger tank was introduced into German service in 1943, it was so powerful that special schwere (heavy) tank battalions were formed to provide maximum impact on the battlefield. In the Waffen-SS, these took the form of special Abteilungen attached to corps headquarters, available to the corps commander for operations over a wide area. In the summer of 1943, I SS-Panzer Corps was created by grouping together SS-Panzer Division Leibstandarte Adolf Hitler (fighting in Russia) and 12th SS-Panzer Division Hitlerjugend (forming in Belgium): to this was added schwere SS-Panzer Abteilung 101, equipped with Ausf E Tigers. Abteilung 101 was organised into a Headquarters Company and three Tiger Companies, each theoretically of 14 tanks, and had integral air-defence in the form of three SdKfz 7/1 quadruple 20mm Flak half-tracks. By June 1944, the unit had 37 Tigers on issue, commanded by SS-Obersturmbannführer von Westernhagen: No.2 Company was commanded by the legendary SS-Obersturmführer Michael Wittmann, a man with 117 enemy tanks already to his credit.

Ordered from Beauvais to Normandy, the unit was hit by Allied air attacks while staging through Paris and did not enter the battle until 12 June.

After Villers-Bocage, the Tigers continued to serve in Normandy, fighting at Cintheaux, Point 140 and Falaise. In October 1944 the unit was retitled schwere SS-Panzer Abteilung 501.

Previous page: The calm, confident figure of SS-Obersturmführer Michael Wittmann (right). Taken before his promotion, this photograph shows Wittmann wearing the cuff title of Leibstandarte Adolf Hitler. After cruising through Morgny (above), Abteilung 101 tank commanders discuss battle tactics (left).

In June 1944 panzer commander Michael Wittmann foiled the attempt by Allied armour to outflank the town of Caen

THE CROMWELL TANK moved cautiously down the rubble-strewn street, its five-man crew straining to catch sight or sound of their quarry. Suddenly, it appeared – a Tiger tank travelling straight towards them. Hurriedly, the Cromwell's commander, Captain Pat Dyas, ordered his gunner to open fire with the 75mm main armament. Two shots were loosed off in quick succession, only to explode harmlessly on the Tiger's frontal armour. A single return shot from the German tank's 88mm gun halted the Cromwell in its tracks. As the crew baled out, they were caught in a withering burst of machine-gun fire; Dyas, despite being wounded, ran for shelter. The Tiger, tracks squealing on the roadway, rumbled past.

It was just after 0830 hours on 13 June 1944 and the Cromwell, one of four belonging to the Regimental Headquarters (RHQ) of the 4th County of London Yeomanry (Sharpshooters) (4CLY), had fallen victim to the greatest tank 'ace' of them all, 30-year-old SS-Obersturmführer Michael Wittmann, commander of No.2 Company of the schwere SS-Panzer Abteilung 101. This unit was the heavy tank battalion of I SS-Panzer Corps and its exploits on 13 June, in the Normandy village of Villers-Bocage, represent one of the most dramatic tank-to-tank engagements of World War II. By the end of the morning, a substantial part of 4CLY had ceased to exist and, although Wittmann's company was virtually wiped out as well, it had succeeded in stopping a British move which had threatened to outflank Caen.

Villers-Bocage, an important road centre, was also the objective of SS-Panzer Abteilung 101

The British attack had developed late on 12 June when General Sir Bernard Montgomery, commanding Allied ground forces in the Overlord invasion which had begun less than a week before, ordered his crack 7th Armoured Division – veterans of the Desert War and among the most experienced troops on the Allied side – to disengage from fruitless assaults on the village of Tilly-sur-Seulles, inland from Gold beach. Only a few miles to the west, American troops seemed to be making good progress down the Aure river valley, implying that a gap existed in the hastily-prepared German defences. If the 7th Armoured Division could push into this gap, moving parallel to the Americans along the Anglo-US interface, and then loop eastwards towards Villers-Bocage, the defenders of Tilly – identified as belonging to the Panzer Lehr Division – would be outflanked and forced to pull back. Once Villers-Bocage had been taken, moreover, the way would be clear for an advance along the Seulles river valley to high ground around Mont Pinçon 10 miles to the south, opening up the prospect of an early breakout from the invasion beaches into the more open terrain beyond. At the same time, a similar attack to the east of the British lodgement area, in the Odon river

valley, would threaten Caen from that direction, catching the defenders in an envelopment which could prove decisive.

The commander of the 7th Armoured Division, Major-General 'Bobby' Erskine, ordered his assault formation – 22nd Armoured Brigade under Brigadier Robert Hinde – to spearhead the move and, late on 12 June, led by 4CLY with men of the 1st Battalion, The Rifle Brigade (1RB) in attendance in Universal (Bren-gun) Carriers and half-tracks, the advance began. The local area, known as *bocage*, was appalling tank country, comprising a bewildering (and menacing) patchwork of sunken, single-track lanes, impenetrable hedgerows and small fields, interspersed with copses. However, by nightfall the road linking Caumont and Villers-Bocage had been reached, opening the route to the east. 4CLY pulled in to a small wood to leaguer for the night and, first thing in the morning, resumed its advance over switchback hills towards Villers-Bocage. At about 0800 hours on the 13th the unit, still with 1RB in support, stormed the

Above right: The panzers of Wittmann's No.2 Company race towards Normandy. Several of Abteilung 101's Tigers were damaged during an air strike on Paris, forcing the unit to enter the battle zone under strength.

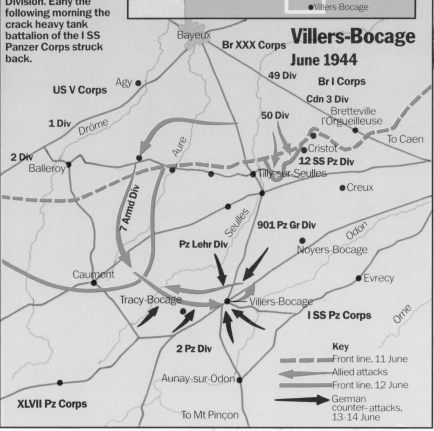

On 12 June 1944, as the Allies fought to secure their toehold in Normandy, the British 7th Armoured Division launched an attack south and eastwards to Villers-Bocage in an effort to outflank the German Panzer Lehr Division. Early the following morning the crack heavy tank battalion of the I SS Panzer Corps struck back.

Villers-Bocage
June 1944

Key
- Front line, 11 June
- Allied attacks
- Front line, 12 June
- German counter-attacks, 13-14 June

village unopposed. The yeomanry commander, Lieutenant-Colonel Arthur, Viscount Cranleigh, left the four RHQ Cromwells parked in the village, jumped in a scout car and pushed ahead with A Squadron and A Company 1RB, aiming to take and hold Point 213, a piece of high ground about a mile to the northeast, on the Caen road. He was understandably wary about the ease of the advance – he had asked for permission to conduct a detailed reconnaissance before taking Villers-Bocage, but had been refused by Hinde, who was pressing for maximum speed – and was worried about reports that a German 'armoured car' had been monitoring his unit's progress, but for the moment, it appeared that the right hook around Tilly was succeeding.

However, the situation was soon to change dramatically, for Villers-Bocage, an important road centre, was also the objective of SS-Panzer Abteilung 101, despatched to the area to plug the gap which clearly existed to the left of Panzer Lehr. Commanded by SS-Obersturmbannführer von Westernhagen, the three companies of Abteilung 101 were immediately deployed to cover the Aure valley: Wittmann's No.2 Company sheltered in woods to the northeast of Villers-Bocage, with SS-Haupsturmführer Möbius' No.1 Company to its right. Early on 13 June, Wittmann decided to conduct a personal reconnaissance towards the village to check on rumours of a British advance.

As Wittmann emerged from the safety of the woods, his force of four Tigers and a single PzKpfw IV (the latter belonging to Panzer Lehr) had a clear view of the Caen road as it snaked out of Villers-Bocage to their right. The sight that greeted them was a column of British tanks and carriers, moving slowly forward and, as they watched, the column halted, with khaki-clad soldiers jumping down to stretch their legs, light cigarettes and, in the established tradition of desert veterans, 'brew up' the inevitable mugs of tea. Wittmann's gunner was heard to mutter 'They're acting as if they'd won the war already', to which his commander replied prophetically, 'We're going to prove them wrong.'

Within less than five minutes, the tip of the British spear had been blunted and destroyed

Leaving the rest of his small force to observe the column, Wittmann moved on alone, cutting behind the British to approach the village from the northeast. Entering Villers-Bocage down the main street, he was suddenly confronted by the four RHQ Cromwells, parked neatly alongside the houses. Wittmann's crew, all Eastern Front veterans, required no orders and three of the tanks, belonging respectively to the commanding officer, the second-in-command and the Regimental Sergeant-Major (RSM), were knocked out in quick succession, their crews machine gunned as they tried to escape. The fourth Cromwell, commanded by Captain Pat Dyas, reversed hurriedly and unceremoniously into a nearby garden, avoiding detection behind the smoke of battle. Unfortunately, neither Dyas nor his gunner were on board and, as the Tiger trundled past, presenting an ideal side-target, they could only curse their luck and quickly scramble aboard. Nosing out as soon as the Tiger had passed, Dyas began to stalk the enemy, hoping for an opportunity to loose off a couple of shots into the less well-armoured engine compartment at the rear. But it was not to be, for as Wittmann reached the western edge of the village he encountered B Squadron 4CLY, waiting for orders to advance. Sergeant Lockwood, commanding one of the squadron's four Sherman Fireflies, fitted with 17-pounder main armament, exchanged fire with the Tiger, registering at least one hit. Wittmann, realising that he was outnumbered, turned round to escape, coming face-to-face with Dyas' ill-fated Cromwell.

Having despatched Dyas' tank, Wittmann motored back to his original position overlooking the road, rejoining the rest of his force. Incredibly, the British column was still in place, presenting a sitting target that was not to be missed. Wittmann's first shot hit a carrier full of ammunition, setting it ablaze and effectively blocking the road. He then sought out the four Fireflies belonging to A Squadron, aware from his earlier experience that they were capable of inflicting damage. Once they had been disabled, he raked the remainder of the column with a devastating concentration of fire. Vehicle after vehicle, unable to manoeuvre on the crowded, narrow road, fell

Right: Decimation on the Caen road. The devastating 88mm guns of No.2 Company enveloped the unsuspecting British column in a holocaust from which there was no escape. Behind the shattered remains of a Bren-gun carrier, a solitary 6-pounder anti-tank gun lies testimony to the last-ditch attempt by the men of A Company 1RB to reverse the tide of battle. Far right: The outmoded Cromwell was no match for the heavily armoured PzKpfw VIE Tiger (inset) which formed the main equipment of Abteilung 101. Note the 'zimmerrit' anti-magnetic mine paste covering the panzer's hull. Below right: Shermans head into Villers-Bocage, with British infantry on the alert for snipers.

to the vicious crack of the 88s, their crews desperately seeking shelter in ditches on either side. Men of A Company 1RB bravely tried to set up a 6-pounder anti-tank gun, but it was swiftly silenced and, as the column devolved into chaos, men were killed or captured by panzer grenadiers belonging to Panzer Lehr. Within less than five minutes, the tip of the British spear had been blunted and destroyed.

Meanwhile Dyas, despite his wound, had alerted Major I.B. Aird, commanding B Squadron to the west of the village. According to some reports, Dyas dragged himself to the blazing hulk of the RSM's Cromwell in the main street to use a radio link that was hanging from the turret; others say he moved on foot to report to Aird personally, having been temporarily patched up by local French civilians. Either way, this was the first clear indication received by Aird that RHQ had ceased to exist and that he was effectively in command. He tried to contact Viscount Cranleigh but, although a brief conversation did take place, in which the latter said that he too was under attack, the radio soon went dead as the commanding officer was captured on Point 213. Aird ordered a troop of three Cromwells and a Firefly under Lieutenant Bill Cotton to drive into Villers-Bocage and make contact with the remnants of A Squadron. He crossed the village and, in an effort to avoid the scene of the RHQ disaster (in case the Tiger was still around), tried to approach the Caen road from the southeast, only to find his way blocked by a steep railway embankment. By then, the sounds of firing had ceased and Cotton pulled back into the centre of the village.

He decided to set up an ambush in case the Germans returned, taking his tanks off the main street and into alleys from which they could fire broadside at any Tigers advancing through the village. They were joined by a single 6-pounder anti-tank gun, manned by soldiers of The Queen's (Royal West Surrey) Regiment and, together, the combined force sighted their guns, squinting along the barrels at houses on the opposite side of the street. They did not have long to wait.

As soon as the one-sided battle with A Squadron had ended, Wittmann rearmed and refuelled before deciding to re-enter Villers-Bocage in company

UNDER FIRE

Wittmann's Tiger attack is vividly described in the Sharpshooter's regimental history:

'For a short time all seemed quiet, and then the most indescribable confusion broke out. Up the street in front, Lieutenant Ingram's Honeys and a dozen half-tracks of the Rifle Brigade were burning. The RHQ tanks started to move backwards down the narrow street. Out of the smoke trundled slowly a German Tiger tank. Major Carr, the second-in-command, fired at it with his 75mm but the shots failed to penetrate the side armour even at this ridiculous range. Almost immediately his tank was on fire.

'The other three tanks of RHQ managed to shuffle into various turnings, but soon the troop leader's tank was on fire and also the RSM's. Captain Dyas watched the Tiger pass him and began to trail it in his tank, but by now it had encountered the more formidable obstacle of B Squadron and decided to beat a retreat. Therefore once more it was head on and there was no escape.'

25

MICHAEL WITTMANN

Born on 22 April 1914 in Vogelthal, Wittmann joined the German Army as a private in 1934, serving in the 19th Infantry Regiment. In 1937 he transferred to the SS, serving in Leibstandarte Adolf Hitler as an armoured-car commander in both Poland (1939) and France (1940). During the campaign in the Balkans (1941), he commanded an assault gun, winning the Iron Cross Second Class, but it was not until the invasion of Russia that his prowess as a tank-destroyer came to the fore. In the advance on Rostov, he destroyed six Soviet tanks in a single battle, earning him the Iron Cross First Class.

In 1942, after an officer training course at Bad Tölz, he rejoined his unit as a tank commander and was given a Tiger in SS-Panzer Regiment I. Over the next few months his tally of kills rose dramatically. Awarded the Knight's Cross on 14 January 1944 and the Oakleaves less than three weeks later, Wittmann's score stood at an incredible 117 enemy tanks destroyed when, in April, he was transferred to command a company in the newly-formed schwere SS-Panzer Abteilung 101. After Villers-Bocage Wittmann was awarded the Swords to his Knight's Cross and promoted to SS-Haupsturmführer, in which rank he assumed command of Abteilung 101 in late July. He died leading his unit into battle on 9 August 1944, by which time his tally was 138 tanks and assault guns and 132 anti-tank guns – all destroyed in the space of less than two years. It is a record unsurpassed in the history of armoured warfare.

SS-Haupsturmführer Michael Wittmann

Wittmann's black tankcrew uniform is capped by an officer's Schirmmütze, with Panzer pink arm-of-service piping, on which a death's head sits below the SS eagle. He carries a Walther PPK pistol and wears the Iron and Knight's Cross, with a Tank Assault Badge.

Below: Disabled by an anti-tank gun, and gutted by fire, Wittmann's panzer lies abandoned. Although he escaped unscathed on this occasion, the reprieve was short-lived. Left: The final reckoning. The scattered remnants of his Tiger, which fell prey to a vicious ambush by five Shermans near the village of Gaumesnil.

with two Tigers and the PzKpfw IV, little realising that a trap had been laid. Moving past the smouldering remains of the RHQ Cromwells, the lead Tiger, commanded by Wittmann, proceeded down the main street, only to be hit by a single shot from the infantry-manned 6-pounder. The left-hand track of the Tiger was broken in the explosion, forcing the tank to slew sideways into one of the buildings. Wittmann and his crew baled out, running for shelter, as the second Tiger, only a few yards behind, dealt with the anti-tank gun, firing 88mm shots into the building from which it had been fired. The structure collapsed, burying the gallant Queensmen.

Almost simultaneously, however, Cotton brought his tanks into the battle, co-ordinating their actions on foot, a radio link in his hand. Sergeant Bobby Bramall fired at the second Tiger from his Firefly, disabling it with a single shot, but Corporal Horne's Cromwell failed to hit the Mark IV bringing up the rear. As it edged past the second Tiger, Horne pulled out of his cover and, with another shot, destroyed its engine compartment. In the absence of supporting infantry, Cotton could not prevent the German crews from escaping on foot, but he was determined to deny them the chance to recover their damaged tanks. In pouring rain, he went from vehicle to vehicle, umbrella in one hand and petrol-soaked blankets in the other. Stuffing the blankets into open hatches and applying a match, he set all three tanks ablaze.

Nevertheless, 4CLY had been badly mauled and, recalling Brigadier Hinde's orders that Villers-Bocage was to be held as long as possible, Aird concentrated B and C Squadrons, with their remaining

With the British advance slowed by tough panzer resistance, RAF Bomber Command used Villers-Bocage as a stage on which to demonstrate its effectiveness. The result was armageddon. Below: The shattered hulls of four German tanks lie amidst the rubble of what was once the peaceful village of Villers-Bocage.

infantry support, in the village. The unit had lost a total of 15 officers and 85 soldiers killed, wounded or missing, together with 20 Cromwells, four Fireflies, three light tanks (Honeys belonging to the Reconnaissance Troop, destroyed with A Squadron and on a separate incursion to the south of the village), three scout cars and a half-track, while A Company 1RB had fared no better. By nightfall, with no reinforcements available, Aird was given permission to pull back to Tracy-Bocage, a village one mile to the west. The Germans, by now fully aware that a dangerous gap existed on the left of their defences, rushed in all available reserves and, before dawn on 14 June, elements of the newly-arrived 2nd Panzer Division, together with a Kampfgruppe (task force) from Panzer Lehr, recaptured Villers-Bocage. Over the next few days, the village was hit by rocket-firing Typhoons of the RAF and, on 30 June, was subjected to a devastating raid by 250 heavy bombers which dropped 1176 tonnes of high explosive. The village ceased to exist.

His Tiger was literally blown apart by five Shermans firing simultaneously from three sides

By then, 4CLY had been pulled out of the line to recover. It took part in the British attack to the east of Caen in late July (Operation Goodwood), but after sustaining further losses, it was clearly no longer a viable unit. On 31 July, at Carpiquet Airfield, it was amalgamated with 3CLY to form 3/4 County of London Yeomanry (Sharpshooters) and taken out of the 22nd Armoured Brigade, a formation it had served with since 1939. Morale among the men remained remarkably high – a tribute to the fighting spirit of Britain's Yeomanry regiments – but the memory of 13 June seared deep. The only consolation was that Wittmann did not survive the battle for Normandy. Awarded the Swords to his Knight's Cross and promoted SS-Haupsturmführer immediately after Villers-Bocage, he went on in late July to assume command of Abteilung 101. On 9 August 1944, he led his unit in an attack on the village of Cintheaux, on the Caen-Falaise road. In typical style, Wittmann was in the thick of the fighting – ranged against Shermans of the 4th Canadian Armoured Division. When the battle ended in German victory, Wittmann was missing. Last seen fighting off three Shermans, it later transpired that he had fallen into a carefully laid trap, in which his Tiger was literally blown apart by five Shermans firing simultaneously from three sides. Wittmann's body was thrown in a shallow roadside grave where it lay, undisturbed, until 1983. It now rests in the German cemetery at La Cambe.

Wittmann's action on 13 June acts as his epitaph, for there is no doubt that it gives him the right to be called the greatest tank 'ace' of World War II. Virtually single-handed, he not only tore the heart out of an experienced British unit but also blunted what could have been a very dangerous outflanking move. If he had failed, 4CLY would probably have advanced as far as the outskirts of Caen, forcing Panzer Lehr to pull back from its positions around Tilly: as it was, his heroic action gave the 2nd Panzer Division time to reach the battle zone. As a result of Wittmann's bravery and fighting skill, the Germans were given the opportunity to continue the battle.

THE AUTHOR John Pimlott is senior lecturer in War Studies and International Affairs at the Royal Military Academy, Sandhurst.

2e DIVISION BLINDÉE

The French 2nd Armoured Division (2e Division Blindée – 2DB) was formed in Morocco in August 1943. Its personnel were from a mixed bag of French units available in North Africa at the time, including both Free French forces that had already seen heavy fighting in the desert and troops who had been loyal to Vichy France until the Allied Torch landings of November 1942. The officer tasked with welding together this diverse force was General Philippe Leclerc (born Vicomte Philippe de Hautecloque), already famous for his actions against the Italians in Libya and with the British Eighth Army in Tunisia.

2DB was given the full equipment of a US armoured division and Leclerc trained his men vigorously until they formed an outstanding fighting force. In April 1944 the division left Morocco for England, where it was attached to General George Patton's Third Army for the Normandy invasion. 2DB arrived in France on 1 August 1944, in time to participate in the breakout, fighting as part of US XV Corps. After taking Alençon and Argentan, the division liberated Paris on 25 August. Its losses made good by French volunteers, 2DB continued to fight with XV Corps, although now under the US Seventh Army, winning an important tank engagement at Dompaire in mid-September and taking Strasbourg on 23 November after a spectacular crossing of the Vosges mountains.

2DB was in action to the very end of the war, taking part in the fighting to eradicate the Colmar Pocket, the clearing of German forces from the Atlantic coast, and finally a dash across southern Germany to Berchtesgaden, Hitler's Bavarian 'Eagle's Nest', which the division captured in the last days of the conflict.

The boldness and flexibility of 2DB's tactics, coupled with its inspired practice of the art of mobile warfare, made it the outstanding French fighting formation of World War II.

Following the liberation of Paris in 1944, the men of the 2nd Armoured Division were determined to be the first Allied troops into Strasbourg

IN MID-NOVEMBER 1944, the French 2nd Armoured Division (2e Division Blindée – 2DB), led by the charismatic General Philippe Leclerc, fought its way grimly into the western foothills of the Vosges mountains in eastern France. A bitter winter was already drawing in. It was getting colder and incessant rain beat down from a low grey ceiling of cloud. Day was barely distinguishable from night and the cheerless weather was matched by the progress of the war. It had ground down to a slow painful advance in the face of stiff German resistance after the brief euphoria of late summer, when it had seemed that the long-awaited victory was almost in sight.

The men of 2DB had felt that euphoria to the full. As the only French division in the Allied forces driving down from Normandy, they received the full adulation of the newly liberated population, making their advance a strange mixture of triumphal progress and bloody warfare. To those men who, like General Leclerc, had joined the Free French at the darkest hour of France's defeat and dishonour four years before, this heroic return was a seemingly impossible dream fulfilled. When the division's tanks liberated Paris on 25 August, the joyous reaction was almost too overwhelming. Major-General Wade H. Haislip, the commander of the US XV Corps to which 2DB was attached, received a letter from Leclerc in which he said he had 'almost lost control of his division and his men were running round getting drunk and going with women and if something didn't happen fast he might never get them out of Paris again'.

For Leclerc, the liberation of Paris had a special personal significance. On 1 March 1941, a force

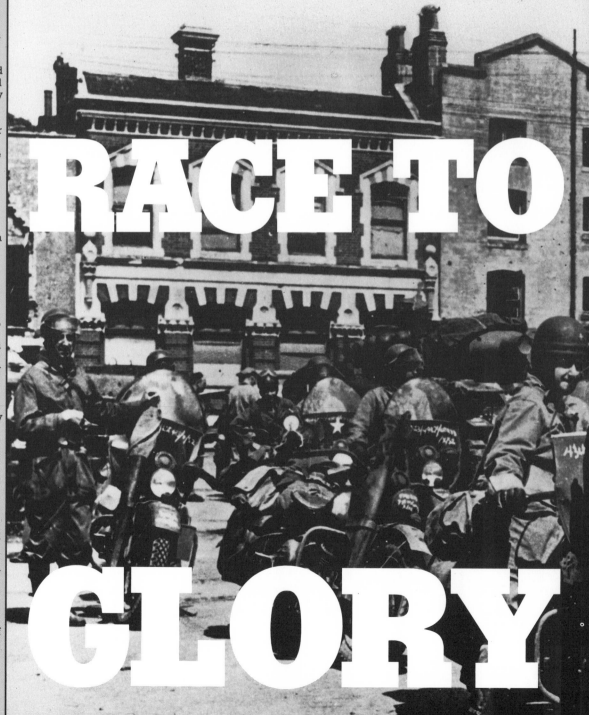

RACE TO GLORY

under his command had achieved the first Free French victory of the war, capturing the Italian fort of Kufra in southern Libya. As the flag of the cross of Lorraine was raised over the fort, Leclerc sent a telegram to Free French leader General Charles de Gaulle in which he pledged: 'We will not rest until the flag of France also flies over Paris and Strasbourg.' One half of this 'Oath of Kufra' had now been fulfilled – but could Leclerc complete the other half of his self-appointed mission?

Strasbourg had a special significance for all patriotic Frenchmen. It was the capital of Alsace, a province seized by Germany in 1871, won back by France in World War I and re-annexed by Hitler in 1940. By mid-November 1944, only the Vosges mountains lay between Leclerc's armoured division and the much-contested city.

But the Vosges were a formidable obstacle. Along the heights, the Germans had constructed a powerful defensive line, the Vogesenstellung. Wherever a pass cleft the steep forested slopes, there were systems of concrete fortifications and concentrations of anti-tank weapons that made an armoured thrust

Right: A brief rest for men of the Free French 2nd Armoured Division on the road to Paris. Top: French troops who have just landed in France express their joy at being home again as they grasp handfuls of their native soil. Above: Their commander, General Philippe Leclerc (on right) shares their pleasure as he steps ashore in Normandy shortly after the D-day landings. Leclerc's priorities, set out in his famous 'Oath of Kufra' of 1941, were the liberation of Paris and Strasbourg. Left: An M3 tank of the 2nd Division mops up German resistance in Paris.

impossible. It seemed that only the slow attrition of artillery bombardment and costly infantry assault could overcome these positions and clear the way for Leclerc's Shermans. But Leclerc was not interested in attrition. He favoured swift attack and belligerent mobility. He also wanted to get to Strasbourg before anyone else.

Leclerc's ADC, Captain Christian Girard, recalled later how the commander faced up to the task, scrutinising a map of the Vosges sector ahead of him:

'The map showed that there was only one gap through which it was possible to send an armoured division, and that was at Saverne. But Leclerc noticed the little lanes and tracks on the right and left of the gap. He had reconnaissance parties go out and from what they reported decided he would use them...He was determined to take Strasbourg completely by surprise and undamaged.'

On 13 November, XV Corps began to push forward into the Vosges as part of a general Allied advance towards the Rhine. To the south of 2DB's position was the rest of US Seventh Army, to which XV Corps was attached, and the First French Army. To the north lay Patton's Third Army. Facing them were the German First and Nineteenth Armies. By the 19th 2DB had advanced far enough into the foothills for Leclerc to activate his plan to outflank the Saverne Gap.

Leclerc knew he could rely on his subordinate officers to show the boldness and flair required

The operation would depend on splitting the division into a number of smaller formations that could function independently – 2DB was already organised to allow such flexible tactics. The division was subdivided into four self-sufficient groups, named after their commanders – Langlade, Dio, Guillebon and Remy – each with its own tanks, armoured cars, artillery, lorried infantry and tank destroyers. In turn, each of these groups was subdivided into smaller fighting units, again comprising all the elements of the division integrated and trained to work together. The commanders of groups and sub-groups had been encouraged to develop initiative and follow the best principles of mobile armoured warfare, to exploit their speed of manoeuvre to avoid frontal attacks on heavily defended enemy positions, maintain the momentum of an offensive at all costs and leave the job of clearing up pockets of resistance to the infantry. Leclerc knew he could rely on his subordinate officers to show the boldness and flair required for an operation whose success depended entirely on speed and surprise.

The plan was to outflank the German defences at the Saverne Gap both to the north and the south. In the northern sector, the Dio group would engage the enemy dug in at Phalsbourg, while a sub-group under Lieutenant-Colonel Rouvillois slipped around the German right flank. In the south, Lieutenant-Colonel Paul de Langlade's group would play the leading role, with a sub-group commanded by Major Jacques Massu taking the difficult mountain route, hopefully to arrive unannounced in the enemy rear.

It was Massu who led off in spectacular fashion on 20 November. The Germans were holding a defensive position on his line of advance at a spot called Saint-Michel, in the Sarre valley. On the morning of the 20th Massu infiltrated part of his force behind the enemy position and, threatened with encirclement, the Germans hastily formed an ill-organised column

and pulled back up into the mountains.

Massu immediately began his advance. The Shermans were soon rumbling up the narrow twisting mountain roads, working their way round hairpin after hairpin in a tortuous ascent. At a turning of the road, the rear of the retreating enemy column appeared above them, labouring up the same mountain side. Chiefly horsedrawn artillery, it was making very slow progress. Massu's tanks steadily gained ground on the Germans in a bizarre slow-motion pursuit. There was no way off the road. With a precipitous drop on one side and a steep slope on the other, the German artillery was doomed.

As the tanks finally caught up with the fleeing rearguard, most of the German troops not unnaturally surrendered. But the artillery still had to be disposed of to clear a way for the French up the narrow trail. With no time to waste, the lead tanks manoeuvred into position alongside the artillery

Right: Leclerc's men receive a warm welcome from French citizens as they drive towards Paris. Below: Shermans of the 2nd Division quell resistance as they roll through the southern suburbs of the capital. Left: The final surrender of General von Choltitz's HQ at L'Hotel Meurisse on 25 August 1944.

The original intention of the Allied commanders in August 1944 was to ignore Paris completely, pushing on to the east and leaving the city to be cleared in a later mopping-up operation. But Resistance fighters inside Paris and the French contingent in the Allied armies forced the generals to change their plans. By 21 August, an insurrection was under way in the city and the German occupying forces were reacting in brutal fashion. It was feared that if the fighting continued for much longer, the Resistance fighters would be massacred and much of the city destroyed.

On 21 August, as the Resistance pleaded for Allied help, General Leclerc sent a small force under Major de Guillebon towards Paris from his position at Argentan, although he was in fact under strict orders not to move. Leclerc's initiative had the full support of the Free French leader General de Gaulle, who wanted his men, not the communists of the Resistance, to take the credit for liberating Paris. Luckily for Leclerc, on 22 August the Allied commanders at last authorised the 2nd Armoured Division to take Paris. On the first day they advanced unopposed to Rambouillet, 30 miles from the city. Then they split into three columns for the drive to Paris. Finding routes around enemy defences wherever possible, Leclerc got his first contingent, under Captain Raymond Dronne, into Paris at dusk on 24 August. The rest of the division arrived the following day and after some sharp fighting in the city the garrison commander, General Dietrich von Choltitz, ignoring Hitler's orders to cause maximum destruction, surrendered on the afternoon of the 25th.

The celebrations that followed added up to one of the wildest parties the world has even seen.

pieces and pushed them, with their horses, off the road. As tank after tank thundered through, the roadside was lined with dead or crippled animals and twisted broken metal. The German prisoners were also left by the roadside, to be dealt with later. Massu had no time to lose. Despite the atrocious weather, his tanks reached Dabo, 20 miles into the Vosges, by nightfall.

Once Leclerc learnt of Massu's quick progress, he set out to exploit the advantage immediately. Massu was supported on his left by another sub-group, commanded by Lieutenant-Colonel Minjonnet, which was moving more directly towards the Saverne Gap to distract attention from Massu's encircling movement. But Leclerc felt that Massu must be reinforced and ordered the Guillebon group to move up to Dabo during the night, ready to continue the advance behind Massu's spearhead the following morning.

It was a wild night of violent rainfall, and progress

along narrow winding roads through the pitch-dark pine forests was a nightmare for the army drivers. The route was soon heavily congested and nippy jeeps, carrying liaison officers up and down the road, added to the danger of accidents. The official history of the US 250th Field Artillery Battalion, which was attached to 2DB, refers laconically to 'a night of misery when our vehicles were caught by darkness, bumper to bumper, on a narrow road in the dense wooded mountains'. A French tank commander gave a more dramatically expressive description:

'It was pouring with rain, had been for days, and we were soaked to the skin. It was pitch dark and some of us had headlights blazing. There were German soldiers covered with mud, slumped all along the sides of the road; there were guns that had been pushed into the water-filled ditches, dead cattle and horses. All manner of vehicles

Below: General Leclerc confers with his officers on the possible routes of the 2nd Division's push to Strasbourg. Leclerc had to contend not only with the opposing German troops but also with certain unsympathetic elements in the American high command. These included General Eisenhower, who did not want the French troops to embark on an unsupported advance to Strasbourg.

and weapons, shot down and to pieces by us as we rushed forward'.

By the following morning, against all the odds, the back-up force was in position behind Massu, who resumed his advance at first light.

Meanwhile, to the north of the Saverne Gap the Dio group had begun its thrust towards the German defences at Phalsbourg, bypassing the town of Sarrebourg and leaving it to the 44th US Infantry Division to clear up. As the main French force engaged the enemy head-on, the Rouvillois sub-group swung away to the left, making for La Petite-Pierre. As with Massu in the south, Rouvillois encountered only scattered German resistance. The enemy was totally unprepared for these fast flanking movements by small mobile forces along roads previously considered unsuitable for tanks. None of the German commanders realised what was happening or understood the threat to the Vosges defensive line.

By 22 November both Massu and Rouvillois were out of the mountains and on to the broad Alsatian plain. Swinging round from north and south, they struck towards Saverne. Meanwhile, Minjonnet pushed along the eastern slopes of the Vosges to the Saverne Gap, in the mountains above the town itself. As if synchronised, at 1415 hours the forces of Massu and Rouvillois converged on Saverne, powering into the main square almost unopposed. Surprise was complete. General Bruhn, the German Regional Commander, was captured in his headquarters with-

out even having time to radio details of the disaster to Strasbourg. At the gap, Minjonnet caused havoc, coming up behind the dreaded 88s and taking them out before their crews had time to turn and face the unexpected line of attack. The concrete fortifications were captured intact.

To the Germans at Strasbourg, all these events were completely hidden in the fog of war. Normal military traffic continued to trundle across the plain up to Saverne, enjoying the cloudy weather that gave immunity from air attack. For the French, the opportunity was too good to miss, as an officer later described:

'We put our tanks in position hidden each side of a road through a village and waited for them. They had no idea we had got through and had cut the road and it was an absolute massacre. We just let them come as close as possible and then shot them to bits – there were all sorts, lorried infantry,

Below: A French gunnery team in action with an M7 Priest self-propelled 105mm gun. The men of the 2nd Division soon proved their mastery of American equipment. They were supplied with various combat vehicles, including the Sherman M4 medium tank and the Stuart M3 light tank.

guns, trucks, staff cars, even the German chief of railways for the region, who was in a camouflaged Citroën. With guns and machine guns we poured fire into them until the roads were absolutely littered with burning vehicles.'

By the evening of 22 November, Leclerc had moved his headquarters forward to Saverne, not only so that he could get closer to the action, but in order to escape from higher command. As far as General Patch, commander of the US Seventh Army, was concerned, Leclerc had authorisation to seize the Saverne Gap, but he was to go no further. Strasbourg was definitely out of bounds. Fortunately for Leclerc, he had an excellent relationship with his immediate superior, General Haislip, who had made it clear unofficially that he would not try to stop the French pressing on to Strasbourg and the Rhine, only warning Leclerc to watch out for a counter-attack from the flanks. Nevertheless, late on the 23rd, Haislip received a direct order from no less a person than the Supreme Commander, General Dwight D. Eisenhower, to hold Leclerc back from any further

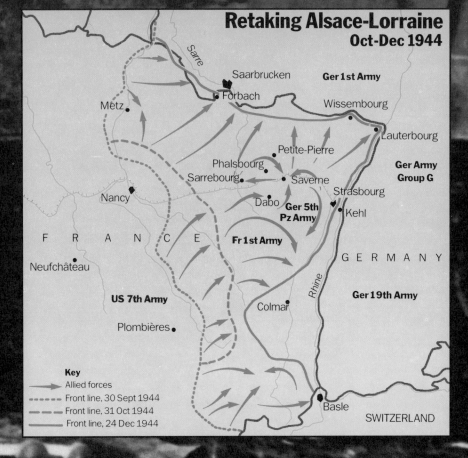

Retaking Alsace-Lorraine
Oct-Dec 1944

Saarbrucken
Forbach
Metz
Wissembourg
Lauterbourg
Petite-Pierre
Phalsbourg
Sarrebourg
Saverne
Strasbourg
Nancy
Dabo
Kehl
Ger 1st Army
Ger Army Group G
Ger 5th Pz Army
Fr 1st Army
F R A N C E
G E R M A N Y
Neufchâteau
US 7th Army
Ger 19th Army
Colmar
Rhine
Plombières
Basle
SWITZERLAND

Key
— Allied forces
- - - Front line, 30 Sept 1944
– – – Front line, 31 Oct 1944
—— Front line, 24 Dec 1944

advance. Throughout the night, US officers up to the rank of general strove to contact the French headquarters. But they were driven by French liaison officers to every point of the compass – except where they knew Leclerc actually was. The French officers considered themselves answerable only to Leclerc, and his orders were that nothing should stop the drive on Strasbourg the following day.

At 0715 hours on 23 November the first tanks coughed, roared into life and swung into position for the advance across the Alsatian plain. Twenty-five miles away lay Strasbourg, defended by a ring of forts but quite unprepared for the lightning blow that was about to fall. The instructions were, as usual, to bypass all enemy strongpoints that could not easily be overcome and to enter the city with all possible speed, pressing on as far as the Kehl bridge over the Rhine, a few miles to the east. The force was to advance in five columns – led by Massu, Rouvillois, Putz, Cantarel and Debray – one for each of the possible routes to Strasbourg. It would be a race to see who got there first, with smaller units within each column operating virtually independently, on the initiative of their officers. The only rule was that the momentum of the advance must never falter.

An American, Lieutenant Tony Triumpho of the 250th Field Artillery noted:

'We three Americans, the only ones to go in that morning, went roaring across the plain in our jeep along with four or five light tanks and a few half-tracks of infantry, altogether about 70 men. We passed working parties and groups of German troops across the plain and they just stood open-mouthed.'

French tanks came rumbling over the cobblestones, unleashing machine-gun fire at anyone in uniform

The first French group to enter the city, led by Rouvillois, achieved total surprise. It erupted bizarrely into the middle of the normal daily life of wartime Strasbourg. German officers were out window-shopping with their wives or sitting in cafés when the French tanks came rumbling over the cobblestones, unleashing bursts of machine-gun fire at anyone in uniform. German bureaucrats standing at tram-stops with briefcases under their arms were confronted by battle-stained French soldiers who, according to one eyewitness, 'looked completely out of place'. No quarter was given as Rouvillois' men thundered through the city.

Obeying instructions, Rouvillois did not stop in the city but drove on towards the Kehl bridge, and it was 600yds short of this objective that stiffening enemy resistance finally halted his onward rush. Behind him, other French units were arriving in Strasbourg. Massu's group had been held up by the Germans at Fort Foch before making a detour to follow Rouvillois' route into the city. The Debray column had taken Fort Joffre after a stiff engagement and moved on to capture Neuhof aerodrome intact. Further to the south, the Putz group took out Fort Kléber, while the

Below: Men and armour of the 2nd Division move through the mist across the Alsatian plain towards Strasbourg. Since the Franco-Prussian War of 1870-1, possession of the city had passed three times between the French and the Germans. After the annexation by the Germans in 1940, many of the streets were renamed by the Nazis. Above: Two members of the 2nd Division fix the sign for 'Adolf Hitler Strasse' to their Sherman tank as a trophy after retaking Strasbourg for France.

Cantarel column was held up at Fort Pétain before finding another road into Strasbourg.

Leclerc himself was soon in the city, but it was too early for celebrations. The German commander in Strasbourg, General von Vaterrodt, had narrowly escaped capture – cups of coffee in his headquarters were still hot when the French troops burst in. He had taken refuge in Fort Ney, and from this and the other unsubdued forts around the city artillery began a somewhat desultory bombardment. 2DB was now seriously vulnerable to counter-attack, should the Germans realise how small a force it was and how far in advance of the rest of the US Seventh Army it was operating. Leclerc urgently requested American troops to be sent up in support, while his men set about reducing the recalcitrant forts. On 24 November, the situation was finally mastered. Fort Ney surrendered and von Vaterrodt was taken prisoner, while across the plain appeared the slouching figures of GIs from the 3rd US Infantry Division, arriving to reinforce the Allied hold on Strasbourg.

The following day, 25 November, Leclerc could at last order a victory parade in the central Place Kléber, despite the presence of Messerschmitts in the sky overhead. It was an emotional moment, the fulfilment of the 'Oath of Kufra' and a symbolic restoration of French honour after so much ignominy and shame. It was also the fitting climax to a truly exceptional military exploit, described by General Haislip as 'the most brilliant operation of the entire war'. Certainly, it would be hard to think of a more daring use of armour or a better exploitation of speed and surprise. The officers and men of 2DB had earned the right to be considered France's foremost elite formation of World War II.

THE AUTHOR R. G. Grant graduated in Modern History from Trinity College, Oxford. He has written extensively on the military campaigns of the 20th century.

In February 1944, encircled by troops of the Red Army, the men of the 5th SS-Panzer Division 'Wiking' made an all-or-nothing break-out from the Cherkassy Pocket

Left: Into action. A panzergrenadier, armed with an MG 34 machine gun, charges forward during a battle on the Eastern Front. The Wiking Division saw action on this front from 1941 to 1945 and maintained a consistently high combat reputation.

SS WIKING

SS-PANZER DIVISION 'WIKING'

Established in December 1940, the 5th SS-Panzer Division 'Wiking' (whose insignia and cuff band are shown above) comprised an artillery regiment and the SS regiments 'Norland', recruited from Danes and Norwegians, 'Westland', recruited from the Dutch and Flemings, and 'Germania', recruited from Germans. A Finnish volunteer battalion was added to the division in February 1941, but in 1943 it was replaced by an Estonian battalion.

In June 1941 the Wiking Division was attached to Army Group South for the invasion of Russia, and it served in the Ukraine and the Caucasus in 1942-43. In November 1942 it was converted into a panzer-grenadier division, and in October 1943 into a panzer division. During the winter of 1943-44 the Wiking Division fought in the defensive battles along the Dniepr and elements survived the battle for the Cherkassy Pocket. In March 1944 the remnants were sent to Poland and, after receiving reinforcements and being refitted, Wiking fought around Warsaw as part of IV SS-Panzer Corps.

In December 1944 the Wiking and 3rd SS-Panzer 'Totenkopf' Divisions were hastily transferred to Hungary in an attempt to relieve Budapest. Despite some desperate fighting in January 1945, Wiking was unable to break through to the city. It was badly mauled in the Soviet offensives to the west of Budapest in February 1945 and was forced to retreat into Czechoslovakia, where it surrendered on 8 May.

The Ukrainian and Belorussian fronts
Dec 1943 – April 1944

On 24 December 1943, the Red Army launched a new offensive on the 1st Ukrainian Front, followed during January by attacks on the fronts further south. The German 1st Panzer Army was trapped in a pocket near Korsun-Shevchenkovskiy. Supplied from the air, the isolated German divisions fought fiercely, and finally on 16 February began a breakout.

Army Group Centre

Brest-Litovsk

Lublin

POLAND

Army Group North Ukraine

2nd Belorussian Front

Chernigov

Desna

1st Ukrainian Front

Army Group South

Kiev

SOVIET UNION

Moshny

Korsun-Shevchenkovskiy

Dniepr

Cherkassy

Vinnitsa

Lysyanka

Gorodishche

2nd Ukrainian Front

Kamenets Podolsky

Kirovgrad

Dnepropetrovsk

Carpathian Mts

Chernovtsy

3rd Ukrainian Front

HUNGARY

Dniestr

Krivoy Rog

Army Group A

4th Ukrainian Front

Jassy

Kishinev

Odessa

Army Group South Ukraine

Sea of Azov

Danube

BLACK SEA

CRIMEA

Key
- Soviet forces
- German forces
- German pockets
- Front line, 23 December 1943
- Front line, 24 January 1944
- Front line, 4 March
- Front line, 21 March
- Front line, April
- Russo-Polish border, 1939
- Russo-German border, 1940

Right: A Wiking panzergrenadier surveys the aftermath of a tank engagement from his dug-out in the shadow of a knocked-out Soviet T-34. Above left: 28 January 1944. Encircled members of the Wiking Division with a self-propelled gun. Above right: A village burns during the bitter fighting for the Cherkassy Pocket.

FOLLOWING A MASSIVE artillery bombardment at dawn on 24 January 1944, the Soviet 2nd Ukrainian Front (a front is the equivalent of an army group), commanded by General Koniev, attacked the vulnerable German salient at Korsun-Schevchenkovskiy along the Dniepr river. On 26 January General Vatutin's 1st Ukrainian Front extended the offensive. Holding the southeastern sector of the German front was the 5th SS-Panzer Division 'Wiking', consisting of two panzer grenadier regiments and a panzer regiment, and the SS-Sturmbrigade 'Wallonien', which was serving alongside the division. SS units were extended along the Dniepr and its tributaries, and from their entrenched positions they had been able to observe Soviet preparations for the offensive. Propeller-driven sledges had moved up, skimming rapidly over the snow, bringing the Red Army artillery and mortars, which immediately had been made ready for action.

Although the joint might of the Wiking Division and the Wallonien Brigade constituted a formidable force on paper, in reality the units were weak on tanks and manpower. Wiking was still being reorganised from a panzer grenadier division into a panzer division. Furthermore, the divisional sector was so over-extended that there were only 20 men to each kilometre. The Soviet offensive broke through the German positions to the northeast and southeast of the Wiking Division, and by 28 January a total of 56,000 men, including four German infantry divisions, two corps headquarters, assorted army troops and the Wiking Division, had been encircled. This pocket was centred around Korsun-Shevchenkovskiy, but the Germans were to refer to it as the 'Cherkassy Pocket', named after a small town to the east which straddled the Dniepr. At the outset, the pocket was 40km wide and 30km deep.

In their trenches and dug-outs, the SS soldiers clung on in stinking mud and water

In many tactical respects the Cherkassy Pocket was a miniature Stalingrad, with the Soviets launching overwhelming attacks on either flank of an over-extended German salient. Having surrounded a sizeable German force, the Soviets repeated their Stalingrad tactic of surrounding the pocket with an inner encirclement of troops, while an outer encirclement prepared to stop German attempts to relieve the pocket. To smash into the Cherkassy Pocket, General Koniev deployed 13 rifle divisions and three cavalry divisions, supported by 2000 guns and 138 tanks. The first attacks were made south of Korsun to clear German units from the area and to 'thicken' the belt between the pocket and the German panzers moving up from the southwest.

The Wiking Division was deployed to the east of Korsun, with divisional headquarters based in the village of Gorodishche. Covering the eastern sector of the encirclement, the division escaped some of the heaviest blows of the initial Soviet attempts to crush the pocket. Nevertheless, for the ordinary SS soldier, conditions were far from easy. Although the area was dotted with small villages and areas of woodland, the bulk of the land was flat and marshy, divided up by streams and tributaries of the Dniepr. After the winter freeze, the thaw had arrived and the whole area had become one vast lake of mud. In their trenches and dug-outs, the SS soldiers clung on in stinking mud and water, and the few roads became impassable as their surfaces were broken up by the passage of vehicles and then washed away by the incessant rain.

Attempts to supply the Cherkassy Pocket by air were doomed to failure. Soviet fighters shot down many of the lumbering German transport aircraft, and the mud and rain destroyed the landing zones.

Many vehicles and supplies were destroyed by Soviet air attacks and artillery fire, and the Luftwaffe's inability to fly in more material meant that within a few days the Wiking Division was short of ammunition and petrol. The Soviets also attempted to destroy the morale of the encircled German troops by forcing comparisons of their position with that of the Germans encircled at Stalingrad. The Soviets dropped propaganda leaflets from the air, promising those Germans who surrendered safe conduct and good conditions. German officers and soldiers, who had been captured earlier in the war, were brought up to the front line to try and encourage desertion. Opposite the Wallonien Brigade's positions, the Soviets placed a powerful transmitter which, according to the military historian Leon Degrelle:

'peddled propaganda every day in honeyed French. A speaker with a Parisian accent charitably informed us of our situation. Then he tried to seduce us, vaunting the marvels of friend Stalin's regime and inviting us to approach the Russian lines holding a white handkerchief in our hands, like sentimental aunties.'

Such Soviet propaganda had little impact on the SS troops, partly because of their discipline, but also because they knew that the Soviets regarded them with particular hatred and would mark them out for special treatment.

As the Soviets began to launch concentric attacks against the pocket, which they combined with continuous artillery and air bombardments, it became increasingly difficult for the commander of the Wiking Division, SS-Obergruppenführer (General) Gille and his staff to control and co-ordinate the various divisional sub-units. Their problems were further exacerbated when the pocket started to contract and the division began to withdraw southwest of Korsun to concentrate for the breakout towards the advancing III Panzer Corps at Lysyanka. Gille was

courtyard of every *isba* hand-to-hand fighting raged amidst the quagmires and the clammy slopes, in the blinding light of millions of sparks from the blazing hovels. We had more than 50 trucks at Moshny, numerous pieces of artillery, anti-tank weapons, anti-aircraft guns, tractors, field kitchens, communications equipment, and the offices of several companies... Drivers, cooks, paymasters, telephone operators, everyone was defending his weapon, his equipment, his skin.'

While the Wiking Division fought a desperate rearguard action to the southeast of the Cherkassy Pocket, the divisional staff were attempting to concentrate the bulk of the division for a retreat to the western end of the encircled area. On 3 February the decision was made to withdraw two-thirds of the troops from combat in order to save all the divisional vehicles and equipment. The remaining troops were to fight a desperate rearguard battle:

'Already the road from Gorodische to Korsun, our last chance to break out, was jammed by an incredible column. Thousands of trucks, spread over 20km, followed three front vehicles and skated in the black frogholes of the road, which

Above and above right: In appalling weather, troops and vehicles of the Wiking Division begin the break-out from the Cherkassy Pocket. Although the snow storms made the going hard for the men, the closing in of the weather forced a halt to the relentless fury of Soviet air attacks. Above, far right: Troops of the Wiking Division and a panzer make a brief halt on the road to Korsun. Right: Tired and unshaven, a panzergrenadier forces a smile for the camera. Bottom: SS-Gruppenführer Steiner, Gille's predecessor at the helm of the Wiking Division. Steiner remained in command until May 1943. He later commanded III SS-Panzer Corps. Main picture: The grim slog across the frozen wastes pushed the German troops to the limits of their endurance.

forced to rely on messengers and unreliable field telephones to keep in touch with his scattered units, which were often little more than a weak company of infantry attached to two or three tanks. During the night of 1/2 February, the Wallonien Brigade withdrew from the village of Losovok to concentrate on Moshny and then follow the Wiking Division in a general withdrawal to the west.

The Soviets harried the retreat, and launched a major attack against the SS troops as Moshny. As scattered companies of the Wallonien Brigade reached Moshny they were amazed to discover a fierce battle raging in and around the village:

'When we reached the village hundreds of men were battling with a terrible fury around our pieces of artillery, which were shooting point-blank at the assailants. On every street, in the

had become a prodigious cloaca. The most powerful artillery tractors struggled painfully to open a passage. This enormous mass of vehicles was an incomparable target for planes. The Soviet machines, like strident swarms of wasps, would circle over the valley and dive down in squadrons.'

In the end, the only way the vehicles could be moved was along the course of a railway line. By dawn on 5 February the Wiking Division had occupied a fortified line from Storoselye to Derenkovez, one which had been prepared in January. The line of defensive positions had been well chosen. It extended from southeast to northwest, atop high crests which overlooked the valley, the bogs, and the canal from Derenkovez to Olshana. The trench system zigzagged, with numerous fire emplacements, for over 30km.

But the SS were weak and exhausted, and this line of defence was the last barrier in the east to cover the general withdrawal towards Korsun: 'Our men were dispersed in tiny groups, each isolated from the others. They were exhausted by the recent battles, by the nights of huddling together, by the icy mists, by the tortuous slogging in pitch-like mud. They had no shelter. Filthy, their faces drawn and worried, they watched the plain where the Soviet advance guard was bustling about.' The Wiking Division delayed the Soviet advance for the next two days, before continuing to withdraw on Korsun along the road from Derenkovez. Obergruppenführer Gille attempted to use his battered units to hold

Herbert Otto Gille was born on 8 March 1897 at Gandersheim. He was commissioned as an officer before 1914 in the 2nd Badischen Feldartillerie and he served as an artillery officer throughout World War I.

He joined the SS-Verfügungstruppe in 1934, and was to serve with the Waffen-SS in Poland in 1939, and France in 1940. In December 1940 he was given command of the 'Wiking' Division's artillery regiment, and he served with great distinction on the Eastern Front. On 8 October 1942 he was awarded the Knight's Cross for personal bravery, and later episodes in his career were to earn him the Oak Leaves, Swords and Diamonds to that award.

In May 1943 he was promoted to SS-Brigadeführer and given command of the SS-Panzer Division Wiking. Gille commanded the division during the great defensive battles of Kharkov, Kovel and Cherkassy in 1943 and 1944, and in August 1944, promoted to command IV SS-Panzer Corps, he fought in some of the bitter battles in Hungary and Austria. Gille was a tough officer with a common touch who was much admired by his soldiers. As commander of the Wiking Division he was able to inspire Danes, Flemings, Walloons and Germans. As a corps commander he was less successful, having been promoted above his ability. In retirement after the war he ran a small bookshop and founded the veterans' magazine 'Wiking-Ruf' (Wiking-Call). He died in 1966 in Stemmen, near Hannover.

vital defensive positions which would enable the withdrawal to continue in an orderly fashion. A Belgian SS officer, Leon Degrelle, witnessed Gille's personal intervention during the fighting on 12 February outside Korsun:

'At 11 o'clock in the morning, while the commander and I were receiving orders at Division, we saw General Gille turn red while on his telephone. He had received catastrophic news. Arbuzinka, which was supposed to serve as a barrier until the next day, had just fallen into the hands of the Soviets. They were advancing at top speed against Korsun itself. The General grabbed his thick baton, jumped into a Volkswagen, and hurried in the direction of Arbuzinka. It was difficult to resist the anger of General Gille. The village was retaken and the barrier re-established.'

On 13 February the Wiking Division withdrew through a burning Korsun and crossed the lake to the southeast on a wooden bridge nearly a kilometre long. Hundreds of vehicles were successfully evacuated over this one single and fragile bridge built by the divisional engineers. But on the far side of the lake, in freezing cold, more and more vehicles broke down in the mud, blocking the way.

Stemmermann was given a directive to ready his forces for an all-or-nothing break-out

By 15 February the Cherkassy Pocket had been reduced to an area of some 60 square kilometres, into which were crammed some 45,000 men. But only about one-third were combat troops, the remainder being personnel of the auxiliary services. The Wiking Division was one of the few German formations in the area still maintaining some degree of cohesion and discipline. It was concentrated around the village of Sanderovka, and there Obergruppenführer Gille attempted to make order out of chaos:

'He kept receiving a continual stream of pessimistic messages from units fighting near ours. Evidently, as is the custom in the army, every one blamed his neighbour for the reverses of his own sector.'

In fact, from about 10 February, General Stemmermann, the overall commander of all the German forces in the Cherkassy Pocket, had been attempting to organise his best units, including the Wiking Division, for a breakout from the area known as Khil'ki-Komarovka southwest towards the bogged-down III Panzer Corps. But III Panzer Corps could not reach the pocket, so Stemmermann was given a directive to ready his forces for an all-or-nothing break-out. Stemmermann's forces had to reach the village of Dzhurzhentsy or Hill 239 under their own power. It was agreed that the attempted break-out would start at 2300 hours on 16 February.

Between 10 and 16 February wet snow had blanketed the mud and piled up into drifts three feet high in gullies and low spots. To the troops in the pocket, the snow at least brought some respite from the air attacks, and it afforded concealment in an area which had now shrunk to a width of about eight kilometres. On the line of exit from the pocket, Stemmermann positioned the 112th Infantry Division and remnants of two other divisions in the north in Khil'ki; the 72nd Infantry Division was placed in the centre; and the Wiking Division in the south. Each division had a regiment with artillery in the vanguard and two roughly regiment-sized units echeloned behind it. The larger second wave of German forces was to

iment was not so fortunate. Passing east of Dzhurzhentsy, it was enfiladed with fire from the village and was forced to turn south; in doing so it then had to cross the Gniloy Tikich river to reach Lysyanka. The SS were forced to abandon most of their equipment, including their rifles, in a desperate attempt to cross the river. Even without their burdens, hundreds drowned in the icy current. As the second wave began to follow the assault regiments, all sense of order broke down. The Soviets then began to pour a mass of machine-gun, mortar and artillery fire into the shrinking pocket. All the vehicles attempting to move forward created a massive traffic jam, and as units intermingled no-one thought of anything except to keep under cover and reach safety. Since the fire from the direction of Dzhurzhentsy and Hill 239 was the heaviest, except for occasional groups which broke through to northern Lysyanka, almost the entire movement veered south to the bend of the Gniloy Tikich. The Wiking Division did its best to cover this movement, and isolated tanks and sections of infantry gallantly blocked the pursuing Soviet troops. But by midday the division had effectively disintegrated, and weapons and equipment were abandoned as hundreds of SS men attempted to swim across the 50ft-wide river.

follow the assault force after a 10-minute interval. Stemmermann had ordered all vehicles destroyed except tanks, self-propelled assault guns, tracked vehicles, and enough horse-drawn wagons to carry men wounded during the break-out.

The attack began on time, an hour before midnight on 16 February. Jumping off in silence and using only bayonets and knives, the three attacking regiments cut through the Soviet outpost line and main screening line before the Russians knew what was happening. The two infantry regiments advanced quickly and with surprisingly few losses, pushing through the Soviet positions between Dzhurzhentsy and Hill 239. But the Wiking Division's panzergrenadier reg-

Top: Weary from their ordeal, survivors from the Wiking Division relax after the break-out. Below: End of the line. A knocked out half-track, bearing the Wiking insignia, lies abandoned in the streets after the struggle for Berlin, which fell on 2 May 1945.

Isolated tanks and sections of infantry gallantly blocked the pursuing Soviet troops

In all, some 30,000 troops escaped from the Cherkassy Pocket, including about 6000 from the Wiking Division. Adolf Hitler was pleased and relieved to have got that many out, but the psychological state of the survivors shocked senior officers. Fear of the Soviets and the possibility of capture had reduced many of the survivors to nervous wrecks. The Wiking Division had lost all its weapons and equipment, and over half its personnel. As the Soviets continued to advance, some 4000 of the divisional survivors were formed into a Kampfgruppe (battle group) and sent back into the line.

The SS-Panzer Division Wiking and the SS-Sturmbrigade Wallonien played a fundamentally important role in the successful German defence of the Cherkassy Pocket and the subsequent break-out. Although there can be no doubt that the Soviet envelopment of the German forces in this pocket and the heavy losses in men, weapons and equipment were major tactical defeats for the Germans, without the presence of the Wiking Division the cost would have been far higher. The panzers of that division were the only armour available to the Germans within the pocket, and the training and fighting spirit of the division were excellent. SS-Obergruppenführer Gille commanded his division effectively and inspired his troops under very difficult circumstances. The appalling weather conditions, unfavourable terrain, the ferocity of Soviet attacks and the lack of food and sleep all produced a terrible strain on the ordinary SS soldier, and yet the remnants of the Wiking Division who escaped from the Cherkassy Pocket emerged with an enhanced fighting reputation.

THE AUTHOR Keith Simpson is senior lecturer in War Studies and International Affairs at Sandhurst. He has a special interest in modern warfare and is the author of *The History of the German Army*.

HOLDING THE LINE

Kharkov, 1943: after the disaster of Stalingrad, the men of the Leibstandarte SS Adolf Hitler had to conduct a desperate defence to prevent the complete collapse of the German armies on the Eastern Front. As part of I SS Panzer Corps, they fought a nightmare series of battles against the Red Army

IN JANUARY 1943, the surrender of the German Sixth Army at Stalingrad was the centrepiece of a massive defeat for the German armies in the south of the Soviet Union. The overextended formations of the Wehrmacht were now terribly vulnerable to the Red Army, which was mounting a series of offensives that threatened to sweep away the shattered remnants of the Army Groups that had marched so confidently eastwards the previous summer. Generalfeldmarschall (Field Marshal) Erich von Manstein, who had been put in charge of the southern armies, desperately tried to persuade Hitler to carry out a strategic retreat, to shorten the line. The Führer refused; but although he was not prepared to see sense strategically, he did send Manstein a crack formation with which to fight this desperate battle for survival – I SS Panzer Corps.

First SS Panzer Corps consisted of 1st SS Panzergrenadier Division 'Leibstandarte SS Adolf Hitler', 2nd SS Panzergrenadier Division 'Das Reich' and 3rd SS Panzergrenadier Division 'Totenkopf'. The Leibstandarte, along with the two other Waffen SS divisions, had spent the previous five months in France, resting and receiving reinforcements of personnel and new weapons. In November 1942 the Leibstandarte had raised a panzer company, later enlarged to a battalion, which consisted of the new Mark VI 'Tiger' heavy battle tanks under the command of SS Sturmbannführer (Major) Joachim Peiper. This panzer battalion was to become the core of the Leibstandarte, and with one other battalion of medium Mark IV tanks, two panzer grenadier regiments and mobile anti-tank and assault gun detachments, the Leibstandarte had grown into a formidable fighting machine of some 15,000 soldiers.

The divisional commander of the Leibstandarte was one of Hitler's original Nazi Party members, SS Obergruppenführer (General) Josef 'Sepp' Dietrich. Under Dietrich the division had fought with determination and ruthlessness on the Eastern Front in 1941-42 and had suffered heavy casualties, but the surviving officers, NCOs and other ranks were hardened and experienced SS soldiers, well able to inculcate new recruits with the fighting ethos of the Leibstandarte.

Temperatures were as low as 20 degrees below zero and snowstorms reduced visibility to a few metres

With the Leibstandarte deployed along the Donets to the east of Kharkov, Hitler ordered I SS Panzer Corps to make a vigorous counter-attack to the southeast against a Soviet breakthrough at the end of January 1943. However, the confused and perilous situation around Kharkov meant that the Leibstandarte was deployed piecemeal in a series of local battles while streams of retreating German, Italian and Hungarian units fled westwards. The Leibstandarte held a bridgehead at Chuguyev with a divisional front in excess of 100km. Dietrich was forced to commit his forces in small detachments to cover

Top: During Hitler's invasion of Poland in 1939 the Leibstandarte SS Adolf Hitler participated in some of the most bitterly contested house-to-house fighting of the war. Surrounded by debris brought down by air and artillery bombardments, a German detachment hacks its way into a town, using what scant cover it can find. Above right: A Waffen SS machine-gun troop armed with an MG34 creeps forward under heavy fire in southern Russia in 1941. Left: Kurt 'Panzer' Meyer, (on left) photographed in 1941, was one of Sepp Dietrich's cadre of elite commanders in the Leibstandarte. The ability of Meyer and his fellow officers to inspire a fanatical fighting spirit in their men turned the Leibstandarte into a devastating war machine.

the line and his soldiers were fighting under the most appalling weather conditions. Temperatures were sometimes as low as 20 degrees below zero and blinding snowstorms reduced visibility to a few metres.

Although the Leibstandarte successfully fought off a series of strong Soviet attacks during the first week of February, the army units in support were less firm, and on the right flank a gap of 60km appeared, a result of the failure of the 320th Infantry Division to maintain its positions. The Leibstandarte, along with Das Reich and Totenkopf, found itself involved in a series of attritional battles from which it was unable to extricate itself. There was a real danger that I SS Panzer Corps would be cut off and encircled.

Between 11 and 16 February, the Leibstandarte fought a series of separate battles, its panzers, panzer grenadiers and support units all deployed in 'ad hoc' formations that attempted to re-establish a continuous front line and to relieve other German units. Dietrich commanded a kampfgruppe (battle group) consisting of detachments from the Leibstandarte and Das Reich which successfully stopped the Soviet advance after launching a three-pronged counter-attack that captured the strategically significant town of Merefa. There was vicious hand-to-hand fighting in driving snow, with senior officers

JOSEF 'SEPP' DIETRICH

One of Hitler's inner circle of trusted Nazis, Sepp Dietrich was appointed commander of Hitler's Leibstandarte (Life Guard) in 1933 after having acted as Hitler's personal bodyguard for several years. After serving in the Bavarian Army from 1911 to 1918 and ending as a tank sergeant, he had worked variously as a butcher and strongarm man before attaching himself to Hitler. He was popular with his men for his undoubted toughness, courage and determination, but was no tactician. 'Decent but stupid,' was the verdict of Field Marshal von Rundstedt. However, Dietrich found young officers like Witt, Meyer, Wünsche and Peiper and trained them into excellent commanders, while his immediate superior in 1943, Paul Hausser, was an excellent tactician, able to compensate for Dietrich's shortcomings while utilising his strengths. Dietrich's campaign successes on both the Eastern and Western Fronts won him rapid promotion. When the Leibstandarte was formed into a division, he became its commander; in July 1943 he became commander of I SS Panzer Corps, then of the Sixth Panzer Army. He was awarded the Knight's Cross in July 1940 for his leadership of the Leibstandarte, with Oak Leaves added in 1941. In common with many SS commanders, Dietrich had a callous attitude towards human life. His force acted as firing-squads during Hitler's purge in 1934, while some 4000 Soviet prisoners were killed on his order at Taganrog in Russia in 1941, and he was tried and sentenced to life imprisonment for the massacre of 84 American prisoners at Malmédy on 17 December 1944, carried out by a battle group under Joachim Peiper that formed one of the units of Dietrich's Sixth Panzer Army.

such as SS Standartenführer (Colonel) Fritz Witt and SS Haupsturmführer (Captain) Hans Becker personally leading their men in combat-group assaults. For their leadership and bravery during these critical days Witt was awarded the oak leaves to his Knight's Cross and Becker the Knight's Cross.

Individual SS soldiers from the Leibstandarte continued to fight when cut off from their units

Soviet attacks continued to press down all along the Donets front, and the Leibstandarte was split up into a series of kampfgruppen which attempted to act as bulwarks against the Soviet tide. Individual elements of the Leibstandarte were combined with those of Das Reich and Totenkopf as the three divisions were decimated in the ferocious fighting. The SS soldiers of the Leibstandarte refused to retreat or surrender even when they became isolated by the enemy, disregarding their wounds, shortages of food and ammunition, and the bitter cold. Possessed by the spirit of Nazism, they were absolutely convinced of their racial and professional superiority to the Russians, and were indoctrinated with the belief that it was incompatible with the ethos of the SS to give in, whatever the circumstances. Even individual SS soldiers from the Leibstandarte continued to fight when cut off from their units by the enemy.

The Leibstandarte could also be relied upon to give strenuous support to other hard-pressed formations. On 13 February, a panzer grenadier battalion under Peiper launched a 40km attack into the Soviet line to relieve the encircled 320th Infantry Division. The battalion effectively protected the remnants of the division and succeeded in bringing them back to the German lines. Such élan and determination on the part of Peiper and his SS soldiers greatly enhanced the Leibstandarte's reputation in the eyes of the army. Again, in the bitter fighting around the village of Bereka, elements of the Leibstandarte's reconnaissance battalion were cut off by the Soviets

Above: Adolf Hitler, accompanied by Reichsführer SS Heinrich Himmler, the head of the SS, examines men of the fighting regiment that evolved out of his personal bodyguard to become the 'Leibstandarte SS Adolf Hitler' and the nucleus of the Waffen SS. Through the efforts of such SS divisional commanders as Sepp Dietrich and Paul Hausser to train a fighting force second to none, Himmler came close to realising his dream of recreating in the Waffen SS the medieval Order of Teutonic Knights.

The Kaiser's army of World War I was built on the principle of strong unit identity, with a hierarchy of regiments rising to a pinnacle in the Guards. When Hitler began to reconstruct the Wehrmacht he retained the fighting qualities of the Imperial period but divested the army of the influence of its conservative Prussian leadership. He thus established a link between his and earlier German armies with decorations such as the Knight's Cross.

Himmler's SS was an avowedly elite organisation. Himmler devised regalia that not only distinguished the various SS formations from each other but also deliberately set them apart from the Wehrmacht.

The ceremonial SS service dagger was worn by all commissioned and non-commissioned personnel after 1936 – its inscription translates as, 'Loyalty is my honour'. The collar patches show the SS runes and the three pips of an Untersturmführer (2nd Lieutenant). Each division of the Waffen SS bore distinguishing marks of the unit such as the cuffband worn by officers of the Leibstandarte SS Adolf Hitler. The standard of the Leibstandarte was carried at ceremonial parades.

Obergruppenführer, Leibstandarte Division, Soviet Union 1943.

Commander of Leibstandarte during the battle for Kharkov, Sepp Dietrich (far left) wears SS officers' service dress upon which is a full range of decorations and insignia. The Leibstandarte cuff-band is worn on the left arm, as is the Waffen SS eagle (distinguished from the army type sewn onto Dietrich's cap). On the flap of his left breast-pocket is the golden party badge while below it lies the Kampfwagen award (dating back to World War I) and a pilot-observer badge in gold with diamonds. The medal ribbon for the Winter Campaign in Russia 1941-42 is attached to a tunic button and directly above it is the Knight's Cross with oak leaves. On his right breast-pocket Dietrich wears the 'Blood Order' ribbon, and on his right arm is a long service chevron. Rank is displayed by the collar patches; the three oak leaves and two pips denoting an Obergruppenführer – equivalent to a full army general.

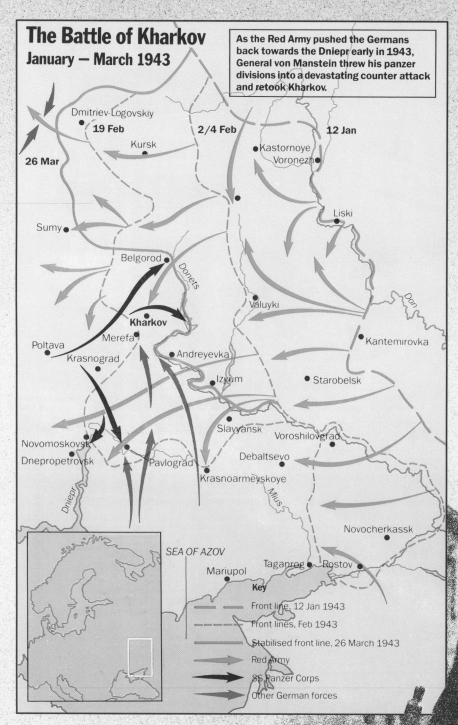

The Battle of Kharkov
January — March 1943

As the Red Army pushed the Germans back towards the Dniepr early in 1943, General von Manstein threw his panzer divisions into a devastating counter attack and retook Kharkov.

Dmitriev-Logovskiy
19 Feb
Kursk
2/4 Feb
12 Jan
Kastornoye
Voronezh
26 Mar
Liski
Sumy
Belgorod
Donets
Don
Valuyki
Kharkov
Merefa
Kantemirovka
Poltava
Andreyevka
Krasnograd
Izyum
Starobelsk
Slavyansk
Voroshilovgrad
Novomoskovsk
Debaltsevo
Dnepropetrovsk
Pavlograd
Krasnoarmeyskoye
Mius
Dniepr
Novocherkassk

SEA OF AZOV
Mariupol
Taganrog
Rostov

Key
Front line, 12 Jan 1943
Front lines, Feb 1943
Stabilised front line, 26 March 1943
Red Army
SS Panzer Corps
Other German forces

Right: A Mark IV tank of I SS Panzer Corps grinds down a shell-shattered street to finish off Soviet resistance in the centre of Kharkov. The faces of the panzer grenadiers and the tank commander clearly show the strain of battle-weary men about to undergo further conflict. Inset: Perhaps Germany's most brilliant tank commander, Joachim Peiper.

but were rescued by SS Sturmbannführer (Major) Max Wünsche leading the 1st Battalion of the Leib-standarte's panzer regiment which had burst through the Soviet lines. For this action, and for personally destroying over 50 Soviet guns, Wünsche was awarded the Knight's Cross

A frozen landscape strewn with destroyed villages, burnt-out tanks and vehicles and the unburied dead

The area over which the Leibstandarte was at war had begun to take on the appearance of a frozen lunar landscape strewn with destroyed villages, burnt-out tanks and vehicles, and the unburied dead lying frozen in grotesque forms. And yet from this war of attrition in nightmarish surroundings came one of the greatest military triumphs of the Waffen SS on the Eastern Front. Although Hitler had categor-ically ordered that Kharkov was to be held at all costs, Obergruppenführer (General) Paul Hausser, commander of I SS Panzer Corps, took the decision to evacuate the town in order to maintain the integrity of his depleted units. By 15 February the Soviets had recaptured Kharkov and I SS Panzer Corps had withdrawn southwest across the Uda river; the Leibstandarte was concentrated to the north of Krasnograd.

What the majority of the Leibstandarte soldiers did not know, however, was that the successful withdrawal from Kharkov had been the initial stage of a proposed counter-attack planned by Manstein, the commander of Army Group South. On 17 February, Hausser told Dietrich and his senior officers of the plan. The Soviets would be allowed to advance, only to be trapped by the Germans in a pocket. This would be the preliminary move of a major counter-offensive. First SS Panzer Corps, along with XLVIII Panzer Corps, made up Manstein's Fourth Panzer Army which was to play an important part in the encirclement plan. On 22 February, the Leibstandarte attacked northeast from Pavlograd towards Lozovaya where it linked up with elements of Army Group Centre moving in from the northwest, encircling a Soviet armoured corps under Popov. Although some Soviet units were able to break out of the

German encirclement, the bulk of the corps was totally destroyed by a massive, concentrated barrage from artillery, tanks, infantry and aircraft. SS soldiers from the Leibstandarte regarded it as a kind of 'duck shoot', with Soviet soldiers fleeing in desperation.

By 6 March the Germans had won a substantial victory, having encircled and destroyed a number of major Soviet formations to the south of Kharkov. For the Leibstandarte, these actions made up for the previous weeks of attritional defensive fighting. Eager to drive home their advantage, the panzer battalions of Mark IV and Mark VI Tiger tanks and the panzer grenadiers in their armoured personnel carriers cruised forward, firing on the move, destroying disabled Soviet tanks and shooting down mobs of running Soviet soldiers.

By 9 March, I SS Panzer Corps was deployed to the north and west of Kharkov. A sudden thaw made movement difficult, with thick mud clinging to the

STALINGRAD AND AFTER

On 22 June 1941, Hitler had launched Operation Barbarossa, the invasion of the Soviet Union, to which he committed three million men and 3000 tanks. In spite of enormous successes, the German Wehrmacht failed in its aims of destroying the Red Army and taking the Soviet capital, Moscow, and was itself almost destroyed by a Soviet counter-attack in the winter of 1941-42. In the summer of 1942, Hitler launched a further series of offensives, concentrated in the south. A drive east towards the city of Stalingrad and a move south into the Caucasus brought great initial gains in territory, but the German armies were now hopelessly overextended. Red Army counter-attacks cut off the German Sixth Army that had reached Stalingrad, and Hitler's refusal to countenance a retreat doomed the soldiers of this formation to defeat. By the beginning of 1943, with Stalingrad about to fall, Erich von Manstein, in command of the southern group of armies, was fighting a desperate series of battles against mounting Soviet offensives. All the German forces in the south risked being swamped. This was no ordinary battle, with fixed front lines, but a fluid struggle over a flat landscape, with the mobility and hitting power of armoured formations holding the key to victory. The distances were vast, and the cold of the Russian winter affected both men and machines. It was into this struggle for survival that I SS Panzer Corps was thrown, around the key city of Kharkov.

MG42 GPMG

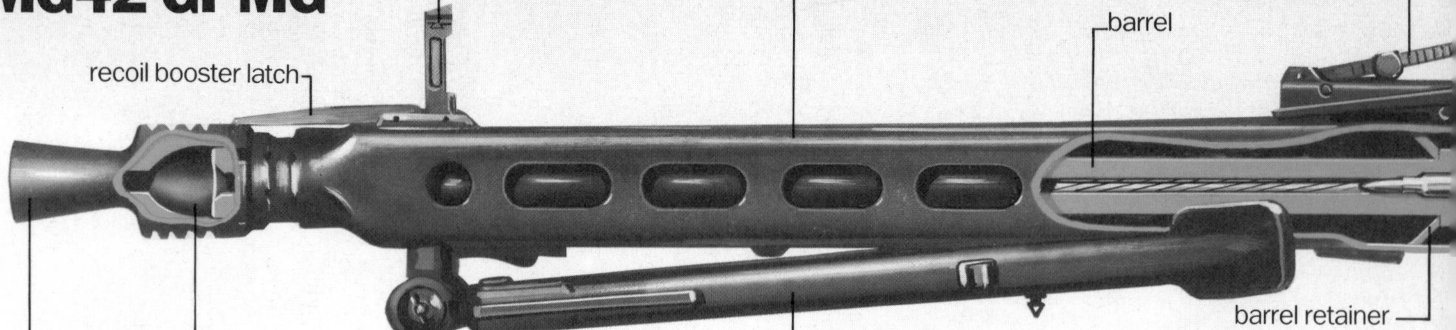

fore sight assembly

barrel housing

rear sight assembly

barrel

recoil booster latch

flash hider

recoil booster

bipod (folded position)

barrel retainer

chambered round

The Maschinengewehr 42 (MG42), introduced in 1942, was probably the most successful GPMG ever built. Its design, utilising many stamped and pressed components, permitted rapid manufacture and by 1945 over 750,000 had been produced. The extremely high rate of fire was achieved via a new short recoil roller-locked breech and a simple barrel change operation that allowed the gun to be fired almost continuously. One disadvantage of the MG42, or 'Spandau' as it was known, was that the high rate of fire caused the gun to vibrate, with consequent loss of accuracy.

wheels of the Leibstandarte's vehicles. Hausser decided to attack Kharkov, deploying the Leibstandarte in the north to cut the Kharkov-Belgorod road and then to probe south, while Das Reich attacked from the west and south. Witt's 1st SS Panzer Regiment soon penetrated the outer suburbs, and on 11 March began to advance towards the city centre to capture Red Square. The previous month's fighting had taken its toll of the Leibstandarte's panzer strength, and on 11 March the division possessed only 23 combat-ready tanks, and not one Tiger was available for service.

Although the Soviet force in Kharkov was surrounded, it defended the city using dug-in T-34 tanks and a complex of strongpoints based in massive departmental blocks. Units of the Leibstandarte had to clear the city in a series of bitter house-to-house fights, and by 12 March the division's heavy armour was reduced to 14 tanks. But the determination of the SS soldiers, and the enthusiastic rivalry of officers such as Witt, SS Obersturmbannführer (Lieutenant-Colonel) Kurt 'Panzer' Meyer and Peiper to recapture prestigious positions such as Red Square, combined to destroy the last remnants of Soviet resistance in a tractor factory on 15 March. On 18 March, Peiper moved north and secured Belgorod. This final part of the four-week German counter-offensive concluded a very successful military operation.

From January to March 1943 I SS Panzer Corps had suffered casualties of 365 officers and 11,154 other ranks, of whom nearly a third were from the Leibstandarte. But the victory at Kharkov was a

firing pin
bolt head
cover
recoil spring
cover catch
stock
safety
grip
barrel return spring
trigger guard
trigger
sear
ammunition belt

Calibre 7.92mm
Length 1220mm
Weight 11.57kg
Feed 50-round belt or 50-round drum
System of operation recoil
Rate of fire (cyclic) 1100-1200rpm
Muzzle velocity 756mps

tremendous boost for German morale, and the Leibstandarte received a major share of the adulation and rewards. Undoubtedly this was helped by Hitler's close interest in 'his' division, and the fact that 'Sepp' Dietrich was an old comrade and a personal friend. The Leibstandarte was awarded a very high proportion of the honours given to the Waffen SS, receiving fourteen Knight's Crosses and higher awards, compared with the 10 awarded to Das Reich and five to Totenkopf.

However, the adulation and rewards given to the Leibstandarte were not merely consequences of Hitler's favouritism or Dietrich's connections. They reflected a genuine admiration by the army and firmly established the Leibstandarte as an elite formation which excelled both at defensive and

Left: The collar insignia of this Leibstandarte recruit identify him as a Volkdeutsche (an ethnic German born outside Germany). Below: Motorcycle troops in southern Russia. The key painted on the side-car is the divisional symbol of the Leibstandarte. Below right: Leibstandarte half-track vehicles under the command of Joachim Peiper forge east past blazing houses. Above right: Fritz Witt (on left) confers with his adjutant near Kharkov.

offensive fighting. The success of the Leibstandarte during the dreadful winter battles of 1943 depended upon the toughness of the SS soldiers, their concept of racial superiority and military professionalism, and the inspiration and example of their field commanders who believed in leading from the front.

Their toughness and racialism, however, had another and much uglier side. As well as leading to bravery and proficiency in battle, they also led to an appalling attitude towards civilians – especially civilians of any of the nations described as inferior in the Nazi hierarchy of races. Soviet sources have estimated that 20,000 men, women and children died

Below: The price of victory at Kharkov. Between the fall of Stalingrad on 30 January and the end of March 1943, I SS Panzer Corps rallied the shaken German forces around the mid Donets and drove back an army that greatly outnumbered them. But by the time the German front had been re-established east of Kharkov SS casualties had reached 11,500, a third of them from the Leibstandarte.

at the hands of the Waffen SS during their occupation of Kharkov – a shocking stain on the record of the divisions involved.

THE AUTHOR Keith Simpson is senior lecturer in War Studies and International Affairs at Sandhurst. A member of the Royal United Services Institute and the International Institute for Strategic Studies, he has a special interest in modern warfare and is currently writing a book on the German Army.

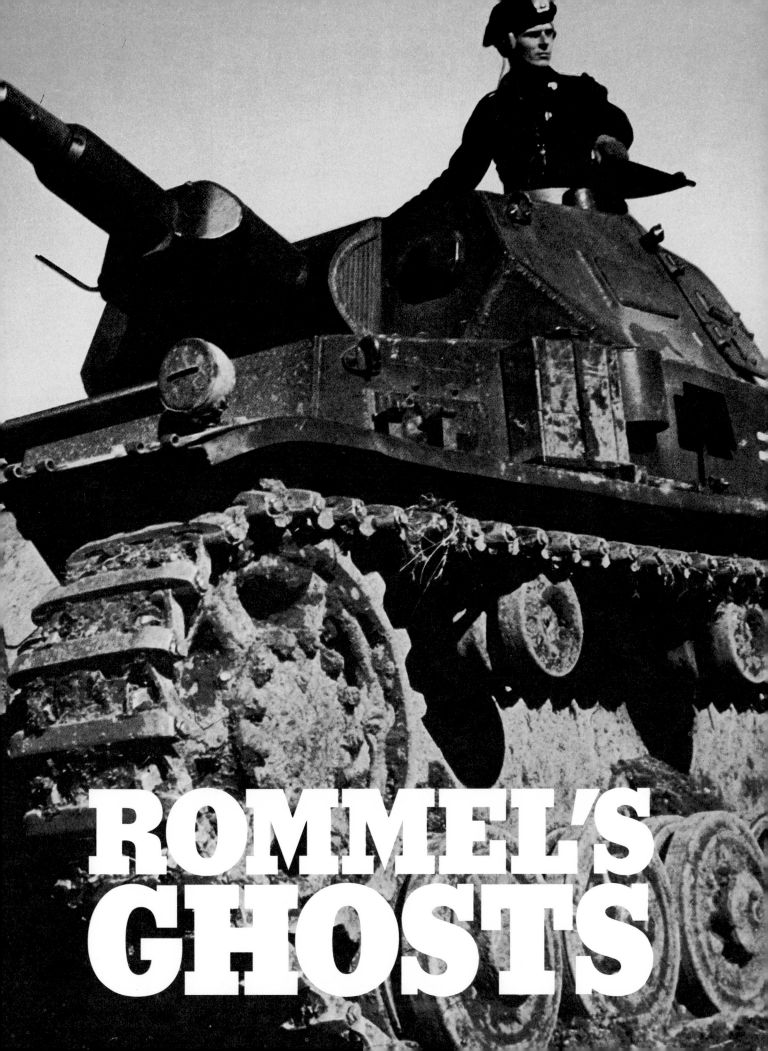

ROMMEL'S GHOSTS

7TH PANZER DIVISION

Before being designated
the 7th Panzer Division, this
formation had begun life as
the 2nd Light Division. The
original wave of light
divisions was formed in 1937
as motorised cavalry
formations and consisted of
two motorised rifle
regiments with a battalion of
light tanks. Support services
included a motorised
artillery regiment armed
with 24 10.5cm howitzers; an
anti-tank battalion with 36
3.7cm anti-tank guns and 12
2cm guns (which were also
used for anti-aircraft
defence); and a motorised
reconnaissance battalion
equipped with motor-cycles
and some armoured cars.
The 2nd Light Division first
saw action during the
invasion of Poland in
September 1939. As a
divisional organisation the
2nd Light was under-
gunned and under-
armoured and following the
Polish Campaign it was
uprated to become the 7th
Panzer Division. In effect
this meant that the tank
element of the division was
increased. Unlike the
majority of panzer divisions
the 7th had one instead of
two tank regiments,
although this was
compensated for to some
extent by having three
instead of two tank
battalions. The panzer
regiment – the 25th –
fielded 218 tanks before
the invasion of France, over
half of which were the lightly-
armoured Czech PzKpfw
38(t) models, the remainder
a combination of PzKpfw IIs,
IIIs, and IVs. Following the
division's triumphant
success in France it took
part in the invasion of the
Soviet Union in 1941. Above:
The divisional insignia of the
7th Panzer Division.

**The German 7th Armoured Division
completely surprised the Allies
when Rommel led it in a bold thrust
through the French lines in May
1940**

At 0532 hours on 10 May 1940, the German 7th Panzer
Division, commanded by Major-General Erwin
Rommel, crossed the Belgian frontier thirty miles
south of Liège. The 7th Panzer Division, along with
the 5th Panzer Division, formed General Hoth's
Panzer Corps, whose objective was to advance
across the wooded and hilly area of the northern
Ardennes providing flank cover for General von
Kleist's Panzer Group of Army Group A, and to seize
the Meuse river crossings between Givet and
Namur. The Germans had calculated that the Allies
would not expect a panzer thrust through the Ardennes and consequently had few good troops in the
area. From the very start of the campaign, Rommel
was determined that the 7th Panzer Division would
be in the forefront of the advance.

Rommel had only been in command of the 7th
Panzer Division from 10 February 1940. His appoint-
ment had been resisted by the German High Com-

mand on the grounds that as an infantry officer he had
no experience with panzers. But Hitler, for whom
Rommel was a favourite, insisted that he be given this
command. Although Rommel had no experience of
armoured warfare he was an acknowledged expert
on infantry tactics, and in his book *Infanterie Greift an
(Infantry Attack),* based upon his experiences during World War I, he had advocated fast, mobile
operations aimed at outflanking an enemy, infiltrat-
ing his positions and paralysing his command.

Initially, Rommel was not impressed by the personnel of his new command. The soldiers were
largely recruited from Thuringia, a German province not noted for producing good troops, and he
thought many of the officers were 'flabby' and lacking the correct National Socialist spirit. During this
period Rommel was an ardent supporter of Hitler
and had commanded his bodyguard during the
Polish Campaign of 1939. But he could rely upon the
professionalism and experience of Colonel Karl
Rothenburg, the commander of the 25th Panzer
Regiment, who was a leading expert on armoured
warfare. A number of Nazi officials were posted to
the 7th Panzer Division, including Lieutenant Karl
Hanke who was a senior assistant to Dr Josef Goeb-
bels and later Gauleiter of Lower Silesia.

In the three months before the invasion in the

Page 51 : A panzer commander surveys the battlefield from a PzKpfw IV, the most powerful tank in the German armoury in 1940. Below left: Rommel and his staff consult their maps during preparations for the division's breakthrough into France. Crossing the Meuse (below) was the first priority, and much of the success of this operation lay in the repeated training exercises insisted upon by Rommel in the spring of 1940 (bottom). Newly appointed to general rank in February 1940, Rommel was determined that his division would be at the point of the panzer spearhead.

West, Rommel worked himself and his subordinates round the clock to bring the 7th Panzer Division up to requirements. He quickly mastered the theory and practice of armoured warfare, and began a comprehensive training programme emphasising gunnery practice and cross-country manoeuvres. He personally briefed all his officers so that they understood what was required of them, and those who failed to meet his exacting standards were sacked. In a remarkably short period of time Rommel grasped the essentials of panzer warfare and brought his soldiers to a much improved level of efficiency.

From the very first day of the war in the West, Rommel led and encouraged from the front. When advance elements of the 7th Panzer Division arrived at Dinant on the Meuse on 13 May, they came under heavy French fire from the opposite bank, and a number of attempts to cross the river were beaten back. Rommel immediately took command of the situation, and ordered that a number of houses be set alight to provide the necessary smoke screen. Over the next twenty-four hours the rifle regiments of the division were able to cross the Meuse at a number of points using rubber dinghies, something they had practised on manoeuvres. Rommel was everywhere, organising the engineers, persuading Hoth to provide artillery support, and shouting himself hoarse encouraging his soldiers.

For a time the situation looked critical as the French counter-attacked the limited number of armoured vehicles on the west bank. In Rommel's own words:

'On arrival at brigade headquarters on the west bank I found the situation looking decidedly unhealthy. The commander of the 7th Motor-Cycle Battalion had been wounded, his adjutant killed, and a powerful French counter-attack had severely mauled our men in Grange. There was a danger that enemy tanks might penetrate into the Meuse valley itself. Leaving my signals lorry on the west bank, I crossed the river again and gave orders for the panzer regiment to be ferried across during the night. However, ferrying tanks across the 100-metre-wide river by night was a slow job, and by morning there were still only 15 tanks on the west bank, an alarmingly small number.'

Whilst organising the tanks on the west bank, Rommel, in a PzKpfw III, came under French artillery and anti-tank fire:

'Shells landed all around us and my tank received two hits one after the other, the first on the upper edge of the turret and the second in the periscope. I had been wounded in the right cheek by a small splinter from the shell which had landed in the periscope. It was not serious though it bled a great deal. I tried to swing the turret round so as to bring our 3.7cm gun to bear on the enemy in the opposite wood, but with the heavy slant of the tank it was immovable. The French battery now opened rapid fire on our wood and at any moment we could expect their fire to be aimed at our tank, which was in full view. I therefore decided to abandon it as fast as I could, taking the crew with me. At that moment the subaltern in command of the tanks escorting the infantry reported himself seriously wounded with the words: "Herr General, my left arm has been shot off." We clambered up through the sandy pit, shells crashing and splintering all round.'

This French withdrawal quickly turned into a rout as troops began to panic

Despite this dangerous moment, the bridgehead over the Meuse held. By 15 May the Germans had crossed the Meuse in two important areas, with Rommel's division in the centre. As a consequence, the French commander of the Ninth Army made a fatal decision to abandon the position along the Meuse and to withdraw 24km further west to a line east of Philippeville. But this French withdrawal quickly turned into a rout as troops panicked in the face of German armour and Luftwaffe attacks.

The 7th Panzer Division quickly brushed aside scattered French units and raced towards Philippeville, with the panzer regiment in the lead, and the divisional infantry following in lorries or on foot, and with its flanks protected by artillery fire and Stuka dive-bomber support. The tanks of the 7th Panzer Division drove along at a speed of 40 km/h having taken the French completely by surprise. At one point, some four miles west of Philippeville, the leading tanks met a column of French motor cyclists coming in the opposite direction who were so shocked at finding themselves in the middle of a German column that they drove their machines into the ditch and surrendered.

Above left: Troops from the division's two rifle regiments advance across French countryside. Left: The 7th Panzer Division pioneered the use of the 8.8cm AA gun as an anti-tank weapon.

Once again, Rommel led the 7th Panzer Division from the front. He travelled in a specially adapted PzKpfw III, and to simplify wireless traffic, he devised a simple idea known as the *Stosslinie*, or line of thrust, which involved drawing a line between two pre-arranged points on a map, so that any point could be described by giving the distance along and from the end point on the line. Rommel encouraged the tactic of having all the available guns of the division firing at a single enemy concentration before directly attacking it.

They were attacked by assault engineers using flame-throwers behind a smoke screen

On 16 May the 7th Panzer Division was ordered to advance through a westward extension of the Maginot Line around Avesnes. The French position here consisted of bunkers and minefields in a wooded hilly area. Rommel managed to get the leading elements of the 7th Panzer Division through this position by guile and firepower. He was able to penetrate the French covering field fortifications by moving the tanks forward without a shot being fired and with the crews outside waving white flags. The startled French troops were too surprised to shoot, and the Germans were through to the bunkers. These were attacked by assault engineers using flame-throwers behind a smoke-screen laid down by the tanks. A hole was blown through the French position and by late the same night the tanks of the 7th Panzer Division had raced through Avesnes and advanced 55km.

Despite the fact that the panzers had outrun the infantry and the supply vehicles, Rommel was determined to continue the advance westwards, exploiting French confusion and collapse of morale. In the previous twenty-four hours the division had suffered 35 killed and 59 wounded, but had captured approximately 10,000 prisoners, 100 tanks, 30 armoured cars and 27 guns. On the morning of 17 May, tanks of

the panzer regiment raced on and captured intact a bridge over the river Sambre at Landrecies. The next day, Rommel attacked and captured Cambrai against a superior French force. His vehicles had raised such a cloud of dust that the French were convinced that they were being attacked by hundreds of tanks rather than a motley collection of mainly soft-skinned vehicles.

Throughout this advance, the leading elements of the 7th Panzer Division were extremely vulnerable to French counter-attack. With ammunition and fuel stocks low, Rommel took audacious risks to confuse and paralyse the French and maintain the momentum of his advance. Much of this advance was due to Rommel's personal leadership and example.

One officer who witnessed Rommel's leadership of the 7th Panzer Division at this time wrote:

'I have never seen anything like the scenes along Rommel's route of advance. His tanks had run into a French division coming down the same road, and they had just kept advancing right on past it. For the next eight or nine kilometres there were hundreds of trucks and tanks, some driven into the ditches, others burnt out, many still carrying dead and injured. More and more Frenchmen came out of the fields and woods with abject fear written on their faces and their hands in the air. From up front came the short, sharp crack of the guns of our tanks, which Rommel was personally directing – standing upright in the command vehicle with two staff officers, his cap pushed back, urging everybody ahead. The spirit of battle inflamed him: he brooked no opposition, from friend or foe. If somebody could not keep up, then let him stand aside.'

Following the capture of Cambrai, the 7th Panzer Division paused to reorganise and to bring up urgently needed supplies. The Allies were now

Above: A Panzerjäger 1, part of Rommel's self-propelled artillery. Based on the PzKpfw I chassis, it provided mobile firepower to accompany the more heavily armoured tanks.
Below: A German reconnaissance plane flies over tanks of the 7th Panzer Division.

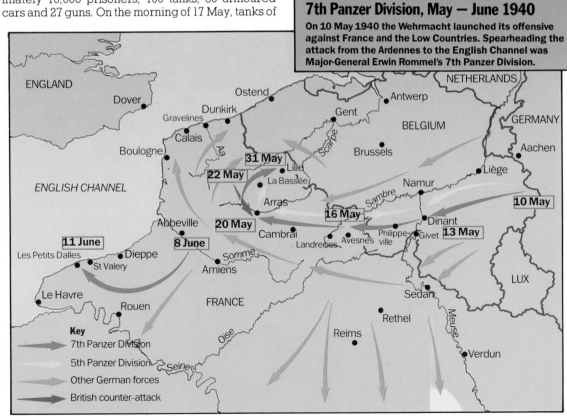

The drive to the Channel
7th Panzer Division, May — June 1940

On 10 May 1940 the Wehrmacht launched its offensive against France and the Low Countries. Spearheading the attack from the Ardennes to the English Channel was Major-General Erwin Rommel's 7th Panzer Division.

Key
7th Panzer Division
5th Panzer Division
Other German forces
British counter-attack

GERMAN TANKS IN 1940

German successes in 1940 were not due to the quality of their armoured vehicles; on the contrary, the tanks fielded by Germany's French and British opponents were in many respects far superior. The majority of German armoured vehicles were poorly gunned and inadequately armoured but they were reasonably mobile and reliable, and it was around these qualities that the panzer commanders developed their Blitzkrieg theories.

The PzKpfw II was developed in the mid 1930s as a stop-gap vehicle to replace the PzKpfw I, prior to the arrival of the more powerful PzKpfw III. Weighing only seven tonnes the PzKpfw II was designated as a light tank but on many occasions was forced into a battle-tank role. Armed with a 2cm armour-piercing gun and a 7.92mm machine gun it relied on its mobility and psychological value more than anything else. More than 1000 took part in the 1940 campaign and many were still in service in a support role as late as 1942.

Hitler's takeover of Czechoslovakia before the war presented the German Army with access to the Czech armaments industry. Large numbers of the Czech LT-38 light tank were assigned to the 7th Panzer Division, to be redesignated as the PzKpfw 38(t). By the standards of the day the PzKpfw 38(t) was a reasonably effective tank, weighing 10 tonnes, capable of a top speed of 42km/h and mounting a 37.2mm main gun. Armour protection consisted of bolted and riveted plates which had only a limited ability to withstand a well-placed armour-piercing shot.

Germany's latest tanks – the PzKpfw III and IV – were just coming into service in 1940 and only a few had been allotted to the 7th Panzer Division. The PzKpfw III was designed as a battle tank, intended to spearhead the breakthrough and be capable of taking on enemy armoured vehicles. Despite its intended function, in 1940 the PzKpfw III was only armed with the infantry 3.7cm gun, possessing a poor anti-tank capability. Weighing 19 tonnes, the tank was reasonably well armoured and had a powerful engine making possible a maximum speed of 40km/h. The PzKpfw IV's role was to support the PzKpfw III, being armed with a low-velocity 7.5cm gun, capable of lobbing high-explosive charges against targets other than armoured vehicles. Similar in general appearance and design to the PzKpfw III, it weighed 20 tonnes and had a maximum speed of 40km/h. Both types were progressively upgunned and uparmoured as the war developed.

faced with a critical situation, because their divisions which had advanced into Belgium were now in danger of being cut off from the main French army by the German thrust from the Ardennes.

On 20 May the 7th Panzer Division attacked south of Arras and although the leading elements made good progress, the motorised rifle regiments were unable to keep up. French tanks and infantry infiltrated the division's lines of communication, and for a few hours defeat seemed possible before the timely arrival of an infantry regiment and some artillery broke up the French attack. As the 7th Panzer Division paused to regroup, the Allies were preparing to attack the German position around Arras. The plan involved a British armoured attack from the northwest and a French armoured attack from the south. But the French part of the plan to the south never fully materialised, and the British attack was an uncoordinated advance by two tank battalions of 74 tanks, supported by two infantry battalions and some French tanks.

At the same time as the British were preparing this improvised attack on 21 May, 7th Panzer Division received orders to advance around Arras towards the northwest to gain the Scarpe river line at Acq. The 7th Panzer Division was to be supported by the SS Totenkopf Division, while the 5th Panzer Division advanced east of Arras. The proposed line of advance for the 7th Panzer Division exposed its right flank to any Allied attack from the north. By 1500 hours leading elements of the 7th Panzer Division were advancing in the area of Ficheux and Wailly to the southwest of Arras, but Rommel found there was considerable confusion with infantry and transport strung out to the rear along the narrow country roads. At 1700 the 7th Panzer Division was attacked by British tanks and infantry. The Germans were taken completely by surprise and units of the 6th Infantry Regiment panicked and fled. What particularly undermined German morale was the failure of their 3.7cm anti-tank shells to penetrate the 3in armour of the British Matilda tanks.

At this critical juncture, Rommel's presence and leadership undoubtedly prevented disaster. At Wailly, Rommel personally organised a stop-line of artillery and anti-aircraft guns to knock out the British tanks:

'It was an extremely tight spot, for there were also

Above: The wide-ranging motorcycle combinations of the reconnaissance regiment provided Rommel with essential information on enemy movements. Below: A shell explodes by a German staff car as the 7th Panzer Division advances deep into France.

several enemy tanks very close to Wailly on its northern side. The crew of a howitzer battery, some distance away, now left their guns, swept along by the retreating infantry. Every gun, both anti-tank and anti-aircraft, was ordered to open fire immediately and I personally gave each gun its target. With the enemy tanks so perilously close, only rapid fire from every gun could save the situation. We ran from gun to gun. The objections of the gun commanders that the range was too great to engage the tanks effectively, were overruled. All I cared about was to halt the enemy tanks by heavy gunfire. Soon we succeeded in putting the leading enemy tanks out of action.'

BLITZKRIEG

The German theory of warfare known as 'Blitzkrieg' (lightning war) was propounded in the 1920s, developed into a practical doctrine in the 1930s and put into practice in the campaigns of 1939, 1940 and 1941. With the victories of the German armed forces in the opening phases of World War II, extravagant claims were made for Blitzkrieg as a war-winning strategy. In essence, however, Blitzkrieg was nothing more than the reassertion of the primacy of the offensive in warfare.

The Germans made this philosophy work because, firstly, they utilised the mobility and fire-power of armoured vehicles and aircraft and, secondly, they ensured that all the various fighting elements in their divisions fought in close-co-operation with each other. On the battlefield, Blitzkrieg involved a breakthrough and deep penetration. Following a short but intense bombardment – using artillery and dive-bombers – the assault would commence, the main weight being concentrated against a weak point in the enemy line. Panzer divisions would spearhead the attack and be responsible for the all-important breakthrough in which armoured columns would advance deep into enemy territory, throwing the opposing forces into confusion. Alongside the panzers would be motorised infantry who would deal with any trouble spots, allowing the tanks to surge forward with minimum delay. At the same time, ground-attack aircraft – protected by air-superiority fighters – would range ahead of the ground troops, destroying enemy communications' centres and disrupting the movements of their reinforcements. The key to success lay in the dynamic interplay of the various elements available to the German commander. Blitzkrieg worked well against unimaginative and slow-witted opponents and in situations where the outcome of the campaign could be decided with relative speed.

The culmination of the 7th Panzer Division's success came with the capture of the British 51st (Highland) Division at St. Valéry. British troops lounge on a PzKpfw II, awaiting despatch to a POW camp (left), while Rommel poses by the vanquished General Fortune (right). Below: Colonel Rothenburg (second left), the commander of the panzer regiment, savours the moment of victory as he stands on the Channel shoreline.

Meanwhile, further south, another part of the British attack overran an infantry and an anti-tank battalion before being stopped by concentrated artillery fire. Tanks from the panzer regiment later attacked the British in the flank and by evening the situation had been stabilised and the British forced to withdraw.

Thirty-six British tanks had been destroyed, but the battle had come as a nasty shock to the soldiers of the 7th Panzer Division, and to the German High Command. The British had achieved much with a scratch force of tanks and infantry without artillery or air support. The initial collapse of German morale was due to their inability to stop British tanks with their anti-tank guns. Rommel had been forced to extemporise and had discovered the effectiveness of the 8.8cm anti-aircraft gun as an anti-tank weapon. Casualties for the 7th Panzer Division on 21 May were 89 killed, 116 wounded and 173 missing, four times the losses suffered during the initial breakthrough into France.

On 22 and 23 May the 7th Panzer Division advanced around the western suburbs of Arras and reached the village of La Bassée on the Aa Canal. Faced with this outflanking movement, the British were forced to withdraw to the canal line running from La Bassée to the coast at Gravelines south of Dunkirk. But on 24 May, Hitler ordered all his panzers to halt along the canal line to enable the supporting infantry divisions to catch up. This pause enabled the British and the French to organise a defence line and to begin the evacuation from the Channel ports.

Rommel used the two days of the halt to repair tanks, re-organise units and bring up fuel and supplies. On 26 May, Hitler lifted his halt order and immediately the 7th Panzer Division began to establish bridgeheads over the canal. By midday on 27 May the division had established two bridgeheads

and tanks were able to cross on a rather shaky pontoon bridge. Hoth placed the 5th Panzer Division under Rommel's orders and gave him the objective of capturing Lille. Rothenburg's tanks broke through towards the town and continued advancing in the dark, their route 'marked by the glare of burning vehicles shot up by his force.' The 7th Panzer Division had advanced so far ahead of the main German force that it came under both Allied and German artillery fire. By 31 May the 7th Panzer Division had blocked the roads to the west of Lille, and trapped half the French First Army. With the arrival of infantry divisions, the 7th Panzer Division was withdrawn for a few days rest.

Rommel was overjoyed with the success of his division and his own personal achievements. On 27 May he had been awarded the Knight's Cross, and he calculated in an interim report on the campaign that the 7th Panzer Division had taken 6849 prisoners, captured 48 light tanks and knocked out 18 heavy and 295 light tanks. 'Not bad for Thuringians!' he commented in a letter to his wife. For the soldiers of the 7th Panzer Division the brief period of rest enabled them to catch up on sleep and write home.

Following the successful evacuation of British soldiers by sea from Dunkirk, Hitler now ordered his armies to strike west and south against the remaining Allied forces. The 7th Panzer Division was attached to Army Group B and was deployed on the extreme right wing between Amiens and Abbeville. The immediate objective of the division was to seize a bridgehead over the Somme. This was achieved by using two railway bridges which the French had failed to destroy. The 7th Panzer Division then began its advance southwards, using Rommel's new concept of the *Flächemarsch* or 'formation drive'. By this method the entire division moved across country in an approximate box formation: tanks on three sides and anti-tank and reconnaissance units at the rear, with the infantry in the centre. The 7th Panzer Division steamrollered across the French countryside – averaging more than 60km a day – blasting aside resistance and striking fear and confusion deep within the French Army. Late in the evening of 8 June the 7th Panzer Division reached the Somme at Sotteville.

Hoth then ordered Rommel to turn to the right and advance towards Le Havre, a movement it

Corporal, 7th Panzer Division, France 1940

An *Unteroffizier* in the tank regiment, this soldier wears the specially designed black uniform – with rose-pink piping – for panzer troops. Headgear consists of the panzer beret, which was standard issue for tank crewmen in the early years of World War II although it was later discarded in favour of the field cap. His decorations include the Iron Cross 1st Class, the ribbon for the Iron Cross 2nd Class and a tank battle badge. German national insignia is worn on the right breast pocket and on the beret. The death's head collar patches were another arm-of-service device for panzer troops, and not simply the prerogative of the Waffen-SS. Of the latter, only the Totenkopf used this device as its divisional insignia.

was hoped would trap several French and British divisions at the coast. On 10 June the tanks of the 7th Panzer Division brushed aside weak opposition and reached the Channel coast at Les Petites Dalles, where Rothenburg drove his tanks through the seawall and down to the sea. French crowds cheered them in the mistaken belief that they were British. To the north, at the port of St Valéry, were several Allied formations, including the British 51st Highland Division, waiting to be evacuated by sea. On the morning of 11 June the panzer regiment occupied the high ground dominating the port. Rommel called on the Allied troops to surrender by 2100 hours, but the British refused, building barricades and preparing to fight it out. At 2100 the Germans bombarded the town with artillery fire and Stuka dive-bomber attacks. This broke the resistance, and the next day Rommel drove into the town and accepted the surrender of 12 Allied generals and over 12,000 troops. This was a triumphant conclusion to the breakthrough battles of the 7th Panzer Division.

Before February 1940 the 7th Panzer Division had been a rather mediocre formation, but after the arrival of Rommel and his ruthless determination to turn it into an elite division, all that changed. He was fortunate to have dedicated subordinates like Rothenburg and Hanke to help him in his task. The hours of training by the division in the three months before the attack in the West were fully justified by results. The rapid advance of the 7th Panzer Division owed much to the drive, determination, bravery and ruthlessness of Rommel, who led from the front and inspired all his soldiers. The campaign of 1940 gave the 7th Panzer Division an *esprit de corps* which was to carry it through much more bloody campaigns.

THE AUTHOR Keith Simpson is senior lecturer in War Studies and International Affairs at Sandhurst. He is a member of the Royal United Services Institute and the International Institute for Strategic Studies.

Set up and trained by Major-General Percy Hobart, the British 7th Armoured Division proved that it was a master of mobile warfare against the Italian forces in North Africa.

THE 7TH ARMOURED DIVISION was not new to fighting in the western desert of North Africa. Its men had been fighting a series of running battles with the Italians for several weeks and now, in early 1941, they and their tanks were exhausted by the harsh conditions. They had fought admirably and were satisfied with their actions, as the first large armoured unit in the British Army they had a lot to prove. The time for reflection, however, would be short-lived; soon, they would be ordered to deliver the *coup de grace* against the retreating enemy.

Less than two months after the opening of Operation Compass, the British plan to drive the Italian Army out of their positions along the Egyptian border, on 9 December 1940, the British Western Desert Force had shattered a significant part of Marshal Rodolfo Graziani's army, and its weary troops were ready for a well-earned rest. Their commanding officers, however, had other ideas; Lieutenant-General Sir Richard O'Connor was ordered by General Archibald Wavell to continue his pursuit westwards; by mounting a large-scale raid against

Benghazi, the major town in Cyrenaica. If his plan was successful, the Italian Tenth Army would be trapped between O'Connor's two divisions and forced into surrender.

In late January 1941 O'Connor ordered the 6th Australian Division to take the coastal town of Derna and the 7th Armoured Division to concentrate on Mechili, prior to the latter unit making a sweeping drive through the desert interior to block any enemy forces making their way to safety along the coast road, the Via Balbia.

At Mechili, however, it was clear that an advance across the Cyrenaica bulge to Beda Fomm, a distance of over 190km, would require the accumulation of at least 3500 tonnes of stores and replacements, to carry out running repairs on all of the division's vehicles, and that the underfed, thirsty and extremely unwashed men would need time to rest up and get themselves into better shape. These basic needs could be achieved in five days but six would have been preferable. In the event, the division was given a mere two hours. One of the men present remembered the fury of activity that accompanied the preparations:

'Every truck had its bonnet open as most of them already had exceeded their useful mileage. Washing operations were everywhere in progress, as far as one gallon of water a man a day allowed. Hair was being cut and vehicles were being unloaded.'

Below left: Although Wavell's offensive against the Italian Tenth Army was originally intended as a large probing raid, early successes encouraged the British to push deeper into Cyrenaica. Inevitably, the head-long pursuit of the enemy placed a great strain on the Western Desert Force's supply services. Here, a group of infantry, armed with short magazine Lee Enfields, are carrying water and more alcoholic refreshment up to the front. Below: A Vickers .303in machine gun, steam rising from its coolant, blasts away at the enemy.

DESERT RATS

OPERATION COMPASS

The Italian dream of a new Mediterranean empire reached its fullest expression in June 1940 when Mussolini declared war on Britain. Over the next few months, the Tenth Army of Marshal Graziani's force built up its strength in the Libyan province of Cyrenaica and, in September, crossed over the Egyptian border.

The British, however, had prepared to meet any invasion. The Middle East Command, under General Sir Archibald Wavell, had over 80,000 men stationed between the Sudan and Palestine. Two divisions known as the Western Desert Force and led by Lieutenant-General Sir Richard O'Connor, faced Graziani in Egypt. O'Connor harassed the Italians as they moved forward and forced them to halt at Sidi Barrani.

The British began to plan a counter-attack and, after receiving reinforcements, the assault, code-named Operation Compass, was scheduled for 9 December. Although intended to be little more than an extended raid, the initial assault proved so successful that Wavell gave his permission for its extension. By late January 1942, Sidi Barrani, Bardia and Tobruk were in British hands and the Tenth Army was in full flight.

Wavell, sensing that a major victory was in the offing, urged O'Connor's force, retitled XIII Corps, to push deeper into Cyrenaica, towards Benghazi. On 4 February elements of the 7th Armoured Division were ordered to head for Beda Fomm as part of a pincer movement to prevent the battered remnants of the Italian Army from escaping.

'Then General Wilson drove up. The enemy were showing signs of quitting Benghazi, of giving up Cyrenaica altogether. The plan was to send an armoured force straight across the desert for a good 200km to cut the road from Benghazi to Tripoli where it ran along the edge of the Gulf of Sirte. There was no time to lose.'

The British advance guard, known as 'Combeforce' after its commander, John Combe, began to move forward on 4 February. A and C Squadrons of the 11th Hussars, supported by a troop of the King's Dragoon Guards (KDGs) that had just arrived in the Middle East, were the first away. Their task was to 'break the trail'. Apart from the information that could be squeezed from the inadequate and often incorrect maps captured from the enemy, the division had little idea of the conditions they would encounter in the desert interior.

Following the armoured cars were 50 A9/A10 cruiser and 40 Mark VIB light tanks of the 4th

7TH ARMOURED DIVISION

The 7th Armoured Division (whose badge is shown above) was the brain-child of Major-General Percy Hobart DSO, MC. Hobart, an enthusiastic proponent of armoured warfare, was plucked from his Whitehall position as Director of Military Training after the Munich Crisis of 1938 and sent to Egypt to form the first ever armoured division fielded by the British Army. Despite the indifference of his senior commanders, Hobart was able to cobble together a Light Armoured Brigade from three Hussar regiments, a Heavy Armoured Brigade from the 1st and 2nd Royal Tank Regiments, and a 'Pivot Group' made up of the 3rd Royal Horse Artillery and the 1st Battalion, King's Royal Rifle Corps.
In late 1938 Hobart took his 'Mobile Force' into the Western Desert to put it through its paces. Despite early problems (which earned them the title 'Immobile Farce') the officers and men were soon learning their trade. Gradually, the separate elements of the force began to learn their trade. The Hussars were taught to form a screen around the main force and gather intelligence, the tanks learnt to manoeuvre for attack and counter-thrust, the artillery to prepare the way for an attack, and the infantry to hold captured ground.
In February 1941, nine months after Italy had declared war on Britain, the 'Mobile Force' was renamed the 7th Armoured Division and became part of 'Western Desert Force' under Lieutenant-General R.N. O'Connor. The division consisted of two armoured brigades, the 4th and 7th, of six regiments in total, a 'Support Group' of infantry and artillery, and logistical and anti-aircraft units.

Armoured Brigade, the only tanks capable of movement after several weeks of constant action. In fact, all the cruiser tanks desperately needed a major overhaul and should have been sent back to base. Each vehicle was stocked with two days' supply of water, just enough petrol to get them to the target area and as much ammunition as they could carry. Behind the tanks came a handful of Royal Horse Artillery (RHA) guns, the 25-pounders of C Battery, 4 RHA and nine portee anti-tank guns manned by men of 106 RHA, and the 2nd Battalion, Rifle Brigade – the only elements of the division's Support Group ready for action.

None of the troops had ever experienced such appalling going. Lieutenant Joly, a commander of one of the leading tanks, remembered the journey:

'For mile after mile, I was faced with a vista of huge, forbidding rocks through which I had to pick my way carefully to avoid the risk of shedding a track. All the time I was being nagged by the Colonel to speed up and press on. In the mind of every one of us was the vision of the Italians streaming out south of Benghazi.

'I found that the fever of the chase kept me at a pitch of excitement throughout the day, despite the many frustrations of the incredible country through which we were passing and the uncertainties of the highly inaccurate maps on which we were forced to pin our faith.

'When the ground improved we accelerated in frantic anxiety to make the best possible time. Where the ground was again cut up by slabs and boulder outcrops, we had to pick a slow laborious route; trying desperately to keep the number of mechanical failures to a minimum.'

By noon on the first day of the drive, the armoured cars had got too far ahead and were on their own but, rather than bring them back, it was decided that some support had to get through to them. The column's wheeled vehicles, which could move just that bit faster than the tanks, were brought up and the RHA batteries and the Rifle Brigade, under Colonel Jock Campbell, were pushed forward.

However, they had a great distance to catch up; by 1500 hours the 11th Hussars had chased a very surprised Italian garrison out of the fort at Msus and were swanning off even further away from any support towards Antelat, with the idea of patrolling nearer the coast road to report on enemy traffic.

The 4th Armoured Brigade was out of the bad country and was making good time through the night

The commanding officer of the Hussars, John Combe, stayed with the KDGs at Msus, to liaise with the support when it arrived. The first man to turn up was Jock Campbell; at midnight in his staff car with its headlights ablaze in order to pick out the 'Thermos' bombs that were left along his route. These nasty little devices had already blown the wheels off some of the vehicles and posed a worrying threat to tank tracks. Despite these dangers, however, the 4th Armoured Brigade was now out of the bad country and was making good time through the night. Lieutenant Joly remembered the drive vividly:

'To me this was a new experience. It was bitterly cold so that my face soon became frozen and raw, and was painful to the touch. Occasionally I glanced down into the turret to reassure myself that I was not dreaming.

'In the eerie light cast by the single red warning bulb, I could see, beyond the glinting metal of the gun-breech, the huddled figure of Tilden. At my feet, crouched forward peering through the gun telescope – his only view of the outside world – sat Holton, on the alert, as he had to be since we were one of the leading tanks of the division.'

Later, the going got worse; in addition to the cold, a fierce wind sprang up bringing with it torrential rain.

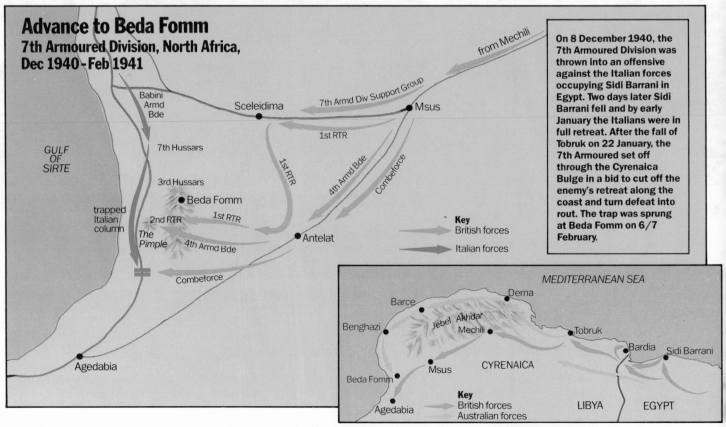

Advance to Beda Fomm
7th Armoured Division, North Africa, Dec 1940 – Feb 1941

On 8 December 1940, the 7th Armoured Division was thrown into an offensive against the Italian forces occupying Sidi Barrani in Egypt. Two days later Sidi Barrani fell and by early January the Italians were in full retreat. After the fall of Tobruk on 22 January, the 7th Armoured set off through the Cyrenaica Bulge in a bid to cut off the enemy's retreat along the coast and turn defeat into rout. The trap was sprung at Beda Fomm on 6/7 February.

from Mechili

Babini Armd Bde

Sceleidima

7th Armd Div Support Group

Msus

1st RTR

GULF OF SIRTE

7th Hussars

4th Armd Bde

1st RTR

Combeforce

3rd Hussars

Beda Fomm

trapped Italian column

2nd RTR

1st RTR

The Pimple

4th Armd Bde

Antelat

Combeforce

Agedabia

Key
British forces
Italian forces

MEDITERRANEAN SEA

Derna

Barce

Benghazi

Jebel Akhdar

Mechili

Tobruk

Bardia

Sidi Barrani

Beda Fomm

Msus

CYRENAICA

Agedabia

LIBYA

EGYPT

Key
British forces
Australian forces

The column was forced to halt, during which time the weary crews carried out essential maintenance on their tanks and then had their first meal in 18 hours – the food was cold, as there could be no fires.

The tanks arrived at Msus on the morning of 5 February, thereby releasing the KDGs with Jock Campbell's infantry and guns south to Antelat, with instructions to block the vital road from Benghazi as soon as possible. The RAF had reported thickening traffic south of the port. At 1400 hours, a single company of the Rifle Brigade was in position on the road, with the 11th Hussars on their right flank and two other companies forming a protective screen around the gun emplacements to the rear. Here, under the enthusiastic direction of Jock Campbell, the RHA batteries were preparing for the most concentrated shoot of their careers so far. They had ammunition for 48 hours, and no-one knew when more would arrive.

The first onslaught was not long in coming. Within half an hour of the riflemen taking up their positions, they saw the head of what proved to be the leading column of the Italian Tenth Army on its way out of Cyrenaica, bowling along towards them. The ensuing action was brief but bloody. The head of the leading column was repulsed, but a mass of enemy soldiery, with their guns, their lorries and their light tanks, built up in front of the British positions as the rest of the Tenth Army came south.

The men knew that every bullet they fired had to find a target and every shell take its toll

The heavily outnumbered British riflemen were saved by the narrowness of their front and their own expertise. The men knew that every bullet they fired had to find a target and every shell take its toll. Even then, there would still be Italian soldiers still willing to fight and, when every shot and shell had been fired, the British would surely lose the battle.

By 1700 hours the Italian column, which had only filled the road initially, had swelled to such a size that its front occupied the entire width of the land between the coast and the foothills. Here, the 11th Hussars were driving their Rolls-Royce armoured cars like cowboys trying to control an unruly herd of cows. The situation was getting out of hand and a group of Italian officers were attempting to mount a serious attack. Fortunately, at this crucial moment, a troop of light tanks of the 7th Hussars bucketted over the last foothills and went into action. Major Younger was with the first unit to arrive:

'At about 1700 hours B Squadron was ordered to find out if Beda Fomm itself, a windmill on high ground, was held. In no time at all the leading troop leader reported it clear and that there was a long column of transport halted on the road away to the west.

'We knew that Combeforce was in position a few miles to the southwest, across the road. In spite of the tanks being low on petrol, B and C Squadrons attacked the column, and only darkness, partly relieved by a burning petrol tanker, saved much of it from being destroyed.'

The resultant sea of flames that spread from the stricken tanker put paid to any thoughts the enemy might have had of mounting a counter-attack.

In the confusion caused by the Hussars lucky hit, six A13s of the 2nd Royal Tank Regiment (RTR) arrived. The sight of these and the 7th Hussar's tanks rampaging up and down the flanks, spread such

panic through the column that hundreds of Italians of every rank threw down their weapons and rushed towards the nearest tank or rifleman to surrender. Indeed, the control of the prisoners became more of a problem than the possibility of a battle developing with those Italians who were still showing signs of hostility.

The night after this battle was spent anxiously by the men of the 7th Armoured Division. Although any attempt by the Italians to break through the British lines was checked by rifle or machine-gun fire from the infantry or the tanks, the situation remained in the balance.

During the night of 5/6 February, the Italian commander, General 'Electric Whiskers' Bergonzoli, formulated a plan which he hoped would enable his trapped army to fight its way through the British blocking force. Artillery had arrived in quantity and 60 tanks of the Babini Armoured Brigade were making their way to the front. Bergonzoli believed that by mounting a feint attack against Combeforce, while his tanks swung off the road at a point known as The Pimple, he would be able to smash through the cordon and then take the British in the flank and rear.

At this stage, Combeforce had plenty of ammunition, but apart from a few drops in the fuel tanks of the armoured vehicles, petrol for retreat or wide manoeuvre was in very short supply. Whatever the odds against them, they were in the position of a hungry boxer; they had to win or starve to death.

Relief, however, was close at hand. The next morning, (6 February), those tanks of the 4th Armoured Brigade which had survived the journey from Msus arrived. With these extra men, the British were able to throw a thin cordon around the vast mass of Italian soldiers. Many of the prisoners had

Below: Desert conference. General Wavell (right) of the Middle East Command discussing strategy with Lieutenant-General O'Connor, the commander of the Western Desert Force.

BATTLE TANKS

The 7th Armoured Division relied on two main types of armoured vehicle during the early months of the Desert War; light and cruiser tanks. The Light Tank Mark VIB weighed 5.3 tonnes and had a maximum armour thickness of 14mm. It was conceived as a mount for mechanised cavalry regiments who were the eyes and ears of the British Army. Despite its poor performance against German armour during the Battle of France in 1940, the light tank was able to hold its own in the desert against the ill-equipped Italians, and could make good use of its high speed (56km/h) to get out of trouble. Main armament comprised .303in and 0.5in machine guns. The tank was withdrawn from service in late 1941.

The British deployed three types of cruiser tank in the campaign: the A9, A10 and A13.

The A9 entered service in 1937 and was designed to carry out general duties within armoured divisions. It was the first British tank to have a power traverse for its main turret which mounted a 2-pdr gun and one .303in machine gun. In addition, two auxiliary turrets each carried a machine gun. The tank weighed 12.2tonnes, had 14mm of armour and a five-man crew. Only 125 A9s were built, remaining in service until late 1941.

The A10 was designed as an infantry support version of the A9, but the addition of heavier armour (30mm) reduced its speed to 24km/h. The design of the A10 was an unhappy compromise; the vehicle was too poorly armoured to perform its intended role and was too slow to be used as a 'fast' tank.

The A13 variant carried similar armament to the A10 (one 2-pdr and a .303in machine gun), they had equal thickness of armour, but was much faster, with a top speed of 48km/h.

Above: British infantry launch an attack against an enemy position. Above right: The fruits of victory; five of the 25,000 prisoners captured at Beda Fomm. The British also captured more than 100 tanks.

made attempts to break out during the night and the tail of the retreating column, over 16km from the British positions, was pushing forward; driven by the men of the 6th Australian Division who had been moving along the coastal road from Derna.

The Italians mounted one more desperate attack that day and came close to breaking the British line after driving 2 RTR from The Pimple, but concentrated fire from Jock Campbell's well-served guns stopped them in their tracks. The scorching heat of the day gave way to the bitter cold of the desert night and both sides pulled back. An uneasy silence fell over the battlefield. Men slept fitfully, their thoughts straying to the horrors that the morning might bring.

Very few men on the British side slept well that night (6/7 February) and most greeted the dawn believing their last moments were at hand. The opening Italian attack seemed to confirm their worst fears; 13 M13 tanks which had been brought up to the front during the night stormed into the Rifle Brigade's positions before the RHA's guns could register. The whole area became a battlefield and a vicious hand-to-hand fight broke out. Smoke and flame engulfed the area and neither side appeared to be gaining the upper hand.

One tank had been stopped by the final shell of the last British anti-tank gun in action

Suddenly, however, a light breeze swept the battlefield and the true picture was revealed. To the astonishment of the breathless riflemen and the tank crews, 13 smoking and twisted wrecks were revealed. Some of the enemy tanks had had their tracks blown off by grenades, others ground to a halt with the death of their crews, shot by men who had

Corporal, 7th Armoured Division, 1941.

The red and yellow slides or flashes on this NCO's shoulder straps and the black lanyard identify him as a member of the 6th Royal Tank Regiment, one of the 7th Armoured Division main units. The black beret and its silver badge (motto: Fear Naught) were the distinctive emblems of the Royal Tank Regiment. The shirt, shorts, socks and short puttees were all standard-issue desert wear.

clambered on to the turrets and fired through their open hatches, and one other had been stopped only a few paces from a command post by the final shell of the last British anti-tank gun in action.

An unsettling hush fell over the battlefield, broken only by the sharp whistle of exploding ammunition

The defeat of this armoured fist was decisive. An unsettling hush fell over the battlefield, broken only by the occasional sharp whistle of exploding ammunition and the crackle of burning vehicles. The Italians had had enough and began to surrender. Joly remembered the scene:

'Gradually I became aware of a startling change. First one and then another white flag appeared amid the host. More and more became visible, until the whole of the enemy column was a forest of waving white flags. They had given up the fight.'

It was a remarkable achievement; the 7th Armoured Division had fought a battle with tanks and trucks so worn out that most would remain where they were until collected as scrap, yet had still managed to catch, and then defeat, the greater part of the Italian Tenth Army – the equivalent of nearly five divisions. Their haul also included a bus-load of Italian ladies, caught powdering their noses and brewing tea in the middle of the battlefield, protected by a lone priest. In this unbelievable, almost surreal scene, their presence seemed oddly appropriate.

The Italian Tenth Army in North Africa had been completely destroyed; over 25,000 prisoners had been taken in the Beda Fomm Battle. Over 1500 wheeled vehicles, 216 guns and more than 100 tanks were also captured. O'Connor sent in a brief message to Wavell; it read, 'Fox killed in the open'.

THE AUTHOR Barrie Pitt is well known as a military historian and edited Purnell's *History of the Second World War* and *History of the First World War*. His most recent work is *The Crucible of War*, a trilogy covering the North African campaign of World War II.

CLASH OF THE IRONCLADS

THE TANK CORPS

When Winston Churchill's Landship Committee produced its first successful prototype in 1915 it was christened the 'tank' in an effort to persuade snoopers that its purpose was merely to transport water. Thus, the men associated with the project were named the Tank Detachment. The codename soon ceased to conceal the weapon's identity, however, and during 1916 the tank personnel were known variously as the Armoured Car Section of the Motor Machine Gun Corps, then Heavy Section, the Machine Gun Corps, and finally Heavy Branch, Machine Gun Corps.

The tank personnel were organised in February 1916 into six companies, each comprising 28 officers and 255 other ranks, and each operating 25 tanks. They were first thrown into action at Flers-Courcellette on the Somme on 15 September, but their first major victory did not come until the Battle of Cambrai on 20 November 1917, when 378 tanks rolled en masse over the German lines.

On 27 July 1917 the Heavy Branch was named the Tank Corps (its badge is shown above) by Royal Warrant, and by the date of the Armistice it had expanded to 25 battalions organised into three brigades. The 1st Brigade had as its nucleus the two companies which had taken their tanks onto the Somme battlefield.

The corps became the Royal Tank Corps on 18 October 1923, a title it retained until the formation of the Royal Armoured Corps on 4 April 1939, when it was redesignated the Royal Tank Regiment. The regiment is still based at Bovington in Dorset, the home of British tanks since 1916.

In April 1918 a historic engagement was fought by the British Tank Corps at Villers-Bretonneux – the first engagement in which tank met tank

NOTHING DISTURBED the still morning air. From their hastily dug trenches around the French village of Villers-Bretonneux, a few weary sentries of the Worcestershire Regiment peered intently into the clearing mist that cloaked the low-lying meadows of the Somme valley a few miles to the east of Amiens. Their ears strained to catch the slightest sound coming from no-man's-land, noises that might herald a renewal of the recent German offensive. The men kept their lonely vigil as the rest of the troops stirred, preparing for another day in the front line. Suddenly, unexpectedly, the silence was shattered, violently and irrevocably: their positions were hit by a devastating rain of high-explosive and gas shells.

At 0600 hours the barrage lifted and the men, shell-shocked figures in a nightmare landscape, clawed their way out of their dug-outs, manned the pitiful remnants of their trenches and prepared to meet the expected onslaught of crack German troops with grenade, machine gun and bayonet. It was not to be. Instead of small groups of grey-clad men moving skilfully from crater to crater, the troops saw and heard the unusual, but by this stage of the Great War unmistakeable, sights and sounds of tanks crossing the wasteland that separated the opposing lines. Though they did not know it, the men were witnessing an historic event: the beginning of an armoured assault that would lead to the world's first tank-versus-tank encounter. It was 24 April 1918.

The events at Villers-Bretonneux in late April marked the final act of the last German offensive in the west during World War I. On 21 March, along a 54-mile stretch of the front manned by the British Third and Fifth Armies, 64 German divisions had launched Operation Michael. Enjoying overwhelming superiority in both men and artillery, the infantry had carved out a salient, some 20 miles deep, by the 26th. The focal point of the attack was the strategically vital town of Amiens, a communications centre lying astride the river Somme.

The appearance of the tanks of Sturmpanzer Abteilungen 1, 2 and 3 outside Villers-Bretonneux caught the British by surprise. The preliminary bombardment had easily drowned out the noisy, lumbering approach of the Germans' A7Vs, great monsters, each weighing 40 tons with a crew of 18, and the 13 tanks committed to the venture, although moving at a snail's pace, were able to close on the British trenches. This sudden armoured onslaught generated the same wholesale panic as had accompanied the first attack with tanks en masse, made by the British at Cambrai in November 1917. Wherever the A7Vs attacked, the defending infantry, hamstrung by their lack of effective anti-tank weapons, broke and fled. By mid-morning a three-mile gap had been punched through the front line, Villers-Bretonneux's ruins were in German hands and a three-strong group of A7Vs, closely supported by stormtrooper detachments, was nosing towards the

Previous page: German troops await the order to advance on British lines at the beginning of the Michael Offensive, and the British Mark IV tank, the weapon which was to stop them in their tracks outside Villers-Bretonneux.

village of Cachy, about 15km from Amiens. It seemed that nothing could prevent the fall of the city and with it the disintegration of the Third and Fifth Armies. Unbeknown to the Germans, however, there was one force that might block their triumphal march: the 1st Battalion of the British Tank Corps.

Resting under the welcome cover of a convenient wood on the road from Villers-Bretonneux to Amiens were the battle-shocked survivors of No. 1 Section of the battalion's A Company under Captain J.C. Brown, MC. Suffering from the effects of a gas attack and several uncomfortable hours in their Mark IV tanks, Brown's men had been pulled out of the line to rest and receive medical attention. Although most of his men were in a sorry state and unfit for battle, Brown was able to cobble together three scratch crews, who quickly prepared their machines for action. One of the crews manned a Mark IV 'male', armed with four Hotchkiss machine guns and a pair of six-pounders mounted in two side sponsons; the others took charge of machine-gun armed 'females'. In a tank battle, the females would have little part to play; only the male's six-pounders could pierce the A7V's armour to deliver a killing shot.

'As the wood was thick with gas, we wore our masks. While cranking up, a third member of my crew collapsed'

Brown's orders were painfully clear. He was to advance on Cachy and prevent any further thrusts towards Amiens. One of his officers, Second Lieutenant Frank Mitchell, later remembered the beginning of the advance on the village:

'As the wood was thick with gas, we wore our masks. While cranking up, a third member of my crew collapsed and I had to leave him behind, propped up against a tree trunk. A man was loaned to me from one of the females, bringing the crew, including myself, up to six instead of the normal eight. Both my first and second drivers had become casualties so the tank was driven by the third, whose only experience was a fortnight's course at Le Tréport (the base camp).'

Mitchell, an able and enthusiastic tankman, had recently reconnoitred the ground around Cachy and was given the task of guiding the other tanks to their objective. Brown was determined to take part in any action that might develop and he joined Mitchell as his tank's 105-horsepower Daimler engine roared into life and its crew took up their battle stations.

The Mark IVs were not the most comfortable fighting platform: they were without suspension, poorly ventilated and fume ridden. Crews could stay in action for no more than a few hours and usually needed a good 48 hours to recover from the experience. The tanks were much too noisy – broken eardrums were an occupational hazard – and orders had to be bellowed above the din of the engines or relayed by hand signals. The interior, a cramped metal box, was crammed with dangerously exposed fuel tanks, the engine and spare ammunition; there was no room for creature comforts. Most tankmen would have preferred to fight in as little clothing as possible because of the stifling heat, but they had to wear cumbersome overalls, a leather helmet and a mail face mask, an outfit that still only offered scant protection against the shards of hot metal which flew off the interior walls when the tank was struck by enemy fire. Burnt and mottled skin was the physical evidence of service in the Tank Corps.

Villers-Bretonneux

On 21 March 1918, the German armies on the Western Front launched Operation Michael — a massive assault by 64 divisions on a front some 50 miles wide between Arras and la Fère. During the next five days, the German offensive secured a 20-mile-deep salient, cutting deep into the Allied front line — and by early April German divisions were within a few miles of their strategic objective, the town of Amiens.

Early on the morning of 24 April, the British trenches east of Amiens were hit by a barrage of high-explosive and gas shells. As the barrage lifted, German A7V tanks lumbered into action, beginning an armoured onslaught that led to the first tank-versus-tank battle in history.

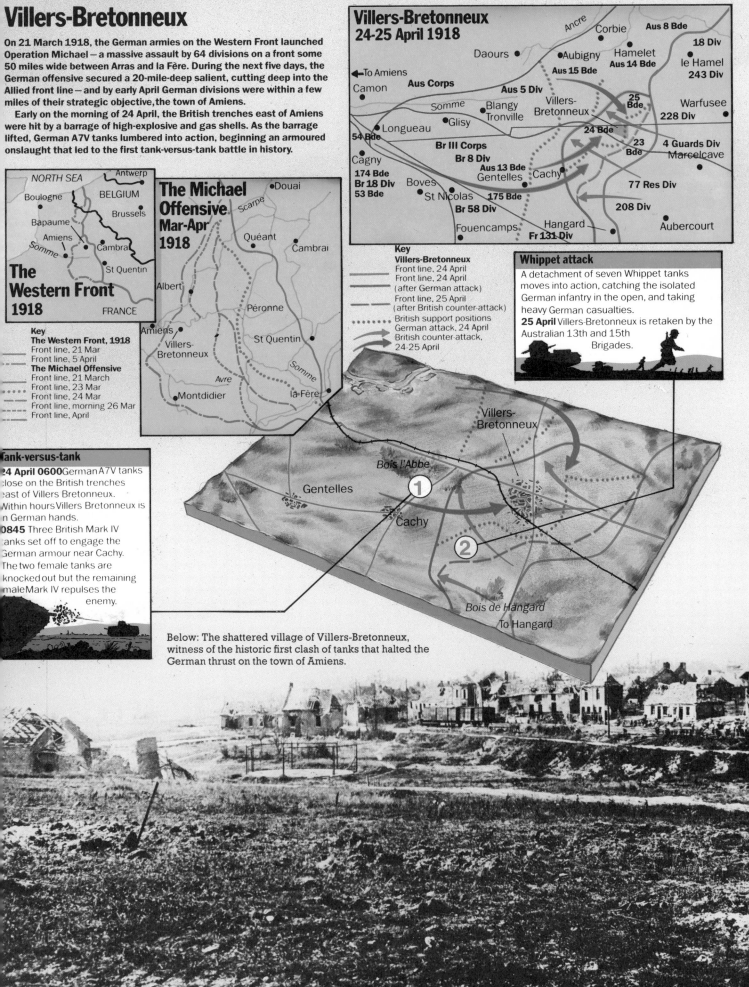

The Western Front 1918

NORTH SEA
Antwerp
Boulogne
BELGIUM
Brussels
Bapaume
Amiens
Cambrai
Somme
St Quentin
FRANCE

Key
The Western Front, 1918
Front line, 21 Mar
Front line, 5 April
The Michael Offensive
Front line, 21 March
Front line, 23 Mar
Front line, 24 Mar
Front line, morning 26 Mar
Front line, April

The Michael Offensive Mar-Apr 1918

Douai
Scarpe
Quéant
Cambrai
Albert
Péronne
Amiens
Villers-Bretonneux
St Quentin
Somme
Avre
Montdidier
la Fère

Villers-Bretonneux 24-25 April 1918

Ancre
Corbie
Aus 8 Bde
Daours
Aubigny
Hamelet
18 Div
Aus 15 Bde
Aus 14 Bde
le Hamel
243 Div
To Amiens
Aus Corps
Camon
Aus 5 Div
Villers-Bretonneux
25 Bde
Somme
Blangy
Tronville
Warfusee
Longueau
Glisy
228 Div
54 Bde
24 Bde
Br III Corps
23 Bde
4 Guards Div
Marcelcave
Cagny
Br 8 Div
174 Bde
Aus 13 Bde
Cachy
Br 18 Div
Gentelles
77 Res Div
53 Bde
Boves
St Nicolas
175 Bde
208 Div
Br 58 Div
Hangard
Aubercourt
Fouencamps
Fr 131 Div

Key
Villers-Bretonneux
Front line, 24 April
Front line, 24 April (after German attack)
Front line, 25 April (after British counter-attack)
British support positions
German attack, 24 April
British counter-attack, 24-25 April

Whippet attack

A detachment of seven Whippet tanks moves into action, catching the isolated German infantry in the open, and taking heavy German casualties.
25 April Villers-Bretonneux is retaken by the Australian 13th and 15th Brigades.

Tank-versus-tank

24 April 0600 German A7V tanks close on the British trenches east of Villers Bretonneux. Within hours Villers Bretonneux is in German hands.
0845 Three British Mark IV tanks set off to engage the German armour near Cachy. The two female tanks are knocked out but the remaining male Mark IV repulses the enemy.

Villers-Bretonneux
Bois l'Abbe
Gentelles
Cachy
Bois de Hangard
To Hangard

Below: The shattered village of Villers-Bretonneux, witness of the historic first clash of tanks that halted the German thrust on the town of Amiens.

BIRTH OF THE IRONCLADS

The tank was born from the need for a bullet-proof machine that was, in the words of Colonel E.D. Swinton, 'capable of destroying machine guns, of crossing country and trenches, of breaking through entanglements and of climbing earthworks'. In February 1915, Winston Churchill set up the Landship Committee to research into the possibilities, and by December the first successful prototype had undergone trials. Named 'Little Willie', it was steered via a rear limber and it featured a specially developed form of track, which gave a degree of manoeuvrability previously unheard of in tracked vehicles.

Little Willie was quite unequal to the conditions on the Western Front, however, and a larger tank was tested in January 1916. Known as 'Mother', or 'Big Willie', this prototype, rhomboidal tank could negotiate trenches up to 11½ft wide, and it was put into production as the Mark I. The two tracks could be controlled independently to gain a form of geared turn, and the steering limber was finally discarded. The armament of the 'male' version consisted of two side sponsons, each containing a six-pounder and a .303in Hotchkiss machine gun, with an additional Hotchkiss carried for defence. It seemed likely that the tank would succumb to a massed infantry attack, however, and so half of the Mark Is were completed as 'females' with the armament of four Vickers and two Lewis machine guns.

The heavy tank was not the only project under development by the Landship Committee. In 1916 a need was perceived for a lighter vehicle which, though sufficiently armoured to withstand machine-gun fire, had enough speed to exploit rapidly gaps created by the wire-crushing Mark Is.

The Medium Tank Mark A, nicknamed the Whippet, was ordered into production in June 1917. Its tracks were the simple tractor type of Little Willie, and steering was effected by speeding or slowing them independently. Armament, consisting of four .303in Hotchkiss machine guns, was fitted into special mountings in a 'fighting compartment', a rigid steel box to the rear.

The three British tanks set off for Cachy at about 0845 hours, making steady but sedate progress. Clear of the wood, they zigzagged their way through an artillery barrage and reached the switch line running from Villers-Bretonneux to the British reserve trench line at 0930. At this point, Brown left the male tank and joined one of the females. The Mark IVs were still searching for a target to engage, when they were informed of the presence of German tanks. Mitchell, commanding the male, was the first man to spot the advancing A7Vs:

'An infantryman jumped out of a trench in front of my tank and waved his rifle agitatedly. I slowed down and opened the flap. "Look out, there are Jerry tanks about," he shouted. This was the first intimation we had that the Germans were using tanks. I gazed ahead and saw three weirdly shaped objects moving towards the eastern edge of Cachy, one about 400yds away, the other two being much further away to the south. Behind the tanks I could see lines of infantry.'

Swinging his vehicle into action, Mitchell ordered his driver to make a right turn and then headed along the length of the switch line in the direction of Cachy. The manoeuvre, carried out by applying the brakes to one track and allowing the other to turn the tank, brought Mitchell on to a heading that ran parallel to that of the nearest German tank, which was moving along at somewhat less than its maximum cross-country speed of four miles per hour. As the range dropped, the lieutenant signalled his men to prepare for battle and his right-side gunner began to range on the nearest A7V.

With the tank weaving to avoid enemy shellfire and deep craters, the gunner, Sergeant J.R. McKenzie, was unable to get in a scoring shot. However, the lead German tank blazed away with some success: a high-powered broadside of armour-piercing shot hit the right side of Mitchell's tank. showering the crew

In retrospect, the action outside Villers-Bretonneux may be seen as a fine demonstration of both the quality of the new British war machines and the calibre of the men who fought in them The Mark IV (a 'female' version is shown below, armed with two machine gu in each side sponson) asserted its tank-killing capacity for the first time, while the 'Whippet' (below left) admirably fulfilled its intended role, taking advantage of the Mark IVs' success to sweep into lines unshielded German infantry with lethal slivers of metal. Mitchell ordered those men not directly engaged to hit the deck and told his driver to take evasive action. The storm of splinters flying across the armoured cabin finally ceased and the Mark IV was gradually driven clear.

As Mitchell withdrew, the two female tanks were also taking a battering. Hopelessly outgunned, they could not pierce the hide of the A7Vs and, while they tried to seek out the enemy's weak spots, both failed and were holed by 57mm shells. A few minutes after withdrawing, Mitchell met up with Brown, who had left one of the females to rejoin the male, and was ordered to pick up a wounded crewman. Driving on, he found the man, who had been hit in both legs, lying in the ruins of a blasted trench; he was placed on the floor of the male. Nearing the Bois d'Aquenne, Mitchell attempted a tight turning manoeuvre to bring the tank back into battle but his driver, inexperienced and ill-prepared for the horrors of combat, could only execute a wide, circling turn. Brown, again appearing out of the fog of war like some fury, demanded to know what was going on; 'Where the hell are you going?' Mitchell replied, 'Back to Cachy.' It was this momentous decision that brought the tank back to the field of battle. The lieutenant later recalled the final encounter with the lead A7V:

'I continued carefully on my route in front of the switch line. The left-hand gunner was now shooting well. His shells were bursting very near to the German tank. I opened a loophole at the top side of the cab for better observation and when opposite our opponent, we stopped. The gunner ranged steadily nearer and then I saw a shell burst high up

Lieutenant, the Tank Corps, Western Front 1918

The point of particular interest in this tank officer's equipment is his steel and leather mask with chain-mail 'veil', the first of two types of face protection issued to guard against hot, steel splinters. Wearing shorts because of the heat inside the tank, he carries a gas mask and a revolver on a 1914-pattern belt. His shoulder straps bear the red slide of the corps' 1st Battalion.

TANK DEVELOPMENT

The Mark II and Mark III tanks which succeeded the large-scale manufacture of the 'Big Willie' type differed only, respectively, in a minor adaptation to the track and in strengthened armour. Only 50 each of these marks were built, but the Mark IV, introduced in March 1917, was to become the most numerous type of the war – over 1000 examples were completed.

Like its immediate predecessor, the Mark IV featured improved armour to withstand the Germans' new armour-piercing weaponry. The barrels of its six-pounders were shortened to keep them clear of the ground on broken terrain and, to reduce the tank's overall width during rail transit, the weapon sponsons were reduced in size and installed on hinges, allowing them to be swung into the tank's interior. Four Lewis guns comprised the secondary armament of the 'male' version, while the 'female', used for direct infantry support and trench clearing, carried two primary machine guns in each sponson and two secondary guns.

The Mark V (shown above left) incorporated an epicyclic gearbox and a purpose-built 150hp Ricardo engine. Unlike the Mark IV, its unditching beams were carried on rails mounted on top of the tank. Introduced in mid-1918, 400 Mark Vs had been built by the Armistice, and they became the standard vehicle of the Tank Corps after the war.

on the forward part of the German tank.

'He obtained a second hit almost immediately, lower down on the side facing us, and then a third in the same region. It was splendid shooting for a man whose eyes were swollen by gas and who was working his gun single-handed, owing to shortage of crew. The German tank stopped abruptly and tilted slightly. Men ran out of a door at the side and I fired at them with my machine gun. The German infantry following behind stopped also. It was about 1020 hours.'

The odds were now less in favour of the enemy. Lining up on the nearer of the remaining pair of A7Vs, the British gunners let fly with their six-pounders. Great plumes of earth, thrown high into the air by the near misses of shells, rained down on the enemy tank. Suddenly, the A7Vs stopped dead in their tracks and then, with their exhausts belching clouds of thick black smoke, began to head off in the direction of the village of Hangard, a few miles south of Cachy.

The timely repulse of the A7Vs prevented the wholesale slaughter of the men of the Worcestershire and Devonshire Regiments who had fallen back under the enemy's armoured onslaught, but the German stormtroopers had still to be dealt with. While Mitchell was fighting his historic action, the Germans had charged through Villers-Bretonneux, and on towards Cachy. To the south, other German forces were holed up in the Bois d'Aquenne, ready to launch a flanking attack. However, the impetus of the German charge and the sudden loss of tank support left the stormtroopers dangerously exposed. Mitchell's tank, damaged by artillery fire soon after his clash with the A7V, could not continue the fight, but if other, faster tanks could put in an appearance, then the infantry might be destroyed.

In the heat of battle, no-one had noticed a British spotter aircraft as it circled over the countryside around Villers-Bretonneux and then departed to the west, heading for a wood three miles behind Cachy. Its pilot had seen the enemy infantry forming up for an attack in a hollow in front of Cachy and was on his way to report his findings to the commander of seven Whippet Medium A tanks from the corps' 3rd Battalion under the command of Captain T.R. Price.

Small though it was, Price's company packed a fearsome punch: each Whippet had a top speed of eight miles per hour over good ground and each three-man crew had charge of four machine guns. Against infantry in the open and away from the fire of enemy tanks and artillery, it could be a devastating combination. Price, knowing that his appearance outside Cachy could have a decisive effect on the course of the battle, ordered his men to move out.

The intelligence provided by air reconnaissance enabled Price to close on the enemy. Finding them spread out in the hollow, seemingly unaware of the Whippets' presence, he placed his command in line abreast, with about 50yds between each tank, and then, in a move reminiscent of the old cavalry days, gave the order to charge. Bouncing across a landscape that had escaped the worst of the pre-assault artillery barrage, the Whippets bore down on the unsuspecting stormtroopers at top speed. Inside, the gunners prepared to open fire.

The Germans were caught out in the open and paid a terrible price. Spraying to their left and right, the medium tanks caused fearful execution. Those men who sought shelter in the field's shell craters suffered horribly, mangled beneath the tracks of the Whippets. Cutting through the enemy line, Price ordered his command to turn about for a repeat performance. Through their vision slits the crews saw only the dead, the wounded and the backs of the survivors as they fled to their own trenches. After the battle, it was established that some 400 enemy infantry, members of the 77th Reserve Division, had fallen to the guns of the seven Whippets. One of Price's tanks had been destroyed and three others had sustained minor damage.

The German thrust on Amiens was over. The crippling losses suffered at the hands of the Tank Corps prevented the enemy from mounting any other attacks against Cachy, and allowed the British to bring up reinforcements that stabilised the situation. Going over to the offensive, during the night of 24/25 April, the 13th and 15th Australian Brigades were able to retake Villers-Bretonneux.

THE AUTHOR William Franklin is a military historian who has contributed to numerous publications. His particular interest is the history of special forces of the 20th century.

Right: Allied troops celebrate the capture of the German A7V 'Elfriede' by A Company, 1st Battalion, the Tank Corps, outside Villers-Bretonneux. Below: Tank crews work over Mark IIIs in the morass of the Western Front. Below right: Tank Corps personnel with 'Elfriede'. The A7V's armament consisted of six machine guns and a captured 57mm Russian gun. Since its 57mm ammunition was not generally available, it made good logistical sense to confine the guns to the tank force. Bottom: A7Vs approach a village. No fewer than 18 men travelled inside each lumbering Sturmpanzerwagen.

In December 1944 Hitler launched a desperate counter-offensive into the Ardennes. In the spearhead was Kampfgruppe Peiper and the battlefield giant, the King Tiger tank

THE SdKfz 251 half-track left the road, lurching over the embankment before careering down onto the railway line. Crossing the track, it strained to mount the opposite bank, spewing mud in its wake before finally disappearing from view. Almost immediately, it was followed by other half-tracks and a company of Panzer IVs which quickly broke down the embankment to

ARDENNES BLITZKRIEG

In mid-December 1944, the sorely pressed Germans unleashed their final Blitzkrieg in the west and some 25 divisions descended on the thinly held Ardennes sector of the front. Kampfgruppe Peiper, a powerful all-arms force, was ordered to grab vital bridges across the Meuse in preparation for an advance on Antwerp. Left: Short of every necessity, the Kampfgruppe survived on captured supplies. Here, a weary member of Peiper's command searches a knocked-out US armoured car for food. Below: Driving a mud-covered Schwimmwagen, a reconnaissance team, often identified as being led by Peiper (left), searches for a way through the enemy's lines.

make a rudimentary roadway. It was late afternoon on Saturday 16 December 1944 and Kampfgruppe (Task Force) Peiper, spearhead of the 1st SS Panzer Division 'Leibstandarte Adolf Hitler', was about to enter the Ardennes battle.

Led by SS-Obersturmbannführer (Lieutenant-Colonel) Joachim (Jochen) Peiper, a 29-year-old veteran of campaigns in Poland, France, the Balkans and Russia, the force was a formidable all-arms group. Its task was to follow a precise route through the Losheim gap in the northern sector of the Ardennes, pushing aside the thin American defensive screen and advancing along the Amblève valley to Stavelot and Trois Ponts. This would open the way to the Meuse river, where bridgeheads were to be seized for other panzer divisions to break out towards Antwerp, the main objective of an overall German plan, code-named 'Wacht am Rhein'. Peiper's role was an ambitious one, dependent for success upon the speed and impact of an armoured Blitzkrieg that would spread confusion in the enemy rear before the Allies could respond.

The Kampfgruppe left its staging area around Blankenheim, to the east of the Belgian-German border, at 0200 hours on 16 December, led by the half-tracks of No. 10 Company of the 3rd SS Panzer-grenadier Regiment and the Panzer IVs of No. 6 Company, 1st SS Panzer Battalion. At first all went well; at 0530 the sky to the west was suddenly set ablaze by the short, sharp artillery bombardment which opened the Wacht am Rhein assault and, as dawn broke on a cold, misty winter's day, sounds of firing could be heard as infantry of the 12th Volksgrenadier Division pushed forward to isolate American outposts and probe for lines of least resistance. But a few hours later, as Peiper's column approached Losheim, the first of a series of problems occurred, the results of which were to

delay the armoured breakthrough and make the build-up of momentum extremely difficult. A bridge over the railway line to the east of Losheim, destroyed by retreating Germans two months earlier, had not been repaired and the road was a solid mass of supply trucks and horse-drawn wagons belonging to the Volksgrenadiers. Peiper forced a way through in his Schwimmwagen command car, calling for field engineers to follow, but little could be achieved. In desperation, he ordered the tanks to clear the road, pushing the trucks into the ditches and fields on either side, while he led the way down the railway embankment to bypass the broken bridge. He was already 10 hours behind schedule.

Emerging onto the Losheim road, it soon became obvious that Peiper's problems were only just beginning, for the Volksgrenadiers had failed to make much headway, pinned down by small pockets of American defenders around the Losheimergraben crossroads less than a mile further on. In a fuel-consuming diversion, therefore, the Kampfgruppe left its prescribed route, moving across country towards the village of Lanzerath, where elements of the 3rd Parachute Division were apparently making

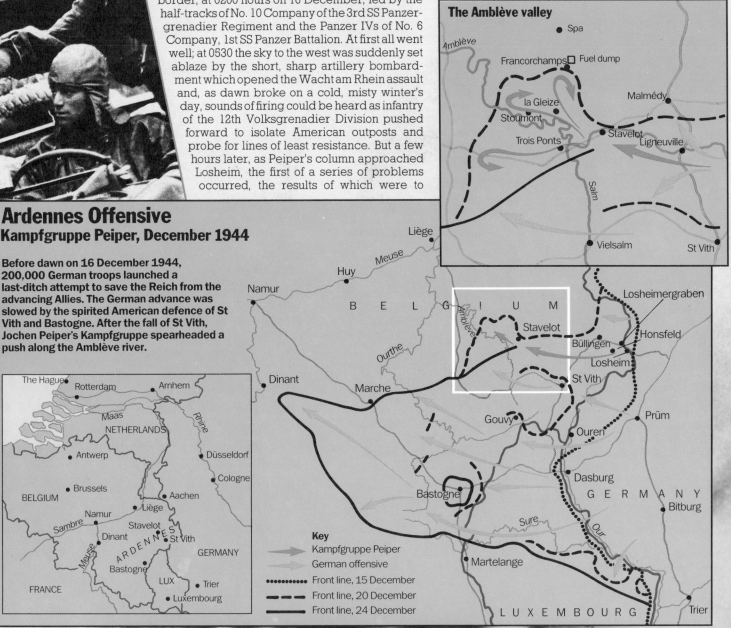

The Amblève valley

Spa
Amblève
Francorchamps ☐ Fuel dump
Malmédy
la Gleize
Stoumont
Trois Ponts
Stavelot
Ligneuville
Salm
Vielsalm
St Vith

Ardennes Offensive
Kampfgruppe Peiper, December 1944

Before dawn on 16 December 1944, 200,000 German troops launched a last-ditch attempt to save the Reich from the advancing Allies. The German advance was slowed by the spirited American defence of St Vith and Bastogne. After the fall of St Vith, Jochen Peiper's Kampfgruppe spearheaded a push along the Amblève river.

Liège
Meuse
Huy
Namur
B E L G I U M
Losheimergraben
Amblève
Stavelot
Honsfeld
Büllingen
Losheim
Ourthe
St Vith
Dinant
Marche
Gouvy
Prüm
Ouren
Dasburg
Bastogne
G E R M A N Y
Bitburg
Sure
Our
Martelange
L U X E M B O U R G
Trier

The Hague
Rotterdam
Arnhem
Maas
NETHERLANDS
Rhine
Antwerp
Düsseldorf
Cologne
BELGIUM
Brussels
Aachen
Namur
Liège
Sambre
Stavelot
Dinant
St Vith
A R D E N N E S
GERMANY
Meuse
Bastogne
LUX
Trier
FRANCE
Luxembourg

Key
→ Kampfgruppe Peiper
→ German offensive
•••••••••• Front line, 15 December
– – – – Front line, 20 December
——— Front line, 24 December

73

better progress. The Panzer IVs of No. 6 Company set out in gathering darkness along unknown tracks, only to encounter a minefield left uncleared by the paras. Despite the loss of three tanks and five half-tracks, Peiper urged his men on, but when he entered the village at 2300 hours, to be greeted by a para colonel who was convinced that American troops were waiting in ambush in woods between Lanzerath and Honsfeld, he decided to halt for the night.

The situation did not seem to improve as the advance was resumed at 0500 on 17 December, for although the para colonel's fears proved unfounded, Peiper had to waste more time and fuel flushing out Americans from defended positions around Buchholz station. Nevertheless, evidence of enemy confusion was beginning to emerge – at 0700 the panzers entered Honsfeld by the simple expedient of joining a column of retreating American trucks – and Peiper could congratulate himself on finally having broken through the initial defensive crust. This should have enabled him to push forward at speed, but yet another problem delayed his advance. The diversions and skirmishes of the previous 24 hours had drained the fuel tanks of the Kampfgruppe, making it essential to capture enemy stockpiles of petrol.

An American fuel dump was known to be at Büllingen, a few miles to the north of Honsfeld, and although this was some way beyond his route, Peiper had no choice but to order another diversion, particularly when he received reports that some of his King Tigers, bringing up the rear of the column, had already run dry. Shrugging aside an attempted ambush by US tank destroyers, the panzers moved forward to capture an airstrip at Morschheck and then the precious fuel. By 0900, American prisoners of war were pouring petrol into thirsty tanks and half-tracks, while reconnaissance units probed north and west to prevent enemy interference. But it was midday, before the Kampfgruppe could resume its advance and even then it took time to get back onto the original route.

Peiper may have gained flexibility and endurance, but he still had to create momentum. A combination of unexpectedly effective defence by small, isolated groups of Americans and the need to make diversions to search for lines of advance or fuel had denied him the chance to build up a Blitzkrieg-style assault and, as he began to realise this, signs of frustration emerged. Already at Honsfeld and Büllingen, American prisoners had been shot out of hand. During the next phase of operations, the Kampfgruppe was to reach new depths of atrocity just to the south of the Belgian town of Malmédy.

Once refuelled, Peiper led his column south to Moderscheid and then west towards his next key objective: the town of Ligneuville, at the head of the Amblève valley. His reconnaissance unit went ahead, opening up a reasonable route through Ondenval to Thirimont, but the most direct approach thereafter was little more than a muddy track. Peiper, therefore, turned north, aiming to join the main road to Ligneuville at Baugnez, a couple of miles outside Malmédy, after which he would turn south towards his objective. Such a move meant that for a

Left: Scenes from the Battle of the Bulge. Enjoying local superiority, the Kampfgruppe scythed a bloody path through the defences with the burnt-out wreckage of US vehicles marking the line of advance. However, the strain of fighting in sub-zero temperatures and the tenacity of the Allied resistance quickly took their toll.

SPEARHEADING THE OFFENSIVE

By early December 1944 the Germans had secretly massed 24 divisions along the Ardennes sector of the western front in preparation for their final offensive against the US and British forces. The high command planned to split the Allies in two by driving north to the Belgian port of Antwerp and south through Luxembourg. Kampfgruppe Peiper was the linch pin of the northern push. This well-balanced column was to lead the race to Antwerp and seize vital bridges over the river Meuse near Liège.

The importance attached to their mission can be judged by the calibre of the troops under Peiper's command and the quality of their equipment. Consisting of 70 tanks of the 1st SS Panzer Battalion, 30 King Tigers of the 501st Heavy Tank Battalion, and the 2nd Battalion, 3rd Panzergrenadier Regiment, the Kampfgruppe contained the cream of Hitler's armed forces. Their leader, Joachim Peiper, a veteran of the bloody battles around Kharkov on the Eastern Front, was widely recognised as a cunning fighter, able to respond to any adversity with great daring and tenacity. Despite the undoubted quality of the Kampfgruppe, its fighting abilities were severely undermined by fuel shortages that forced Peiper to waste valuable time searching for US petrol dumps and allowed the Allies to organise a devastating response.

Below: Smiling paras hitch a lift on a King Tiger during the early phase of the onslaught. Bottom left: German infantry loot winter equipment from dead GIs. Bottom right: Vast stockpiles of petrol were destroyed by US troops to slow the Kampfgruppe down. Far right: Inspecting a 'tamed' Tiger. Starved of vital fuel, these leviathans failed to maintain the momentum of the advance.

short distance he was travelling parallel to the main road, less than 1000yds to his left, and it was as the lead tanks probed north from Thirimont at about 1330 hours, that they saw an American column moving away from them along the road to Ligneuville. Opening fire, they destroyed the leading truck and, as panzer grenadiers dismounted to clear the road, American troops began to surrender. They were in no position to offer resistance, lacking heavy weapons and suffering the full effects of surprise.

As the panzers wound round the Baugnez crossroads, panzer grenadiers gathered in about 120 prisoners and herded them into a nearby field. Leaving two Panzer IVs to stand guard, Peiper lost no time in pushing on towards Ligneuville, particularly as he now had reports that an American headquarters was stationed there. As the column disappeared down the road, the prisoners were suddenly subjected to machine-gun fire and 85 men of Battery B, 285th Field Artillery Observation Battalion were killed. It was the single worst atrocity against POWs in northwest Europe during the campaign of 1944-45 and, as the bodies were discovered soon afterwards by American troops advancing out of Malmédy, it ensured a hardening of Allied resolve that was to prove crucial in the following days.

Peiper, unaware of this development, entered Ligneuville at 1430. A small group of Shermans crippled the leading Panther outside the Hôtel des Ardennes, but was quickly forced to withdraw. Nevertheless, a bridge over the Amblève river was seized intact and Peiper, by now under considerable pressure from his divisional commander, SS-Oberführer (Brigadier) Wilhelm Mohnke, lost no time in pressing forward to Stavelot. At first, the way seemed clear, and the column passed through the villages of Pont and Lodomez without incident; but it was beginning to get dark and snow was falling heavily. This part of the advance was a gamble, for Peiper had no way of knowing if Stavelot was defended, yet he needed to capture the town and its bridge across the Amblève if he was to reach the road to Trois Ponts and more American fuel dumps.

In fact, Stavelot was protected by nothing more than a group of 13 men from Company C, 291st Combat Engineer Battalion, but their actions late on 17 December were perhaps the most important factor in stalling Kampfgruppe Peiper. Led by Sergeant Hensel, the engineers set up an ambush position to the east of the town, where the road skirted a cliff with a steep drop on the other side, and when the first of Peiper's tanks approached, it was destroyed by a single bazooka shot. In total darkness, Peiper called a halt for the night, enabling the Americans to send forward more troops to bolster local defences.

When the Kampfgruppe resumed its advance at 0800 hours on 18 December, it had to fight to gain control of Stavelot, and although the Americans were overwhelmed before they could destroy the vital bridge, yet more delays had been imposed. Peiper was forced to push through towards Trois Ponts as quickly as he could, ignoring the existence of a fuel dump just a few miles to the north at Francorchamps.

It was a major miscalculation, made worse by the fact that by now the Americans were beginning to discern the pattern of the German advance. As Peiper left Stavelot to be guarded by a small detachment of panzers, the first elements of the US 30th Infantry Division were moving towards the town from the north, intent upon containing the threat.

Trois Ponts proved to be the turning point in the battle, however, for it was essential for Peiper to capture its bridges across the Amblève and Salm rivers if he was to reach open country on the road to the Meuse. By midday on 18 December, he should have been carving out his bridgeheads somewhere between Huy and Liège, so speed was vital, but once again the advance was stalled by hastily-prepared American defences. In this case, men of Company C 51st Combat Engineer Battalion were responsible,

priming the bridges for demolition and deploying a single 57mm anti-tank gun to cover the Stavelot road where it narrowed to pass beneath a railway viaduct. At 1045 the leading Panther nosed forward towards the viaduct, only to be destroyed by a lucky shot and, although the gallant gun-crew was wiped out, the road was blocked. Thirty minutes later, the Amblève bridge was blown and, as Peiper heard the explosion, a crucial decision was made. Instead of continuing into Trois Ponts, the Kampfgruppe turned right towards La Gleize, hoping to find an alternative crossing further up the river. The panzers were by now desperate for petrol – one of the King Tigers, its fuel tanks dry, had to be abandoned just outside Trois Ponts – and Peiper was being channelled onto minor roads where the chances of capturing American stockpiles were minimal. The destruction of the Salm bridge at Trois Ponts at 1300 reinforced the point.

The leading Panthers followed the Amblève, moving through La Gleize to the southwest. They were lucky: in mid-afternoon a bridge was found intact at Cheneux and the tanks began to cross. But their luck did not hold. Suddenly there was a break in the weather, an Allied spotter plane flew over and, despite frantic orders from Peiper to scatter the panzers under cover, fighter-bombers swept down to hit tanks and half-tracks in a devastating attack. One of the King Tigers slewed across the bridge, blocking it for over two hours, and although Peiper did not give up – he sent surviving panzers to seize yet another bridge, across the steep-sided Lienne river at Habiemont, in a final attempt to break clear – it was obvious that time had run out. US combat engineers reached Habiemont first and, as the Panthers approached, they blew the bridge. At 1630, with the light of a third frustrating day beginning to fade, Peiper accepted the success of the American

TIGER II

When the mighty Tiger II (King Tiger) entered service with the German Army in late 1944, it was the most potent main battle tank in existence, able to out-fight any Allied opposition.

Like the Tiger I, the King Tiger had an all-welded hull, but its armour was thicker, up to 185mm, and sloped to deflect anti-tank rounds. The Tiger II packed a fearsome punch: the long-barrelled 88mm gun and two 7.92mm MG34 machine guns.

Although the King Tiger was a first-rate piece of engineering, its sheer weight and size undermined its battlefield performance. The tank's maximum speed, 38km/h, was often cut by half over difficult terrain, and even with full fuel tanks its range was just over 100km. The high-velocity gun was a cause of complaint; wearing out quickly, it had to be changed frequently.

Despite these shortcomings, the arrival of the King Tiger came as a nasty shock to the Allies. Even when deployed in penny packets, it was able to take on and beat much larger forces.

By the end of the war some 500 models had been produced. Despite heavy Allied bombing, Henschel, the manufacturers, were taking only two weeks to complete a single unit; only shortages of fuel ended the King Tiger's reign of terror.

blocking moves and fell back to La Gleize.

By now, the Americans were intent on destroying Peiper's force, sending elements of two divisions to surround La Gleize and interdict the vulnerable supply line at Stavelot. By nightfall on 18 December, a battalion was preparing to attack Stavelot from the north, while an equivalent force entered Stoumont, to the west of La Gleize, inflicting a significant defeat on Peiper's reconnaissance unit. Peiper pulled his perimeter tight, concentrating his remaining force, about 2000 men and 200 vehicles, into a pocket which included La Gleize, Cheneux and the eastern outskirts of Stoumont. It was just as well that he did, for early on 19 December Stavelot was attacked. The battle for the town was to take another 48 hours to resolve in favour of the Americans, but to all intents and purposes Peiper was cut off.

He refused to give in, however. At 0700 on 19 December, a counter-attack was mounted towards the Amblève bridge at Targnon, a few miles beyond Stoumont and, despite initial problems, some progress was made. But as news of the Stavelot battle filtered through and American defences hardened around Stoumont station, Peiper was forced to pull back, sending the remains of his reconnaissance unit to reinforce the threatened supply link. They failed to make much headway, weakening the Kampfgruppe at a time when American units were rapidly closing in. Deploying the remnants of 1st SS Panzer Battalion at Stoumont, the King Tigers at La Gleize and anti-aircraft units around Cheneux, Peiper waited for the inevitable attack.

The American plan was for the 82nd Airborne Division, supported by tanks, to secure a line from Stavelot to La Gleize while two regiments of the 30th Infantry Division continued to squeeze in from the flanks. A co-ordinated assault began at 1830 hours on 20 December, when men of one regiment seized the sanatorium at Stoumont, initiating a savage hand-to-hand battle which extended well into the night. Peiper's panzer grenadiers held on, but it did them

On 19 December, elements of Peiper's column carried out one of the worst atrocities seen during the campaign in northwest Europe. On the outskirts of the Belgian town of Malmédy, 85 US prisoners of war were murdered in cold blood. Below: Pictorial evidence of the killings. News of Malmédy did much to stiffen the resolve of the American units battling for survival in the Ardennes and signalled the end of the Kampfgruppe. As the scattered pockets of resistance slowed the German attack, Allied commanders plotted a devastating counter-stroke. The US 82nd Airborne Division pounced on La Gleize and Stavelot, interdicting Peiper's line of retreat. Below left: Paras bring in a young SS trooper for interrogation. After suffering heavy losses, Peiper ordered his men to make their own way back to friendly lines.

little good. During the night US patrols began to infiltrate the German perimeter, and attempts by other elements of 1st SS Panzer Division to break through at Stavelot failed. Peiper was by no means finished, however, and at dawn on 21 December he pre-empted an American attack at Stoumont, inflicting heavy casualties on one unit; but time was running out. As the American pressure increased and air strikes became more frequent, Peiper was forced to pull in his perimeter even more. Stoumont and Cheneux fell on 23 December; at 0100 on the 24th, the remains of the Kampfgruppe, less than 800 men, were given permission to make their own way to safety. Very few succeeded.

Indeed, by 24 December the tide had begun to turn throughout the Ardennes sector, as Allied forces closed in to counter the German thrusts. Kampfgruppe Peiper had been destroyed, worn down by blocking moves, ground and air attacks and supply deficiencies. Peiper's failure to build up the momentum so essential to an armoured thrust, guaranteed his ultimate defeat.

THE AUTHOR John Pimlott is senior lecturer in War Studies and International Affairs at the Royal Military Academy, Sandhurst. He has written *Strategy and Tactics of War* and edited *Vietnam: the History and Tactics.*

DUEL
IN THE DESERT

The 15th Panzer Division of Rommel's Afrika Korps proved itself a devastating fighting force when it took on the British in North Africa

TO THE FEARFUL Italian colonists of Libya, the arrival of a lone Heinkel 111 bomber at Castel Benito on 12 February 1941 seemed to be merely another part of the fleet of German aircraft which, over the last few days, had been ferrying much-needed supplies from Sicily in an operation to establish a Luftwaffe base near to Tripoli in North Africa. From the aircraft, however, there stepped a German general, slight in stature, quick and dynamic in speech and manner, who was destined to change the whole course of events in the Desert War. The officer was Erwin Rommel, a man who had made a career of soldiering since World War I, and had played a distinguished part in the Wehrmacht's Blitzkrieg on France in May

Below: A PzKpfw IV of the 15th Panzer Division rolls past one of its victims: a British Bren-gun carrier. German tanks were not always superior to the Allies' machines, but, under Rommel's leadership, the tactical approach of his tank crews outclassed that of the British.

1940. Two days later, the 5th Light Division, the first unit of his new command, that became the Deutsches Afrika Korps (DAK), began to disembark at Tripoli.

In early 1941 the Axis war effort in North Africa was on the verge of collapse. Italian settlers lived in a permanent state of panic, and the reason was plain to see: their army – or what little remained of it after a devastating series of defeats at the hands of a tiny British force, under General Wavell – was in no position to withstand any new offensive. Indeed, the soldiers who had survived no longer had either the means or the will to continue the fight. Hitler knew that he could not allow the British to gain complete control of North Africa, since to do so would expose the Axis southern flank to attack, and might undermine the defences of his newly-won European Empire. He was, however, unwilling to commit any large formation of the Wehrmacht to the cause and opted to send a small force under the command of an experienced senior officer to retrieve the situation.

Rommel was acutely aware that his troops, thrown into a totally unfamiliar theatre of operations that required an entirely different approach to warfare, would not only have to overcome the British but also the desert. The North African desert – an area of stark contrasts – was a beautiful, but savage place. For the most part, the forthcoming battlefield was an

THE 15TH PANZER DIVISION

The heart of 15th Panzer was the two battalions of the 8th Panzer Regiment. Each battalion comprised three companies, with 20 tanks, divided between four troops, per company. Originally, PzKpfw IIs predominated, but these were replaced gradually by the more powerful PzKpfw IIIs and IVs.

In addition to an artillery regiment of three battalions, equipped with 24 10.5cm and 12 15cm guns, support for the tanks was provided by the 15th Infantry Brigade (Motorised). The brigade's two infantry regiments, the 115th and 200th, each had three battalions of three rifle companies, plus a machine-gun company of 150 men with 18 guns and six mortars, an engineer platoon and a signal section. The 13th company of each battalion had nine 7.5cm, 10.5cm and 15cm infantry-support guns, while the 14th fielded 12 3.7cm anti-tank guns.

The 33rd Reconnaissance Battalion (Motorised) provided the eyes and ears of the division and contained one heavy troop and four light troops of armoured cars. Infantry support was provided by three motorised infantry companies and an artillery company. Additional back-up came from the 15th Motor Cycle Battalion. Finally, apart from two signal and engineer battalions, the 15th Division also contained an anti-tank and an anti-aircraft battalion.

empty, waterless waste; scorchingly hot by day and bitterly cold at night. There was little natural vegetation to give shade from the merciless sun, except where a few hardy farmers had irrigated the baked earth of the coastal strip or around the few principal towns. In the hinterland, water was an even more precious commodity. Although a handful of wells supported tribes of nomads and later were to save many lost soldiers from a lonely, agonising death, most men had to carry what they needed, and nothing did they need more than water.

Movement on any scale was a perilous affair and not to be undertaken lightly; great expanses of soft, shifting sand could swallow both men and wheeled vehicles, and even tanks were easily bogged down. Only one all-weather road, the Via Balbia, traversed the 1600km from Tripoli to the Egyptian border, and it was only on this single surface that traffic could move as swiftly as in Europe. Rommel, like the British, recognised that control of this highway, following the Mediterranean coast and linking the widely-spaced towns of the Italian colony, was the key to any offensive.

Further inland native *trigh* (tracks), of limited value for large-scale movement, criss-crossed the desert. Barely adequate even when in good condition, the slightest downpour would turn them into impassible quagmires. At points where two or more *trigh* met, there was usually some sort of landmark; a

Left: Good reconnaissance in the desert could make the difference between victory or defeat. Here, two men in a camouflaged observation post scour the horizon for signs of the enemy. The man on the left is using trench-glasses while his comrade, with goggles to protect his eyes from the sun and dust, keeps a careful watch for any unusual movement behind the position. Below: A 15cm artillery piece at the moment of firing. Bottom: A column of PzKpfw IIs cruises along a desert track. Although seriously under-gunned with only a 2cm main gun, their high speed and long range made them ideal vehicles to carry out patrols.

bir (well) or *sidi* (the grave of a Moslem saint). These junctions were to play an important part in the Desert War as they were used as points of reference in a landscape devoid of distinctive natural features. Strategically important, these man-made features were often fortified and held by a garrison or acted as advance supply depots. Sense of direction, however, lost all meaning when violent sandstorms could obliterate all reference points, and mirages made a mockery of attempts at judging distances.

The Wehrmacht did nothing to protect their vehicles from the scouring effects of dust and sand

Because the Germans had no recent experience of desert warfare, and their allies failed to provide either adequate or accurate information, the Afrika Korps was ill-prepared for the task in hand. In the early months of the war the Germans had to rely on Italian reports based upon their battles with the British in Egypt, but they were soon found to be grossly inaccurate, lacking vital details and maps. The first Afrika Korps units were supplied, in consequence, with unnecessary or badly-designed equipment. The most glaring mistake was the Italian recommendation that the Germans should not send diesel engines to North Africa. Although it was widely recognised that they were superior to petrol driven engines under desert conditions, and the Italians themselves had developed a successful tropical-pattern diesel engine, they had failed to inform their partner. The German Army did nothing to protect their vehicles' motors from the scouring effects of dust and sand, and paid a high price for their lack of foresight during their first months in the desert. Many tanks were put out of commission and the average life of a tank engine was between 1000 and 2000km – about half that of the more reliable British armour. It was not until special filters were rushed into service that the Germans could match the endurance of their opponent.

The second most important omission from the Italian reports was the need for special camouflage skills in the open desert. The first Afrika Korps vehicles to arrive were covered in standard European greys and greens as the Wehrmacht did not possess paint appropriate to North Africa. A makeshift solution was found: tanks were sprayed in oil over which sand was thrown. The greatest need, however, was to break up the outline of stationary vehicles and their shadows. Tank crews were taught

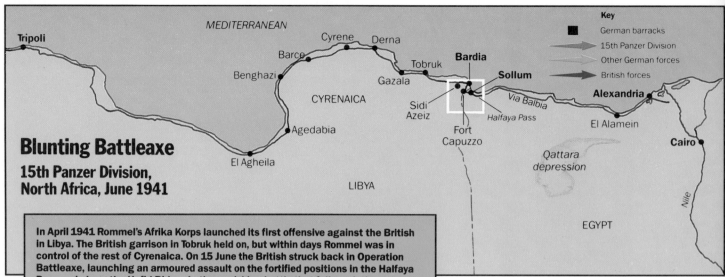

Blunting Battleaxe
15th Panzer Division, North Africa, June 1941

In April 1941 Rommel's Afrika Korps launched its first offensive against the British in Libya. The British garrison in Tobruk held on, but within days Rommel was in control of the rest of Cyrenaica. On 15 June the British struck back in Operation Battleaxe, launching an armoured assault on the fortified positions in the Halfaya Pass and along the Hafid Ridge. In the punishing battle that followed, the newly-arrived 15th Panzer Division suffered heavy casualties. But on 17 June, after regrouping, the division began an outflanking manoeuvre to the south, engaging its opponents south of Fort Capuzzo and forcing them to withdraw.

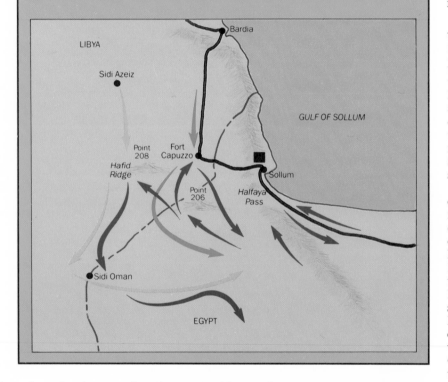

to make extensive use of netting covered in camel thorn when not on the move, and infantry learned to dig slit-trenches into the side of dry river courses. Although never fully effective, these simple but time-consuming precautions did provide a measure of protection against low-flying aircraft.

If the desert placed a great strain on the equipment of the Afrika Korps, it tested also the stamina and spirit of the German soldier. Initially, the High Command made no special arrangements for the welfare of its troops in the field, but experience soon showed that the normal methods of feeding and hygiene were unsuited to desert conditions. Substitutes for the German soldier's basic foodstuffs were issued; beans instead of potatoes and biscuits in place of bread. It was found that butter and margarine turned rancid in the heat, and olive oil was issued as a replacement. With the exception of the occasional piece of cheese and cans of tinned beef, only

Above right: An 88mm gun in action during the early stages of Rommel's attack. This much-vaunted weapon, although suffering from a high profile that made it hard to conceal in the desert, ended the Matilda's reputation as the 'queen' of the battlefield. Its high rate of fire and long range made the '88' far more effective than any anti-tank gun possessed by the British. **Right: Rommel (left foreground) and his generals inspect the front line at Sollum – the 'Desert Fox' always led from the front.**

locally-produced foodstuffs were available. In general, the diet was monotonous and lacked Vitamin C.

The men of the Afrika Korps were sent to North Africa dressed in a pattern of clothing developed in late 1940: jacket, breeches, sun helmet and boots. Practical experience, however, showed that the uniform was badly designed – the jacket was too tight, the breeches restricted movement and the sun helmet gave little protection against smallarms fire and shrapnel. Only the boots stood up to the rigours of the desert campaigning. Experience soon taught the men that it was possible to fight even in the hottest months, if clothing was light, loose and comfortable. Standard issue clothing was replaced or amended to suit individual needs.

Rommel, although aware of the Afrika Korps' lack of battle readiness and the shortcomings of much of its equipment, decided to go over to the offensive as quickly as possible. His plans were based on his estimation of Wavell's ability to respond to any attack by the elements of the Afrika Korps he had to hand. Rommel surmised, correctly as events were to show, that the most recent defeat of the Italians on 7 February had totally exhausted the British. After a series of limited attacks against enemy outposts in March, Rommel felt confident enough to plan a major offensive against the weakened British Army that was holding a series of passes along the coastal plain. On 4 April the order to attack was given: the objective was the recapture of the Libyan province of Cyrenaica. A few days later, after a series of sharp defeats for the British, the Afrika Korps was poised to cross the Egyptian frontier. It had forced Wavell's men to retreat over 800km, and only Tobruk, the sole deep-water port between Tripoli and Alexandria, remained in Allied hands. Both sides, however, were exhausted by the battles and stood back to await the arrival of reinforcements.

It was on this dramatic stage that one of Rommel's finest units, the 15th Panzer Division, made its desert debut. The division had lain impotent at Naples in the first weeks of April, but by the end of the month its armoured spearhead, the 8th Regiment, arrived in Tripoli.

Wavell, aware of the division's arrival, pushed forward the plans for his own offensive, code-named Operation Battleaxe. Reinforcements were hurried to North Africa, and on 12 May the convoy carrying the 'Tiger Cubs', 238 Matilda and Crusader tanks

DEUTSCHES AFRIKA KORPS

Following the severe defeat of the Italians in North Africa in 1940-41, Hitler ordered the despatch of a German force under General Erwin Rommel to salvage the situation. The newly-formed Deutsches Afrika Korps (DAK) arrived in Africa in February 1941. After fighting a series of battles along the Mediterranean coast between early 1941 and July 1942, the DAK succeeded in pushing the British forces back to the gates of Alexandria.
The arrival of Montgomery and the steady build-up of the British and Commonwealth army, however, allowed the British to regain the upper hand, and after the decisive Battle of El Alamein in October/November 1942, the Afrika Korps was forced into a

docked at Alexandria. Much work, however, needed to be done before they would be ready for action; they had to be modified to suit desert conditions and their crews prepared for combat. And during the few weeks remaining before the attack, Rommel was far from idle.

Behind the bristling shield of '88s', the panzers waited, silent and menacing

Forbidden to unleash the full force of his panzers due to the acute shortage of supplies, he opted for a strategy of mobile defence to defeat the imminent British offensive. To this end, Halfaya Pass, a meandering gorge, was turned into a fortress. Throughout the long hot days of early June, his anti-tank gunners dragged their powerful 88mm guns into position. Dug in, so that only their sleek, camouflaged muzzles poked over the parapets of their emplacements, these weapons were sited to cover every approach to the pass. Inland, Point 206, guarding the approach to Fort Capuzzo, and Point 208, on Hafid Ridge, were fortified in a similar manner. Behind this bristling 'shield', Rommel deployed the 200 tanks of his armoured 'sword'. The men of 15th Panzer waited, silent and menacing, behind Fort Capuzzo while their comrades of the 5th Light Division garrisoned Sidi Azeiz to the west.

As dawn broke on 15 June, the normally silent desert reverberated to the throaty growl of the engines of the tanks belonging to the British 4th and 7th Armoured Brigades. As the cold morning mist cleared to reveal the great plumes of dust thrown up by the closing British armour, the German gunners manned their weapons. They did not open fire, but allowed the tanks to continue their headlong dash into Rommel's carefully-prepared first line of defence – minefields. In an instant, the steam went out of the British attack; their tanks, bogged down in the minefields, unable to either advance or retreat, were sitting ducks and rich pickings for the deadly '88s'. Round after round struck home. So great was the slaughter at Halfaya Pass, the British rechristened it

final, but stubbornly-contested retreat westwards. Operation Torch, the Anglo-American landings in Morocco and Algeria on 8 November 1942, opened up another front and the Afrika Korps was finally forced to capitulate on 12 May 1943 in Tunisia.

ARMOURED ADVERSARIES

The battles fought around the Egyptian border in June 1941 were the first direct confrontation between major armoured units of the British Army and the Afrika Korps. These actions proved to be not only a test of tactics and the battlefield use of tanks, but also an acid test of rival armour design. Although the Afrika Korps was provided with quantities of PzKpfw IIs and IVs, it was the PzKpfw III that formed the mainstay of the 15th Panzer Division. The first full production model of this tank, the Ausf F, appeared in early 1940 and was armed with a 3.7cm main gun. Later that year, however, the Ausf G, equipped with a more powerful short-barrelled 5cm gun, entered production. Both these versions fought in the early desert battles.

The 3.7cm gun of the Ausf F, however, lacked the punch to penetrate the frontal armour of British infantry tanks and its own armour was particularly vulnerable to the British six-pounder anti-tank gun.

The PzKpfw III's main adversary on the British side, the Matilda, was a comparatively heavily-armoured but slow-moving infantry support tank. In 1940 the Matilda was almost invulnerable to anti-tank fire, but the use of German '88s' in an anti-tank role soon ended its reputation as the 'queen' of the battlefield. In the end, the Matilda's slow cross-country performance and inadequate armament made it less effective than the faster German tanks.

'Hellfire Pass'. Elsewhere, the burning wreckage of Matilda and Crusader tanks told the same story and, although the 4th and 7th Brigades had made some headway at Fort Capuzzo and Hafid Ridge, Wavell's offensive was over. In one bloody, vicious day the Afrika Korps had destroyed over half of his Tiger Cubs.

Although the bitter actions on the 15th had cost Rommel a fair proportion of his infantry and guns, his tank force was as fresh as it had been at the start of the battle. The men of the 15th Division were rested, they had eaten well and had time to prepare both themselves and their tanks for action. They did not have to wait long – at dawn the division's 8th Panzer Regiment was ordered to retake Fort Capuzzo by frontal assault. As part of a diversionary attack to the south, the 5th Light Division was sent against Hafid Ridge.

At 0500 hours the regiment's Panzer Mark IIs, IIIs and IVs roared into life. Their crews steeled themselves for battle. The tanks rolled forward at 24kph; it was the turn of the Afrika Korps' tanks to prove their mettle in the face of a storm of shot and shell. Rommel believed that by a combination of fire and movement his tanks would swamp, and then destroy the British defences. He did not, however, reckon on the skill of the British anti-tank gunners, who poured a devastat-ing rain of fire onto the 8th Regiment. Time and time again the German tanks advanced, but the defenders stood firm. Six hours later the regiment was on the point of total annihilation – only 30 tanks had come through the barrage unscathed – and was forced to concede defeat.

Rommel, however, then displayed the genius that marked him out as one of the greatest commanders of World War II and earned him the nickname of the 'Desert Fox'. Although his forces had received a severe mauling, he knew that the British were at the end of their tether and that one bold stroke would finish them off. He ordered the 8th Regiment and 5th Light Division to regroup to make a wide, sweeping thrust into the desert to outflank the British at Fort Capuzzo and Hafid, and then to push on to relieve the hard-pressed garrison at Halfaya.

Throughout the night of 16/17 June the men of the 15th Division worked on their tanks; crews struggled to repair damaged tracks, engines were cleared of sand and weapons were cleaned. By early morning, the division was ready for action, and at 0900 hours the order to advance was given. At first nothing barred their way. The British were caught off balance – elements of the 7th Armoured Brigade had withdrawn across the Egyptian border to refuel and rearm, leaving only a handful of Matildas of the 4th Brigade at Fort Capuzzo to aid the hard-pressed men of the 22nd Guards Brigade. The British commander at Capuzzo recognised that his troops were in danger of being surrounded and ordered an immediate withdrawal, to be covered by his armour.

To the tank crews, survival not victory was the order of the moment

As the Matildas raced south to keep the line of retreat open, the panzers of the 15th Division pushed north to close the trap. A few hours later the two forces collided. In this desperate struggle, as each side sought to gain the upper hand, the thicker armour of the Matildas, their guns and the skill of their crews, were an equal match for the German tanks unsupported by their '88s'. At long range. each side's shells would bounce off the enemy's armour with a deafen-

Opposite page, top: The smashed and burnt-out wreckage of Matilda tanks. Their valiant stand against the might of the 15th Division on 17 June gained time for the British infantry at Fort Capuzzo to escape Rommel's trap. Opposite page, below: PzKpfw IIIGs, with the short 5cm gun, pursue the defeated Allies. Above: The crew of a 10.5cm leFH (*leichte Feldhaubitze*) 18 await the order to fire. Unpacked shells litter the ground around the gun.

Corporal, 15th Division North Africa 1941

The basic DAK uniform was standard German tropical kit. However, clothing discipline was much less strict in the desert than in other theatres of war. This man is wearing a *Bergmütze* (peaked field cap), a light-weight tropical field service jacket with 'death's head' insignia on the lapels and a pair of flared 'riding breeches'. The latter narrow below the knee to button tightly round the calves and are tucked into lace-up boots. Like much of the clothing supplied to the Afrika Korps, the boots and jodhpurs were uncomfortable to wear in the desert and were soon 'lost' or replaced.

ing, metallic roar. To the crews, drenched in sweat, their sight blinded by dust and their throats parched for lack of water, survival rather than victory was the order of the moment. Hidden by the folds of the ground or thick clouds of sand, tanks would blunder into each other; then it was time for a speedy manoeuvre and a steady aim. Life depended on hitting the enemy before he could line up on you. The battle raged with unheard of intensity for six hours—it gave the British infantry time to retreat across the Egyptian border and delayed Rommel's arrival at Halfaya until 1600, but the cost was grievously high. The Matildas had been severely punished for their brave stand; very few returned to the British lines.

By the evening of the 17th, Rommel had won a decisive victory and Wavell's Operation Battleaxe had been defeated. In its first large-scale offensive the Afrika Korps lost only 25 tanks totally destroyed while the British lost 87 of their Tiger Cubs, with, many more left on the battlefield. The crushing of Battleaxe was much more than just the defeat of another British force, for it also gave birth to the legend of Rommel's invincibility in the minds of both the British soldier and his commanders. The subsequent removal of Wavell and the senior officer of the 7th Armoured Brigade served only to reinforce this belief. Although the men of the 15th Panzer Division did not believe they had fought with superior equipment, they could feel justifiably proud of their ability to return to the fray after suffering heavy losses, and they must have sensed that, in the Desert Fox, they had a commander worth more than a division of the enemy.

THE AUTHOR James Lucas served with the Queen's Own Royal West Kent Regiment during the North African Campaign and is currently Deputy Head of the Department of Photographs at the Imperial War Museum, London.

THE 79TH ARMOURED DIVISION

Formed in October 1942, the 79th Armoured Division (whose insignia is shown above) was reorganised in March 1943 and converted into an assault formation, tasked with a highly specialised role during the D-day landings of June 1944. Equipped with specialist vehicles and weapons, the way in which the division's organisation changed during the course of the war made it a unique formation. When on active service, the 79th fought in dispersed groups, providing armoured assistance for conventionally organised divisions.

During the Normandy landings, the 79th fought within an area 200 miles wide and 150 miles deep.

Over such a large battlefield, however, a sophisticated organisation was required to ensure the effective operation of centralised control, communications, re-supply and maintenance systems. The 79th Armoured Division thus comprised four main elements: an armoured brigade equipped with DD tanks and divided into three tank regiments; an armoured engineer brigade equipped with AVREs; a second armoured brigade equipped with minesweeping flail tanks; and a CDL brigade. After D-day, the division expanded to include a brigade equipped with flame-throwing 'Crocodile' tanks, another brigade fitted out with 'Buffalo' tracked amphibious assault vehicles, and an armoured personnel carrier regiment.

The division built up a distinguished record during the fighting from D-day to the end of the war, seeing action at Caumont, Villers Bocage, Caen, Falaise, the Rhine crossing, the Ruhr pocket and on through northwest Germany.

HOBART'S FUNNIES

During the Normandy landings of June 1944, the 'funnies' of the 79th Armoured Division were tasked with breaching the formidable German defences of the 'Atlantic Wall'

ON THE MORNING of 20 August 1942 a group of high-ranking German officers looked with satisfaction towards the sea front at Dieppe, to the piles of dead bodies and wrecked Churchill tanks that marked the destruction of the Canadian 2nd Division in the previous day's battle. The Allies had mounted a large-scale raid on the French channel port of Dieppe on 19 August, and it had ended in disaster. None of the objectives had been achieved and casualties were heavy: over 3300 men were killed, wounded or captured out of the 5000-strong Cana-

The Sherman Crab (below and main picture) was used by the 30th Armoured Brigade, 79th Armoured Division, during the Normandy landings. The 43-chain flail drum was powered from the main engine, and wire cutters were situated beneath the rotor arms. Above left: A Sherman Duplex Drive (DD). The canvas screen displaced the tank's volume and enabled it to float. Far left: Valentine Mk III and MK VIII tanks, on which the DD principle was first tested.

dian force, and the 30 tanks that comprised the assault's heavy armour lay stranded on the shingle beach or trapped amid the concrete road blocks on the promenade. A humiliating blow for the Allies, Dieppe nonetheless provided them with lessons of real military value, to be learned and put to good the effect some two years later in Normandy.

Combined Operations Headquarters compiled a report based upon a detailed analysis of the Dieppe raid, and one of its main findings was the need for overwhelming close-support fire power 'during the critical stages of the attack'. Dieppe had illustrated the inability of the conventional tank to meet this requirement; for an assault on a fortified coast a whole range of armoured vehicles would be needed. These would have to be capable of protecting the men and equipment whose job it was to smash and clear a way through the enemy's defences. Integrating the special skills of the engineer with those of the tankman, a new formation was called for and found in the shape of the 79th Armoured Division. Under the command of maverick tank enthusiast, Major-General Percy Hobart, the 79th had only recently been formed, and was currently being trained from scratch for front-line service. Hobart was called to the War Office in March 1943, where the Chief of the Imperial General Staff, General Sir Alan Brooke, offered him the job of converting his division for this new role.

When not flailing, the Crab could fire its main armament and act in a conventional role

Hobart set about transforming the 79th Armoured Division with all his customary enthusiasm, and a programme of rapid expansion was put into effect. In addition to the existing specialist units that were being incorporated into the division, other armoured units were also sent to the 79th for training in the handling of amphibious tanks – including three tank battalions from the US Army.

In the period leading up to the Normandy landings the 79th deployed most of its resources in the development of four highly specialised armoured fighting vehicles (AFVs), popularly known as 'funnies'. These were the DD tank, the Crab, the AVRE and the CDL. The DD (Duplex Drive) was the best of a number of designs submitted to the War Office for an amphibious tank. It took the form of a conversion kit for a standard Sherman tank, enabling it to be launched from a parent ship up to 5000yds from the coast, and yet capable of 'swimming' ashore. An incidental advantage of the DD design was the collapsable canvas screen surrounding the tank that hid it from view – German defenders thus confused the tanks with small open boats and deemed them not worth firing at. On D-day itself, the DD-equipped tanks almost doubled the strength of the heavy armour that landed on the British sector.

Once ashore, the Crab mine-sweepers came into their own. The Normandy beaches were extensively mined and any attempt to clear them could be expected to encounter devastating fire from the German defenders. The solution was the bullet-proof mine-sweeping Crab which, like the DD system, was based on the Sherman tank. A rotary flailing device was fitted to the front of the tank, its flailing chains setting off the mines at a safe distance ahead of the tank. When not flailing, the Crab could fire its main armament and act in a conventional armour role.

79th Armoured Division
D-day, 6 June 1944

Port-en-Bassin
Arromanches
Gold
Le Hamel
La Rivière
Asnelles
Juno
Courselles
ENGLISH CHANNEL
St Aubin
Bernières
Sword
Langrune
Luc
Lion
Ouistreham
Douvres
Houlgate
Cabourg
Bayeux
Seulles
Creuilly
Esquay
Hermanville
Merville
Dives
Périers
Sallenelles
Varaville
Biéville
Benouville
Robehomme
Lébisy
Ranville
Bures
Mue
Caen
Orme
Bretteville
Dives

Key
- - - Allied front line, 2400 hours
→ Allied assaults

Advancing out from the minefields to deal with battlefield obstacles and defences were the AVREs (Armoured Vehicle Royal Engineers). These were Churchill tanks with their main gun removed and replaced by a 12in spigot mortar. Designated the Petard, but commonly known as the 'flying dustbin', the AVREs were capable of lobbing these high explosive charges to a distance of 80yds. Concrete walls and emplacements could be breached with 'flying dustbins', and their dramatic effect sometimes encouraged engineer tank commanders to extend their duties and charge forward in the assault role. In addition, the AVREs carried or towed a whole range of devices to deal with particular problems on the battlefield. Sea walls could be spanned by SBG (Small Box Girder) bridges; anti-tank ditches would be filled in with fascines carried on the tank's hull; and roller 'carpet layer' AVREs laid a continuous track enabling heavy vehicles to cover soft ground on the beaches.

Secrecy was vigorously imposed concerning the activities of the 79th Armoured Division, and never more so than with the CDL tanks. Given the deliberate misnomer of Canal Defence Lights, the CDLs were Matilda and Grant tanks fitted with special turrets containing a high-intensity arc light. This was capable of lighting up a frontage of 350yds at a range of 1000yds. Much work was done in developing the CDL, but it was eventually decided not to deploy them for the Normandy landings. However, they were used to good effect later in the war, notably during the crossing of the Rhine in March 1945.

By the spring of 1944, the 79th was shaping up as a fighting formation and trials were laid on for the Allied commanders – including Field-Marshal Bernard Law Montgomery and General Dwight D. Eisenhower – who invariably left the proving ground highly impressed by the division's potential. Hobart stressed to his officers and men the key role they were to play in the coming battle – if they failed to overcome the German defences the Allied infantry might never be able to break out from the beaches, leaving them in a hopeless position to deal with the inevitable enemy counter-attacks.

The Allied assault was to be launched across a front of 45 miles, with five divisions landing between Varreville and Ouistreham. Along this section of the 'Atlantic Wall' the Germans had constructed a strong system of defensive positions, with guns of all calibres protected within reinforced concrete emplacements. In addition, there were anti-tank ditches and walls, minefields, coils of barbed wire and beach obstacles loaded with Tellermines. Natural obstacles such as cliffs had been fortified, and the maximum use had been made of normal sea walls within the general coastal defence system. The Allied plan was fraught with danger but Eisenhower, as Supreme Allied Commander, had two main advantages: aerial supremacy and the element of surprise achieved during the landing itself. To the leading waves of the invasion was assigned a massive weight of armour, with the task of overwhelming the defences during the first few hours. A spearhead role was given to the DD tanks and the LCTs carrying

the specialised armoury of the 79th Armoured Division. The three divisions in the British sector all had special assault teams provided by the 79th, under the immediate command of Hobart's deputy, Brigadier Nigel Duncan.

For the 79th Armoured Division the battle for the Normandy beaches took the form of small, often isolated actions by the individual assault groups. Each group met varying degrees of resistance, but all of them were actively engaged in opening a way forward through the German positions. The men of the 79th had been among the first to hit the beaches, and a common theme in accounts of D-day was the relief felt by the infantry on coming ashore to see the assault groups ahead of them clearing a way through the minefields and knocking out German gun emplacements. Whenever the Allied infantry were pinned down or unable to overcome a particular obstacle, a tank of the 79th would be called for to resolve the deadlock.

Arriving on the beaches in the vanguard of the assault, it was inevitable that many of the 79th's tanks

② Dropping the brushwood bundle into the ditch below, the AVRE begins to topple forward...

③ The heavy frontal armour, independently-sprung wheels and roomy interior of the Churchill AVRE ease the crew's discomfort on impact with the ground.

④ Extremely manoeuvrable, and able to turn on its axis when in neutral, the AVRE negotiates the fascine with ease – the result is the modern equivalent of medieval siege warfare.

① After laying a Small Box Girder Bridge (SBG), an AVRE carries a fascine to the crest of the obstacle.

In the wake of the Normandy landings, as Allied forces advance south along the Falaise road, a Sherman Armoured Recovery Vehicle (ARV) tows a crippled tank through Bourgébus, south of Caen.

would be knocked out. At La Rivière on Gold Beach, a well-sited 88mm anti-tank gun, firing from a huge pillbox, shot up two AVREs until a Crab worked its way outside the gun's traverse to within 100yds of the enemy strongpoint. The Crab let fly a shell from its 75mm main gun that went straight through the embrasure and silenced the German gun permanently.

Of the three beaches on the British sector, Sword Beach, west of Ouistreham, was considered one of the hardest to secure. Here, at the eastern edge of the Allied landings, the fight to dislodge the Germans revealed the ability and courage of the 79th's assault teams. The leading tanks of the first team waded ashore under heavy fire, and the two Crabs at the front flailed up the beach until one was hit. The second carried on alone until a clear lane was opened, although a party of sappers had to complete the clearance by hand in spite of being sniped upon. Number 2 team arrived on schedule, but suffered heavy casualties – both Crabs were knocked out. However, a narrow gap had been made in the enemy defences. An anti-tank mound proved a major problem, especially when the team's SBG bridge was rendered useless. Captain G.C. Desanges clambered out of his tank and, aided by Sappers Price and Darrington, placed demolition charges against the mound. Smallarms fire was heavy and one bullet hit and killed Desanges, but Lieutenant A.J. Nicholson ran forward to join the group – just managing to light the fuse before he too was hit and wounded. The explosion blew a hole through the mound, and a bulldozer was employed to forge a channel through the remains. By this time, the team's AVREs had all been knocked out. Number 3 team encountered similar difficulties: its two Crabs were rendered inoperable by German gun fire and the lane had to be completed by assault sappers. The Crabs of Number 4 team cleared a lane with few problems until an 88mm anti-tank gun put four rounds into the leading Crab. Its loss was avenged by a Crab from Number 1 team. Manoeuvring into position, the Crab put a shell into the German gun and silenced it. The four teams had all opened mine-free lanes, and now moved up to take on the main defences, firing on enemy-held houses with their machine guns.

Ouistreham was proving a major obstacle to the commandos who had been tasked to capture the town, and in the afternoon 79 Squadron of the 79th Division was asked to lend assistance. The dry narrative of the squadron log provides an insight into the variety of tasks that the men of the 79th were called upon to perform:

'1500 hours: Commanding Officer 4 Commando reports to Squadron Leader that the lock gates and bridge at Ouistreham are held by the enemy and asks for assistance. 1530 hours: Squadron Leader moves off the 10 AVRE's. Enemy is surprised and west bank is taken although enemy blows the east span of the bridge. 1630 hours: After intense Besa machine-gun and Petard fire the enemy surrenders; six officers and 51 other ranks taken prisoner, with three anti-tank guns captured. Squadron takes up positions on the west bank with Bren posts on the east bank. Locks and remainder of bridges are inspected for demolition charges and are made safe. 2000 hours: Four AVREs move up to support 2nd Royal Ulster Rifles at Benouville while the remainder hold the lock gates until relieved by a new wave of infantry the following morning.'

During the night their positions were bombed and mortared but, undeterred, the sappers instigated active patrolling that brought in a large number of German prisoners – in one instance a lone sapper captured 20 Germans with just one Bren gun.

D-day totally vindicated the concept and effectiveness of the 79th Armoured Division

At the close of D-day the Allies had gained a firm hand-hold on Occupied Europe. In the following days and weeks this would be expanded until the dramatic break-out virtually destroyed the German Army in France. Much of this success was undoubtedly a consequence of the activities of the 'funnies' on D-day. The problems encountered by the American forces on Omaha Beach can be cited as proof of this. There, the Americans rejected the offer of specialist armour – with the exception of some DD tanks. Even these were launched too far from the beach and in the rough seas of the day, 90 per cent of them foundered. The infantry of the US V Corps was therefore forced to land first, without tank support that was only brought in piecemeal during later waves of the assault. Despite the fact that the German defences were not particularly strong on Omaha Beach, the result of the US policy was that American troops were only able to penetrate inland about 100yds from the water's edge – at a cost of over 2000 casualties.

D-day totally vindicated the concept and effectiveness of the 79th Armoured Division, and for the remainder of the war the division was to play a prominent part in the set-piece battles designed to break into the German homeland. New vehicles were continually added to the 79th, and by the end of the war it had expanded enormously, containing a total of 17 regiments with four times as many AFVs as a standard armoured division.

THE AUTHOR Adrian Gilbert has edited and contributed to a number of military and naval publications. His book *World War I in Photographs* covers all aspects of the Great War.

Following successful trials with a flamethrower installed in a Valentine tank, the device was incorporated into the Churchill Mk VIII in 1943. Known as the 'Crocodile', it entered service in 1944, seeing action with three regiments of the 31st Armoured Brigade, 79th Armoured Division, during the campaign in northwest Europe. Below: A Crocodile flamethrower from the 79th Armoured burns the area surrounding Belsen concentration camp. The ground was riddled with germs, and needed to be thoroughly scorched to reduce the risk of an epidemic breaking out. A 6-ton armoured trailer behind the Crocodile carried 400 gallons of napalm. The pressurised fuel was pushed through a link-bar and along the belly of the vehicle, and the fire was then directed by means of a projector in the hull gunner's position. Effective to a range of 120yds, the flame could be directed against enemy emplacements in 80 1-second bursts. The Churchill's 6-pounder main armament remained operational on the Crocodile variant, and the combination of fire and shells proved deadly to German defences.

In the frozen wastes of the Demyansk Pocket, the men of the 3rd SS-Panzer Division 'Totenkopf' held out against ferocious attacks by the Soviet Red Army

DURING THE NIGHT of 7/8 January 1942, in the midst of a blizzard and with the temperature at 40 degrees below zero, the Red Army launched a major offensive against the right flank of the German Army Group North. Three Soviet armies attacked the front of the German Sixteenth Army between Lakes Ilmen and Seliger to the south of Leningrad. Simultaneously, the Soviet Third Shock Army attacked round the southern edge of Lake Seliger on the extreme right flank of the Sixteenth Army and then swung northeast. The Soviet aim was to encircle and destroy the Sixteenth Army, uncover the entire right flank of Army Group North and split it from Army Group Centre. The Red Army very nearly achieved its objective, but was prevented from doing so by the fighting power and determination of the 3rd SS-Panzer Division 'Totenkopf (Death's Head).

The Totenkopf Division had participated in Army Group North's offensive towards Leningrad from 22 June 1941. When that offensive ground to a halt in the first week of November, the Totenkopf, as part of the Sixteenth Army, had dug in along the edge of the Valdai hills between Lakes Ilmen and Seliger. The area was heavily wooded and the SS soldiers had hastily begun to construct a fortified line. Over the next two months the Totenkopf had to face appalling weather conditions and continuous harrying attacks by the Red Army and from partisans. In sub-zero temperatures the SS soldiers found it impossible to dig in, and bunkers and trenches could be constructed only by using explosive charges. The Soviets had burnt down every dwelling in the area, and the Totenkopf was attacked by aircraft, bombarded by artillery, and ambushed by partisans. The division was seriously under strength, having suffered over 50 per cent casualties since June 1941, of

In the snow-bound, sub-zero wastes of the Eastern Front an SS soldier surveys the landscape for signs of a renewed Soviet attack.

DEATH'S HEAD
DIVISION

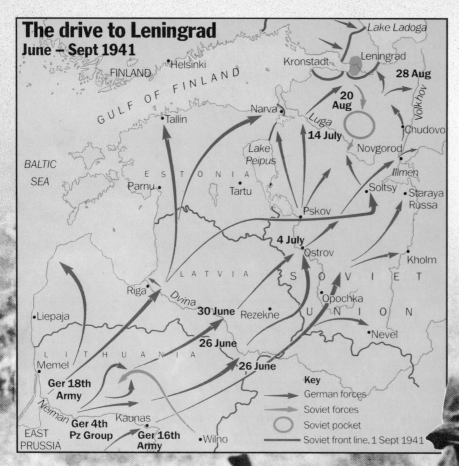

The drive to Leningrad
June – Sept 1941

Key
- German forces
- Soviet forces
- Soviet pocket
- Soviet front line, 1 Sept 1941

Right: Troops of the Totenkopf resting near Demyansk. Far Right: Theodor Eicke, commanding officer of the Totenkopf.

which only half had been replaced. Short of heavy weapons, the SS soldiers shivered in their bunkers until the Soviet offensive in January 1942.

The Totenkopf Division received only a glancing blow from the northern thrust of the Soviet offensive, which hit the army divisions on either flank. Within 24 hours the Soviets had effectively destroyed one of these divisions and had broken through some 30km to the rear. With the Soviet offensive south of Lake Seliger moving northwards, it was obvious that the two prongs would quickly meet and thus encircle the Sixteenth Army. Faced with this crisis, General Ernst Busch, the commander of the Sixteenth Army, looked to the Totenkopf to prevent a disaster.

Although many army officers viewed both the Totenkopf Division and its commander, SS-Obergruppenführer (General) Theodor Eicke, with extreme distaste, they recognised that the SS had formidable fighting qualities. To Eicke's dismay, Busch began to deploy individual units of the Totenkopf to bolster up weak points in the Sixteenth Army's defences. On 9 January, five battalions of the Totenkopf were sent to the vital road and rail junction of Staraya Russa to hold it at all costs. A few days later, two further battalions of the division were sent southeast to Demyansk.

Hitler refused to allow any units of the Sixteenth Army to withdraw in the face of encirclement, and, as a result, the army was split in two, with II and X Corps, along with the bulk of the Totenkopf Division, eventually encircled by 8 February after four weeks of bitter fighting. West of the River Lovat, the five battalions of the Totenkopf, along with army units, fought a savage battle against repeated Soviet attacks and succeeded in stabilising the German line. From 8 February 1942, the German forces in what became known as the Demyansk Pocket, consisted of two corps, with units of six divisions, includ-

ing most of the Totenkopf, a force of some 95,000 men and 20,000 horses. Surrounding this motley force were 15 fresh and well-equipped Soviet divisions and a number of armoured and ski units. Hitler forbade any attempt at break-out, and ordered that the trapped divisions should stand fast and wait for relief from the area of Staraya Russa. Hitler's decision was partly based upon Göring's claim that the Luftwaffe could supply the pocket by air. Initially, the Luftwaffe was able to supply 'Fortress Demyansk', but by the end of February the supplies flown in met only half the minimum requirement.

The Totenkopf came under the command of II Corps, which quickly recognised the value of this SS division. Soviet pressure on the Demyansk Pocket threatened to destroy it in a number of places, and once again the Totenkopf was deployed to bolster the German defences. The Totenkopf was split into two regimental Kampfgruppen (battle groups), one under Eicke's command, the other under SS-Standartenführer Max Simon, each reinforced by army units. Simon's Kampfgruppe was deployed to the northeastern side of the pocket to prevent the Soviet Thirty-Fourth Army from achieving a break-in. Eicke's group consisted of about 4100 men and was deployed at the western tip of the pocket to prevent any widening of the gap between the German front line across the River Polist and the encir-

3RD SS-PANZER DIVISION 'TOTENKOPF'

Among the 18,000 SS troops who participated in the Polish campaign in September 1939 were 6500 members of the SS-Totenkopfverbände (concentration camp guards). The men had been recruited by the notorious SS-Obergruppenführer (General) Theodor Eicke, who devised the unit's skull and cross bones badge (above), and their role was to liquidate political opponents and to deal with partisans. After the campaign, Hitler agreed to establish an SS division based around the SS-Totenkopfverbände, and thus the SS-Totenkopf Division was raised at Dachau concentration camp in November 1939, with Eicke as its commander. The Totenkopf Division participated in the 1940 campaign in France, where some of its SS soldiers murdered 100 prisoners of the Royal Norfolks in the atrocity of Le Paradis. For the invasion of the Soviet Union in June 1941, Totenkopf was attached to Army Group North. During the winter of 1941/42 it was engaged in the savage fighting in the Demyansk Pocket, and only withdrawn to be re-equipped as an SS panzergrenadier division in October 1942. In February 1943, as part of II SS-Panzer Corps, the division helped to recapture Kharkov, and it fought in the battle of Kursk in July.

During the summer it was re-equipped as an SS panzer division. In August 1944 it fought in the battle for Warsaw as part of IV SS-Panzer Corps, and in December it formed part of the relief force sent to Budapest. In March 1945 it fought in the defensive battles around Vienna before surrendering to the Americans on 9 May 1945.

cled units. The Totenkopf was so short of men at the beginning of February that Eicke recalled all wounded men from hospital and deployed supply and administrative personnel with the Kampfgruppen.

Throughout February and early March, units of the Totenkopf were engaged in an uninterrupted series of bitter engagements, repulsing attack after attack by Red Army divisions. Among the burnt-out villages and in frozen trenches SS soldiers fought on. The weather conditions were absolutely appalling, with the German and Russian soldiers fighting in chest-deep snow and in temperatures that averaged 30 degrees below zero. The SS soldiers faced not only continuous infantry attacks but Soviet artillery fire and ground attack by Red Air Force planes. Furthermore, on at least two occasions the SS troops were strafed by the Luftwaffe because the Soviet and German positions were so close to each other.

The ferocity of the fighting between Soviet and SS soldiers was such that in the few cases where the Russians overran SS positions it was usually only after every Totenkopf soldier had been killed. But the savage nature of the fighting also reflected the ideological hatred between the SS and the Russians. Many of Eicke's SS men were former concentration camp guards or had been indoctrinated by Eicke to regard the Russian soldier as a communist sub-human. It was therefore considered inconceivable for the SS to give up ground before the Russians. Eicke was a hard, brutal, callous man, and he trained his SS soldiers in his own likeness. They were taught to be hard, to accept pain and suffering, and to expect heavy casualties. For them, war was a racial struggle, a matter of the survival of the fittest, and in the Demyansk Pocket the Totenkopf soldiers proved that they were tougher and more ruthless than either their comrades in the German Army or their Soviet opponents. The SS rarely took prisoners and shot Russian civilians without a qualm. However, the intensity of the fighting was reflected in the division's casualties, and by the third week of February 1942, Eicke's Kampfgruppe, which was defending a 12km front, had been reduced to 36 officers, 191 NCOs and 1233 soldiers.

Eicke faced considerable frustrations throughout this period because he was unable to exercise command and control over all his divisional units. He was also aware that senior army officers inside the pocket continually used his SS units to strengthen the defences and bolster up weak and demoralised army units. As a consequence, the Totenkopf was taking proportionally higher casualties to army units, and Eicke resented what he believed was the sacrifice of SS men for the failures and incompetence of the army. He was also angered at the failure of the Luftwaffe to supply the pocket and suspected that the

Below: In the fighting for the Demyansk pocket Totenkopf troops man a 2.8cm s.PzB 41 gun on a light airborne carriage. How they came by this rare weapon, normally issued to paratroopers, is a mystery. Totenkopf, however, were fortunate in having a particularly resourceful divisional supply officer who was able to lay his hands on supplies and equipment from a variety of sources. Right below: A Totenkopf patrol, caught in the harsh glare of a Soviet flare, keeps a low profile during a reconnaissance mission to probe the Demyansk perimeter. Right inset: Protection against the sub-zero temperatures on the Eastern Front. The Totenkopf soldiers did not relish the bulky winter-warfare issue since it reduced their mobility, but in temperatures of 30 degrees below, frostbite was an enemy to be reckoned with.

army was not giving the Totenkopf its share of the food, ammunition and supplies. And yet the SS soldiers had more winter clothing than the army troops, thanks to supplies received at the beginning of January. Ironically, SS soldiers of the Totenkopf complained that their winter clothing was too bulky and thus reduced their mobility. But such complaints had to be weighed against the fact that wearing fur-lined boots and gloves and thick parkas reduced the number of cases of frostbite and exposure. Eicke was also fortunate in that his divisional supply officer was a resourceful man who 'acquired' equipment and supplies from a variety of sources and who arranged cargo priority drops with the Luftwaffe.

The main hardship for the Totenkopf soldiers in the Demyansk Pocket resulted from a serious shortage of shelter. The Soviets burnt down most of the villages with artillery fire and air strikes, and attempted to burn the SS out of their bunkers by using incendiary bombs. By the end of February, Soviet penetration attacks against Eicke's positions on the western side of the pocket had split the Kampfgruppe into small units, which became increasingly isolated from one another. It was impossible to evacuate the wounded to hospital, and the slightly wounded and the sick remained in the firing line. On 28 February Eicke lost contact with neighbouring army units and his SS soldiers appeared to be in a hopeless position.

The fighting conditions were desperate, recalling those at Ypres in the autumn of 1917

But, in fact, the Soviets were becoming desperate in their attacks, not realising just how near the Germans were to collapse. They were also desperate to destroy the pocket before the spring thaw turned the frozen ground into an impassable mire. Finally, in the first week of March, things began to improve for the Totenkopf. Milder weather began to reduce the number of Soviet attacks, and some 400 SS reservists were flown into the pocket, along with supplies of food, ammunition and medicine. On 20 March, Soviet attacks on Eicke's Kampfgruppe temporarily ceased. Eicke calculated that between 3 February and 20 March his Kampfgruppe had fought one Red Army division, five brigades, one ski regiment and four ski battalions, and a naval rifle brigade. The Totenkopf claimed to have inflicted over 22,000 casualties, but at a serious cost. At the end of March the Totenkopf had some 9600 SS men scattered throughout the Demyansk Pocket and at Staraya Russa. But although the Soviet attacks against the pocket had all but ceased, there remained the problem of achieving a link-up with the German forces to the west.

Hitler categorically refused to allow a withdrawal from the Demyansk Pocket, and so plans had to be made for a relief force from X Corps to attack east, some 32km from the River Polist. From the beginning of March, German reinforcements were moved into the area of Staraya Russa, and five divisions, making up X Corps under General Walther von Seydlitz-Kurzbach, prepared to attack. Hitler agreed that a simultaneous attack by units in the western part of the pocket towards Seydlitz's advancing divisions could be made to achieve a quick success. As Eicke's Kampfgruppe was positioned in the western sector of the pocket, it was ordered to spearhead the breakout, codenamed Operation Gangway. Reinforcements from four infantry divisions formed part of Eicke's Kampfgruppe, and they were to attack westwards once Seydlitz's offensive had reached the River Lovat at Ramushevo.

At 0730 hours on 21 March, X Corps began its offensive to link up with the Demyansk Pocket. Under a considerable Luftwaffe umbrella the offensive made excellent progress in the first 48 hours, driving the Red Army back from the River Polist. But the Soviets withdrew to prepared defensive positions along the River Lovat, and by 28 March X Corps laboriously had to reduce one Soviet strongpoint after another. This cost time and lives and caused Operation Gangway to be postponed repeatedly.

In fact, it took X Corps another fortnight to destroy and break through the Soviet defences west of the River Lovat. These delays were very frustrating for the units of the SS and army within the pocket, who had to conserve their ammunition and supplies for the postponed attack. It was not until X Corps captured Ramushevo on 14 April that Operation Gangway began. Although Eicke's Kampfgruppe attacked the Soviet units to the west, they became bogged down almost immediately in the full spring thaw. Instead of advancing across frozen terrain and areas of water, it was a quagmire where roads and tracks were running like streams. The fighting conditions were desperate, recalling those at Ypres in the autumn of 1917. Eicke's Kampfgruppe took six days to fight slowly towards Ramushevo, averaging about 2km per day. On 20 April a company of SS soldiers reached Ramushevo and the next day they fought across the swollen river. Finally, on 22 April, some 73 days after the encirclement of the Demyansk Pocket, X Corps had linked up and supplies

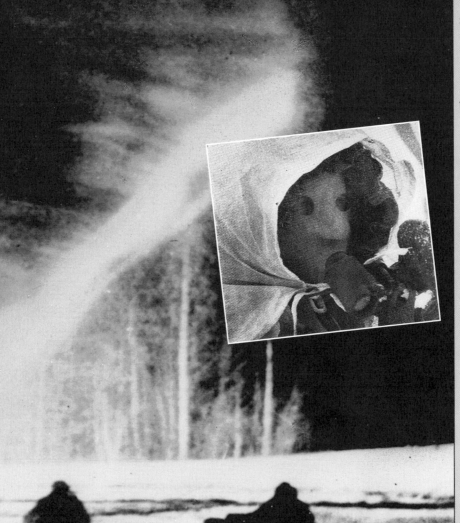

DOCTRINE OF THE WAFFEN-SS

When Heinrich Himmler was appointed commander of Hitler's SS (Schutz Staffeln or 'protection squads') in 1929 they comprised no more than 280 men. By 1933, membership had risen to 33,000, and by the end of World War II the SS had become one of the most vital elements of the Nazi military organisation. Himmler's recruits were encouraged to see their decision to join as 'the expression of a voluntary determination to continue the present political struggle upon another level.' Insisting on high standards of physical prowess and 'impeccable' racial credentials, Himmler created a desire in young Germans to belong to an elite formation that contained the best fighting men in the Nazi empire, one which surpassed the German Army both in military effectiveness and in heartfelt commitment to Nazism. Their rewards came, not in personal privileges or preferential rates of pay, but in the knowledge that they were the iron backbone of Hitler's armies. The training of SS personnel was geared to create men totally dedicated to the performance of the Führer's will. Discipline within the SS battalions could be extremely harsh, and the SS officers and NCOs inculcated their men with a savage racial contempt for their non-Aryan enemies. An SS soldier was judged by his hardness; his readiness to kill and inflict pain and suffering on others, and his ability to endure hardships himself. The fighting force created by Himmler and his lieutenants set a standard of sheer military effectiveness that has seldom been surpassed. But it must also be emphasised that they created a force of unprecedented wilful brutality which, during its career, both on and off the battlefield, committed some of the worst atrocities against soldiers and civilians of World War II.

Main picture: With machine gun and a plentiful supply of ammunition at the ready, Totenkopf infantry advance in an assault vehicle.

SS Rottenführer, 3rd SS-Panzer Division 'Totenkopf' – Demyansk 1942

This SS soldier wears makeshift winter camouflage over a standard issue greatcoat and boots. On his left collar he wears rank insignia while his right collar bears the death's head patch. His main armament is a 7.92mm MG34 machine gun, fitted with a drum magazine, and in addition he carries a pistol in a holster and a pair of stick grenades tucked into the belt. Also on the belt, he is equipped with a spare-parts set for the machine gun.

was publicly displayed by the award of 11 Knight's Crosses to personnel of the division. Eicke was awarded the oakleaves to his Knight's Cross, and among his officers awarded the Knight's Cross were SS-Sturmbannführer (Major) Karl Ullrich, who commanded the engineer battalion; SS-Sturmbannführer Franz Kleffner, who commanded the reconnaissance battalion, and SS-Sturmbannführer Otto Baum, who commanded an infantry battalion. Among the rank and file, the Knight's Cross awarded to SS-Oberscharführer (Senior Sergeant) Ludwig Köchle was for outstanding bravery and initiative as an assault trooper in destroying six Soviet strongpoints and machine-gun positions.

But such a formidable fighting performance and such personal bravery had cost the Totenkopf heavy casualties. By the end of May 1942 the division had a strength of 6700 out of an establishment of 17,000, and the majority of these were from the supply and administrative units. The survivors of the Demyansk Pocket were exhausted, undernourished and sick. Eicke requested that the Totenkopf be withdrawn from the front to be reinforced and reorganised. But Hitler regarded the Totenkopf as the one reliable unit he had around Demyansk and he refused to allow it to be withdrawn. Instead, the Totenkopf remained within what had been the Demyansk Pocket, but was now a salient, linked by a 5km-wide corridor at Staraya Russa with the rest of Army Group North. From May until October 1942 the Totenkopf Division remained at Demyansk, continually pulverised by Soviet attacks. Only in August did Hitler reluctantly agree to withdraw what was left of the formation and reorganise it.

began to move across the River Lovat, officially ending the siege.

By any standards, the SS-Totenkopf Division had displayed outstanding bravery during the battle of the Demyansk Pocket. Broken up into three Kampfgruppen, one serving outside the pocket at Staraya Russa, the SS soldiers had not only endured the most appalling weather but had fought aggressively against the Red Army. The ferocious reputation of the Totenkopf was recognised in contemporary Soviet and German Army reports. The Red Army would probably have destroyed the Demyansk Pocket had it not been for the fighting ability of the SS soldiers of the Totenkopf. Furthermore, Eicke's Kampfgruppe had played a decisive role in the successful break-out. Hitler's recognition of the role of the Totenkopf and the bravery of its SS soldiers

THE AUTHOR Keith Simpson is senior lecturer in War Studies and International Affairs at Sandhurst. He is a member of the Royal United Services Institute.

Top left: Sturmbannführer Max Seela, who led a small group which held out for over a month at Staraya Russa, enduring almost continuous air and ground attack. For this action he was awarded the Knight's Cross. Top right: Two of Totenkopf's recipients of the Knight's Cross – Otto Baum (left) and Karl Ullrich. Far left: Sturmmann Fritz Christien destroyed 13 Soviet tanks. Below: A Marder III tank destroyer.

In American military history, there is no operation more decisive in its impact than the seizure of the bridge at Remagen.

SECOND-LIEUTENANT Karl Timmermann, the 22-year-old commander of Company A, 27th Armored Infantry Battalion, could hardly believe his eyes. Called to the head of the column by the urgent cry of one of his platoon commanders, Second-Lieutenant Emmet J. ('Jim') Burrows – 'Hey, Tim, take a look at that' – he had been presented with a panoramic view of the river as it snaked past the small town of Remagen, some 300ft

below his vantage point. 'Dammit, that's the Rhine,' he exclaimed. 'I didn't think it was that close.' With the distinctive spires of the St Apollinaris Church on the left and the low hills of the Ahr river valley on the right, it was a picturesque sight, but Timmermann's attention was soon riveted on one particular feature: the Ludendorff railway bridge, spanning the Rhine just beyond Remagen. It was 1256 hours on 7 March 1945 and, incredibly, the bridge was still intact.

Timmermann's company – less than 70 men, mounted on half-tracks and closely supported by four M-26 Pershing tanks of No. 1 Platoon, Company A, 14th Tank Battalion, under Lieutenant John Grimball – was acting as 'point' to Task Force Engeman, an

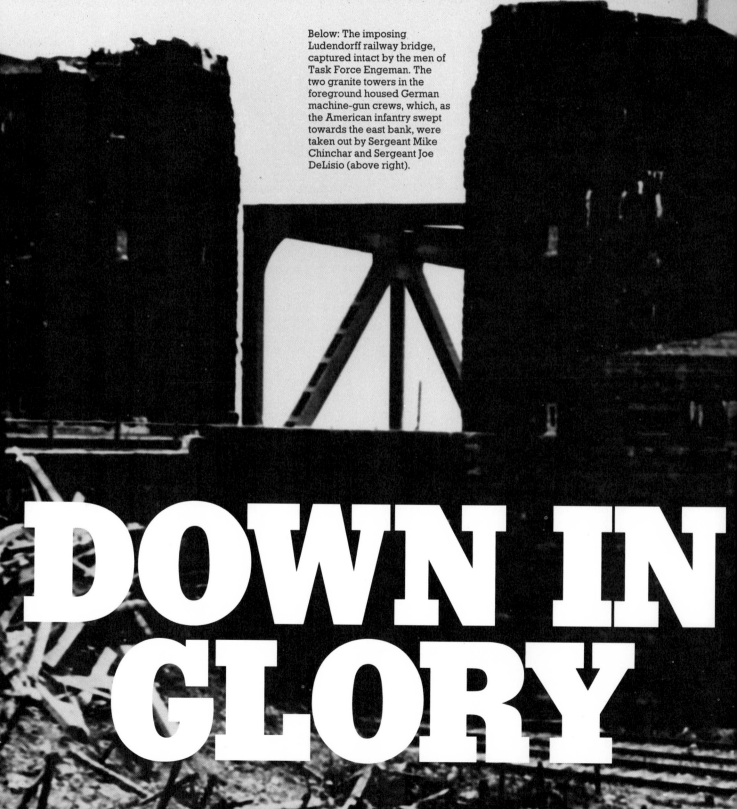

Below: The imposing Ludendorff railway bridge, captured intact by the men of Task Force Engeman. The two granite towers in the foreground housed German machine-gun crews, which, as the American infantry swept towards the east bank, were taken out by Sergeant Mike Chinchar and Sergeant Joe DeLisio (above right).

DOWN IN GLORY

all-arms formation belonging to Brigadier-General William Hoge's Combat Command B (CCB) of the 9th US Armored Division. The Task Force, commanded by Lieutenant-Colonel Leonard Engeman, Commanding Officer of 14th Tank Battalion, had left the town of Stadt Meckenheim, about 20 miles to the west of the Rhine, at 0820 that morning, under orders to capture Remagen before turning south along the west bank of the river to link up with other elements of 9th Armored on the Ahr. Part of a general move by Lieutenant-General Courtney Hodges' US First Army, the intention was to close to the Rhine all along the central sector of the Allied line, prior to assault crossings to the north and south. No mention was made of the Ludendorff bridge, partly because a crossing in this sector was not part of the plan, but also because no-one expected it still to be standing. However, its existence had been acknowledged: late on 6 March the commander of the 9th Armored Division, Major-General John Leonard, had been told unofficially that if he seized the bridge, his name would 'go down in glory'. He had merely grunted in reply, convinced that the opportunity would not arise.

Engeman had organised his Task Force with speed rather that fighting ability in mind, since German resistance was crumbling fast. Timmer-mann and Grimball, together with a platoon of combat engineers under Lieutenant Hugh Mott of Company B, 9th Armored Engineer Battalion, led the column, followed by the rest of 27th Armored Infantry and Companies A and D of 14th Tank Battalion, the latter (with the exception of Grimball's platoon) equipped with M3A4E8 Shermans and M5 light tanks respectively. Assault guns and half-track mounted mortars completed the formation. At first, progress had been slow – piles of rubble in the streets of Stadt Meckenheim had delayed the start of the advance and roadblocks (fortunately unmanned) in the villages of Adendorf and Arzdorf had forced the Americans to move cautiously – but once the column had broken out onto the Werthhoven road at 1020, the half-tracks and tanks built up an impressive turn of speed. The column arrived at the Waldschlosschen Inn, and it was from here that Timmermann had raced forward in response to Burrows' call.

As soon as Timmermann saw the bridge, he called up his battalion commander, Major Murray Deevers, who arrived, with Engeman, at about 1300 hours. Their first reaction was to call for an artillery strike, using shrapnel to prevent any movement of enemy troops from the far bank, but this was refused, chiefly because of the range. This forced Engeman to concentrate on his primary objective – the seizure of

THE 9TH US ARMORED DIVISION

Formed on 15 July 1942 from the 2nd Horsed Cavalry Division, the 9th was a 'triangular division', containing three tank, three armoured infantry and three self-propelled artillery battalions, backed by self-contained support services. After training in the United States, the division moved to Europe in 1944, staging through the United Kingdom before entering France via the Normandy beaches in August. Under the command of Major-General John Leonard, it fought in the Battle of the Ardennes in December. In late February 1945, the division advanced from the Roer river across the Cologne plain towards the Rhine, as part of the US First Army's Operation Lumberjack.

Divided into the three normal Combat Commands – A, B and R (Reserve) – the division initially fought according to battalions, but problems of co-ordination led the commander of CCB, Brigadier-General William Hoge, to organise special all-arms Task Forces, invariably named after their senior officers, for the final drive to the Rhine on 6/7 March. Task Force Prince, commanded by Lieutenant-Colonel William Prince of the 52nd Armored Infantry Battalion, was tasked with the main attack on 7 March, aiming towards the Ahr river, while Task Force Engeman, commanded by Lieutenant-Colonel Leonard Engeman of the 14th Tank Battalion, was to protect the left flank and clear Remagen. Engeman, with the whole of 27th Armored Infantry Battalion and two companies of 14th Tank Battalion at his disposal, set out from Stadt Meckenheim at 0820 hours on 7 March 1945.
Above: Insignia of The 9th US Armored Division.

Remagen
7 March 1945

During February 1945, as German resistance began to crumble, the Allied armies on the Western Front advanced from the German border to the Third Reich's last line of defence: the River Rhine. By 7 March the 21 Army Group under General Montgomery had established a line along the river from Rheinburg to Düsseldorf, and it was poised to drive into Germany's industrial heartland — the Ruhr. Further south, the US 1st and 3rd Armies under Hodges and Patton advanced on Bonn, Remagen and Koblenz. Soon after midday on 7 March, as lead elements of the US 9th Armoured Division neared Remagen they sighted an intact bridge over the Rhine. Some four hours later the first bridgehead across the Rhine was in Allied hands.

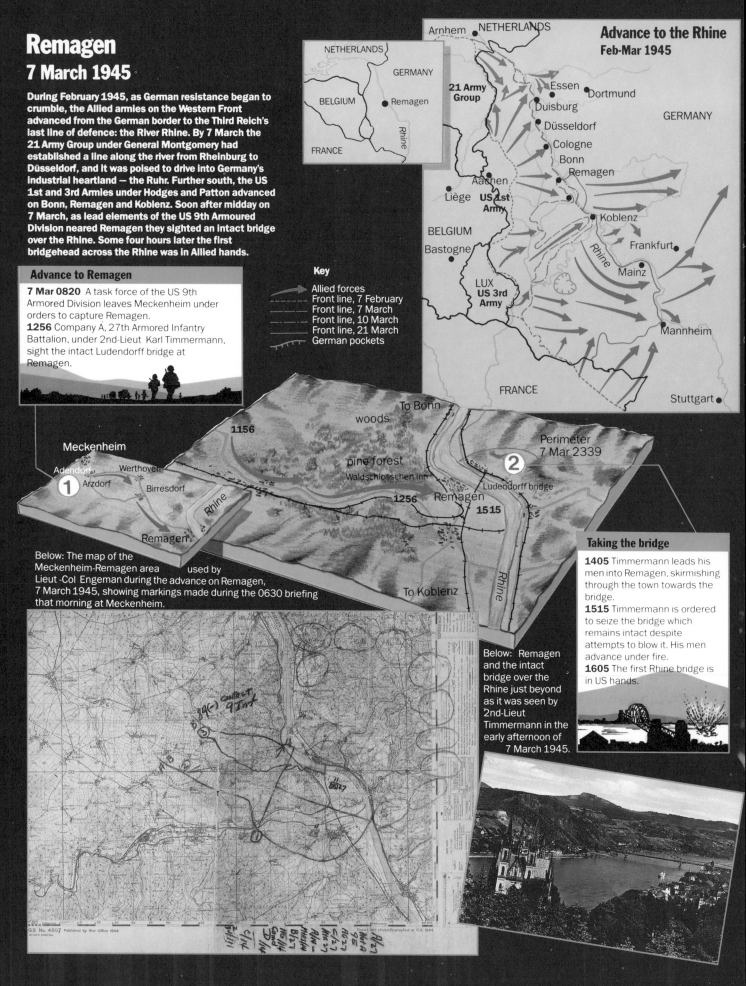

Advance to Remagen

7 Mar 0820 A task force of the US 9th Armored Division leaves Meckenheim under orders to capture Remagen.
1256 Company A, 27th Armored Infantry Battalion, under 2nd-Lieut Karl Timmermann, sight the intact Ludendorff bridge at Remagen.

Key

→ Allied forces
‑ ‑ ‑ Front line, 7 February
— ‑ — Front line, 7 March
— ‑‑ — Front line, 10 March
——— Front line, 21 March
⌢⌢⌢ German pockets

Advance to the Rhine
Feb-Mar 1945

NETHERLANDS
Arnhem
GERMANY
BELGIUM
Remagen
Rhine
FRANCE

21 Army Group
Essen
Dortmund
Duisburg
Düsseldorf
GERMANY
Cologne
Bonn
Remagen
Aachen
Liège
US 1st Army
BELGIUM
Koblenz
Bastogne
Frankfurt
Mainz
LUX
US 3rd Army
Rhine
Mannheim
FRANCE
Stuttgart

To Bonn
woods
1156
pine forest
Waldschlosschen Inn
Meckenheim
Adendorf
Werthoven
Arzdorf
Birresdorf
Rhine
Remagen
1256
Remagen
1515
Ludendorff bridge
Perimeter
7 Mar 2339
To Koblenz
Rhine

Below: The map of the Meckenheim-Remagen area   used by Lieut -Col Engeman during the advance on Remagen, 7 March 1945, showing markings made during the 0630 briefing that morning at Meckenheim.

Taking the bridge

1405 Timmermann leads his men into Remagen, skirmishing through the town towards the bridge.
1515 Timmermann is ordered to seize the bridge which remains intact despite attempts to blow it. His men advance under fire.
1605 The first Rhine bridge is in US hands.

Below: Remagen and the intact bridge over the Rhine just beyond as it was seen by 2nd-Lieut Timmermann in the early afternoon of 7 March 1945.

G.S. No. 4507 Published by War Office 1944

the town of Remagen – and as a preliminary he ordered Timmermann, together with the commander of Company C, 27th Armored Infantry, Lieutenant William McMaster, to conduct a personal reconnaissance down the hill into the western outskirts. Timmermann and McMaster set off at 1320, following a narrow track to the left of St Apollinaris and were gone for about 30 minutes. When they returned, having found no signs of enemy defences, Engeman had set up a command post overlooking the main road down into Remagen. The obvious plan would have been to continue the advance 'in column', but the main road was a tank commander's nightmare – a narrow, twisting avenue, dominated by steep-sided banks – and Engeman was determined to avoid casualties. Instead, he decided to send Timmermann's company on foot down the track on the left to clear the outskirts of the town, after which Grimball would drive down the road and join them. For convenience, rather than through any intention at this stage to seize the Ludendorff, the huge granite towers at the western end of the bridge were designated as the objective.

Timmermann briefed his squad commanders as they stared down over Remagen and then led them, in single file, along the track by the side of the church. Once at the river bank, his three platoons split up and moved towards separate objectives: No.1 Platoon under Sergeant Mike Chinchar (20 men) on the right, aiming for the railway station; No.2 under Burrows (15 men) in the centre, advancing through the town; and No. 3 under Sergeant Joseph DeLisio, with Timmermann in attendance (30 men) on the left, following the river bank. They set off at about 1405 hours, skirmishing through the houses and dodging from doorway to doorway. Chinchar's men encountered a small enemy patrol, which was hit by rifle fire and dispersed, before seizing the station. Burrows had more difficult problems, caused by a machine gun located in a building close to the Town Hall, but this was silenced by a single shot from Grimball's lead tank when it appeared down the main road at 1420. Timmermann and DeLisio made steady progress, arriving at the town cemetery close to the bridge towers just after 1500. By then, Grimball's four tanks were already in position on the towpath, laying

Below right: Captain Willi Bratge, commander of the locally-raised bridge defence company. Below centre: Bridgemaster Jakob Kleebach. When explosive charges laid by Kleebach failed to destroy the bridge, the way was clear for an American assault. Main picture: The bridge secured, American infantrymen leaguer in the Erpeler Ley tunnel. German defenders had earlier gathered here in a last-ditch attempt to halt the advance of Second-Lieutenant Timmermann's three platoons. Below left: German resistance crushed, US armour is free to move across the Rhine. These were among the last tanks to cross the bridge before it was closed to traffic.

LUDENDORFF BRIDGE

The railway bridge at Remagen, built in 1917 as part of a plan to link the Western Front with the powerhouse of the Ruhr, was named after the Chief Quartermaster General at that time, General Erich Ludendorff.

Of box girder construction with a single central span, it was over 1000ft in length, carrying two railway tracks from the flat river plain of the Rhine on the west bank, into the steep basalt cliff of the Erpeler Ley on the east. Once inside the Erpeler Ley, the tracks turned sharp left to emerge parallel to the river, joining the main north-south network in the village of Erpel. By early March 1945, the rails on the bridge had been surrounded by wooden planks and earthen approach ramps built at either end to allow vehicles to cross.

Badly damaged by an attempted demolition on 7 March, the bridge was closed to traffic by the Americans four days later, by which time pontoon bridges had been built. Engineers then tried to repair the central span, but the structure was unable to take the strain. Weakened by the effects of German counter-attacks, which included heavy artillery and V-2 rockets, the bridge collapsed at 1500 hours on 17 March (below), killing 28 American servicemen. It was never rebuilt. Today, the granite towers on both banks stand as mute testimony to the events of March 1945.

down suppressive fire across the bridge to prevent any sudden enemy move. German troops could be seen sheltering in a tunnel on the far bank, where the railway entered a large basalt cliff known as the Erpeler Ley, and some fire was being directed against the Americans from 20mm flak guns across the river. Generally, however, the enemy was strangely quiet.

This was hardly surprising, for the sudden appearance of American troops in Remagen had taken the Germans completely by surprise. The commander of the locally-raised bridge defence company, Captain Willi Bratge, was fully aware of Allied pressure along the Ahr valley – but he had insufficient troops under his command to guard against an attack from a different direction. On paper, the bridge should have been adequately protected by a German force of nearly 1000 men – a mixture of *Volkssturm* (Home Guard), Hitler Youth, Russian 'volunteers' and Luftwaffe anti-aircraft crews, as well as Bratge's own company and a squad of engineers under Captain Karl Friesenhahn – but there were probably no more than 60 of these on duty on 7 March. Many of the local men had stayed at home to protect their families, the Russians had taken every opportunity to desert and most of the Luftwaffe crews had been withdrawn, leaving just two four-barrelled 20mm flak guns under Leutnant Karl Peters to defend the bridge. To make matters worse, Peters had been ordered to move his guns from the west bank over the bridge early on 7 March – a process still incomplete by midday – and the only mobile patrol, under Sergeant Rothe, had been dispersed by Chinchar's platoon as the latter neared the station at 1420. Rothe himself had been badly wounded and was crawling painfully back to report the contact.

Bratge faced even more daunting problems as the day wore on. Despite receiving permission to prepare the bridge for demolition, his Bridgemaster, a local man called Jakob Kleebach, had only managed to find 600kg of an inferior industrial explosive, and although this had been strapped to the girders of the central span by the time the Americans arrived, it was unclear if the blast would be enough to collapse the structure entirely. In desperation, Friesenhahn had used some of the explosive to mine the earthen approach ramp on the west bank. Theoretically, Bratge should have received orders from the local defence commander – a major-general based in Cologne – but early on 7 March, unknown to Bratge, responsibility for all Rhine crossings between Cologne and Koblenz had been transferred to the nearest fighting general. In the case of Remagen, this was Major-General Otto Maximilian Hitzfeld, commanding LXVII Corps in the Ahr valley, and Hitzfeld, sent his adjutant, Major Hans Scheller, to take command of the bridge. Scheller was shocked by the inadequate defences he found as he entered Remagen, but there was little he could do. After a swift tour of the bridge, he returned to the tunnel on the east bank, where Friesenhahn was awaiting permission to detonate the charges. Under orders from Hitzfeld to keep the bridge open for as long as possible as an escape route for LXVII Corps, Scheller hesitated. He had still not given the order when the first of Grimball's tanks appeared on the west bank.

By 1500, the Americans had not taken the decision to seize the bridge, although it was obvious that a unique opportunity existed to do so. Thirty minutes earlier, Brigadier Hoge had arrived at Engeman's command post on the hill, urging the Task Force commander to clear Remagen and 'get to the bridge' as quickly as possible, but it was not until approximately 1520 that he issued precise orders to cross the river. By then, Engeman had made his own decision, travelling by jeep to the bridge towers and ordering Deevers to send the infantry across. Timmermann received his instructions at 1515 – his response was a heartfelt 'What if the bridge blows in my face?' – and was gathering his squad commanders for a

Main picture: Perched high on the Erpeler Ley, an observer from the US First Army surveys the Ludendorff bridge, six days after its capture. The Germans had not deployed any heavy armament on this natural defensive feature and Task Force Engeman exploited this mistake with ruthless efficiency. Left: Second Lieutenant Karl Timmermann, the commander of Company A, 27th Armored Infantry Division. Below left: A US Army soldier uses a traffic control telephone to direct supplies and ammunition across a pontoon bridge between Remagen and Erpel.

THE FIRST ACROSS THE RHINE
CONSTRUCTED BY
• 291 ENGR C BN
• 988 TDWY CO
• 998 TDWY CO
THE LONGEST TACTICAL BRIDGE BUILT

briefing when, at 1517, Friesenhahn detonated the charges on the approach ramp. For a moment, the Americans thought that the bridge had been blown. When it became apparent that this was not the case, Timmermann ordered Chinchar's platoon to take the lead, followed closely by those of DeLisio and Burrows, with engineers from Mott's platoon accompanying them onto the bridge to clear any remaining explosives.

The infantrymen ran towards the ramp crater at about 1535, scrambling across the rubble to reach the level of the bridge. Some may even have started across when, at 1550, a second explosion occurred, far more powerful than the first. Once Friesenhahn's initial delaying move had been executed, the urgency of the situation was apparent even to Scheller. He immediately ordered the main charges to be blown. Unfortunately, when Friesenhahn turned the key of the electrical firing mechanism, nothing happened. He tried again, with similar results, and then called for a volunteer to race onto the bridge – by now under fire not only from the tanks on the west bank but also from assault guns and mortars on the hill – and use the manual back-up system. Sergeant Faust of the engineers stepped forward and, in a remarkable act of bravery, ran out to the manual-firing box, seizing the flare pistol from within and igniting the fuze. He just made it back to the safety of the tunnel when the charges went off. However, as the smoke cleared and debris fell into the river, the Germans were horrified to see the bridge still intact. Although the central span was twisted and a huge hole had appeared in the flooring, it had not collapsed.

Chinchar reached the east end first, entering the left-hand tower to silence a machine gun

As soon as this became obvious to Timmermann's men, they calmly carried out their orders. Sergeant Anthony Samele, leader of the first squad of No. 1 Platoon, turned to Chinchar and said quietly, 'C'mon Mike, we'll just walk it over', and together with Private Art Massie and Lieutenant Hugh Mott, they stepped out onto the bridge. Chinchar turned to Massie and ordered him to 'leapfrog' the others as far as the hole in the planking, and, amid machine-gun fire from the eastern towers, the tunnel and a sunken barge in the river to their right, men of all three platoons began to zigzag their way across. Grimball did all he could to help, firing at the eastern towers with his 90mm main armament, but to all intents and purposes the infantry were on their own. Chinchar reached the east end first, entering the left-hand tower to silence a machine gun, and DeLisio did the

same in the right-hand tower. This left Sergeant Alex Drabik, a squad leader from No. 3 Platoon, to be the first American actually to set foot on the east bank. Drabik ran forward thinking that DeLisio was in front of him and, with his rifle held high, dodged left, following the earthen approach ramp as it fell towards the road at river level. Other men followed close behind, some of whom fired into the tunnel entrance to prevent a German counter-attack. Timmermann sent Burrows off to the left to find a route up the Erpeler Ley, and ordered a squad to trace the exit of the tunnel in order to cut off the enemy escape route. By 1605, about 75 Americans, drawn from Timmermann's company and Mott's engineer platoon, were safely across, and the first of the German defenders had been taken prisoner. Mott himself, in company with two of his sergeants, was still on the bridge, cutting cables and throwing undetonated charges into the river.

The arrival of the Americans created panic among the Germans in the tunnel, particularly when it was discovered that the exit along the railway had been blocked. Bratge searched in vain for Scheller (it later transpired that he had escaped before the exit was closed, intent on reporting in person to Hitzfeld), and as the American pressure increased, at approximately 1630 he decided to surrender. By then, Engeman had ordered Company C of the 27th Armored Infantry to reinforce the men on the east bank, while Hoge had started the laborious process of reporting his success to higher commanders and requesting urgent support. By nightfall, the bridge was firmly in American hands, with fresh divisions converging on Remagen from all directions. The bravery of Task Force Engeman had been matched by a remarkable display of command flexibility.

It has been estimated that the seizure of the bridge shortened the war by as much as a month, thereby saving a significant number of casualties on both sides. This was small consolation to the German defenders – Scheller, Peters and two engineer officers ultimately responsible for the protection of crossing points in the Remagen sector, Majors Strobel and Kraft, were court-martialled and shot on 12/13 March – but to the men of Task Force Engeman, prepared to risk all in the prosecution of the war, this is a fitting tribute. Before 7 March, they were just ordinary men doing a nasty job to the best of their ability; after that date, they were heroes whose names, justifiably, went 'down in glory'.

THE AUTHOR John Pimlott is senior lecturer in War Studies and International Affairs at the Royal Military Academy, Sandhurst. He has written Strategy and Tactics of War.

Following the capture of the Ludendorff railway bridge by Task Force Engeman, a series of German counter-attacks were launched – using ground forces, aircraft and even frogmen. However, their chances of success were small. A deep psychological blow had been struck to German civilian and military morale. Until 7 March, the Germans had been convinced that the Rhine would act as a natural barrier to enemy advances from the west, and, although the main Allied crossings took place to the north and south later in the month, there can be no doubt that the sudden appearance of American forces in this central sector weakened German defences overall. Below: An historic moment, as troops of the 9th US Armored Division move over the Ludendorff bridge, preparing to reinforce the bridgehead on the east bank. Task Force Engeman had played a crucial part in securing the Allies' first bridge over the Rhine.

ROYAL ARMOUR

If NATO and Warsaw Pact forces clash on the North German Plain, Britain's armoured regiments will be at the forefront of battle

Below: The 17th/21st Lancers – nicknamed 'The Death or Glory Boys' – present the business end of their Chieftain main battle tank to the camera.

SINCE THE EARLY Tank Mark I of World War I, conceived as a means of breaking the deadlock of trench warfare, revolutionary advances in technology have produced sophisticated armoured vehicles whose capabilities determine the strategy of every modern army.

Stationed in West Germany and numerically outnumbered by at least four to one, NATO's main battle tanks, including the British Chieftain and Challenger, guard Western Europe against the threat of a Warsaw Pact shock offensive. Military analysts may disagree as to the effectiveness of heavy armour on the modern battlefield, but these weapons would almost certainly be the first into action during the initial stages of a conventional conflict. The spearhead of British defence forces in this area rests firmly in the hands of the Royal Armoured Corps – the 'mailed fist' of NATO's heavy armour. If the T-64s and T-72s of the Soviet arsenal start rolling westward towards the Rhine, Britain's armoured regiments will be tasked with defence and local counter-attack.

Few military organisations can have survived such dramatic alteration, while still retaining their traditions and ancient customs, as the British cavalry regiments. Despite all the upheavals and mechanisation of the last 70

THE ROYAL ARMOURED CORPS

The cavalry component of the British Army comprises three main groupings, the Household Cavalry, the Royal Armoured Corps and the Yeomanry. The latter is the smallest of the three, consisting of two regiments only, in the armoured role – The Royal Yeomanry Regiment and The Queen's Own Yeomanry. The second grouping is provided by the Household Cavalry, made up of The Life Guards and The Blues and Royals.

By far the largest grouping of cavalry regiments, however, is the Royal Armoured Corps, comprising 17 regiments: The Queen's Dragoon Guards, The Royal Scots Dragoon Guards (Carabiniers and Greys), 4th/7th Royal Dragoon Guards, 5th Royal Inniskilling Dragoon Guards, The Queen's Own Hussars, The Queen's Royal Irish Hussars, 9th/12th Royal Lancers (Prince of Wales's), The Royal Hussars (Prince of Wales's Own), 13th/18th Royal Hussars (Queen Mary's Own), 14th/20th King's Hussars, 15th/19th King's Royal Hussars, 16th/5th The Queen's Royal Lancers, 17th/21st Lancers, 1st Royal Tank Regiment, 2nd Royal Tank Regiment, 3rd Royal Tank Regiment and 4th Royal Tank Regiment.

In its modern role, the cavalry is responsible for providing the manpower for two battle formations – the armoured regiment and the armoured reconnaissance regiment. The flexibility of these two formations is greatly enhanced by the fact that most regiments are capable of exchanging roles and equipment in order to fulfil either commitment.
Above: The insignia of the Royal Armoured Corps.

Main picture: Closely monitored, three Chieftains advance through open terrain. During Exercise Lionheart, in September 1984, British tank crews demonstrated their professionalism to their NATO colleagues by always 'buttoning down' when engaging the 'enemy'. A troop of three Chieftains ploughs through muddy terrain. The tank's gun barrel is wrapped in a thermal sleeve to prevent warping, and a muzzle reference system ensures that the sights are kept aligned with the centre of the barrel.

years, the cavalry regiments deliberately maintain a strong link with their origins. For example, the Queen's Own Hussars maintain a drum horse to carry replicas of the magnificent kettle drums captured at the Battle of Dettingen in 1743. Such proud customs have ensured the preservation of all that is best in the British regimental system, with its family ties and sense of 'belonging'.

The 1st and 4th Armoured Divisions would be deployed side by side to confront enemy forces

Since the end of World War II, and the establishment of NATO in 1949, the British armed forces have become an integral part of a much larger European defence organisation. This post-war development has been accompanied by sweeping changes in the armed forces, with once-rival cavalry regiments being amalgamated. Today, these cavalry regiments comprise 15 of the 19 regiments in the armoured component of the British Army – the Royal Armoured Corps (RAC). Established on 4 April 1939, the RAC now forms approximately eight per cent of the total strength of the army and includes the four regiments of the Royal Tank Regiment (RTR). Although the latter does not possess a 'cavalry' past, its four units have rapidly acquired historical associations and traditions of their own. Indeed, at Villers-Bretonneux in April 1918, its predecessor, the Tank Corps, achieved victory in the first-ever engagement of tank against tank.

The Royal Armoured Corps currently operates two types of armoured unit – the armoured regiment and the armoured reconnaissance regiment. While the latter exists in several different forms, it is the former which, as part of the 1 (BR) Corps in West Germany, comprises the main striking force of the British Army of the Rhine (BAOR).

BAOR contains the bulk of the British Army's combat forces, and is committed to NATO as part of the European standing forces responsible for defending the West against any attack from the Soviet/Warsaw Pact bloc. It has two main formations that would be fully mobilised in the event of a prolonged period of political tension. The first of these, 1 (BR) Corps, provides British forces with their main combat echelon, while the second, the British Support Corps (BRSC), is tasked to protect the rear of 1 (BR) Corps as it advances to meet the enemy, as well as to maintain supply routes back to the Channel ports.

1 (BR) Corps has four divisions, three of which are armoured and would provide the corps with its battle 'teeth' in any major conflict. The fourth division, the 2nd Infantry Division, is based in the United Kingdom and would only travel to Germany in the event of war. This leaves the 1st, 3rd and 4th Armoured Divisions permanently based in Germany, ready to move into action against a suspected Warsaw Pact offensive.

Together with units from The Netherlands, West Germany and Belgium, 1 (BR) Corps comes under the command of the NATO Northern Army Group (NORTHAG), and is supported by the 2nd Allied Tactical Air Force (2 ATAF), containing squadrons from each of the four countries in addition to units from the United States Air Force.

1 (BR) Corps is responsible for the defence of a

sector of the German border running south from Hanover to the Harz Mountains. Much of this area is open plain and ideal tank terrain, although hilly and broken ground does prevail in some areas to the south. Along this defensive line, the 1st and 4th Armoured Divisions would be deployed side by side to confront enemy forces. The 3rd Armoured Division would position itself behind the other two divisions, to provide a mobile reserve in the case of a breakthrough by the enemy, while the 2nd Infantry Division would guard the rear and provide support for the BRSC.

The armoured regiments in BAOR are exchanging their Chieftain main battle tank for the new Challenger

Designed to exploit available resources rather than follow any established military precepts, the British armoured division represents a feat of extremely complex military organisation. Its primary combat forces consist of three armoured brigades (apart from the 3rd Armoured Division which has two), although the make-up of each differs according to its mission. Artillery, engineer, helicopter and transport support are also provided, in addition to the usual 'admin' services of maintenance, military police, stores and medical units. Whereas some armoured brigades have two armoured regiments and one mechanised infantry battalion, others have one armoured regiment and two mechanised infantry battalions. In all cases, the infantry are transported on the FV 432 armoured personnel carrier.

There are two types of armoured regiment within the modern Royal Armoured Corps – the Type 57 and

Left: Maintenance on one of the Chieftain's road wheels. Far left: At present, jerrycans are used for forward replenishment, enabling the tanks to be refuelled in their tactical positions.

computer-based Integrated Control System of the dern Chieftain (left), uses a er rangefinder and orporates external sensors ich take into account wind ed, temperature and gun nion angles.

Type 43. These titles denote the number of tanks in any given regiment, depending on whether the regiment comprises three or four squadrons. There is a tendency, however, to move towards the more compact and combat-flexible Type 43 regiment. One of the main considerations behind this development is the current modernisation programme, whereby the armoured regiments in BAOR are exchanging their Chieftain main battle tank for the new Challenger. Eventually, it is intended to use this new weapon as the basis of 12 Type 43 regiments, in place of the existing 11. Some regiments within 1 (BR) Corps have already completed the transition from Chieftain to Challenger, but the majority are still equipped with the older battle tank.

The Type 57 armoured regiment, still the backbone of 1 (BR) Corps' combat forces, has six main elements: regimental headquarters (RHQ), headquarters squadron and four armoured squadrons. Responsibility for ensuring that the tanks can keep moving while in the field falls on the shoulders of the Light Aid Detachments (LAD) from the Royal Electrical and Mechanical Engineers (REME). Indeed, the sheer logistics of maintaining the efficiency of an armoured regiment at combat readiness necessitate the employment of extra personnel to perform invaluable support services. In addition to REME, therefore, each Type 57 regiment includes personnel from the Royal Army Medical Corps (RAMC), Royal Army Pay Corps (RAPC), Army Catering Corps (ACC) and an instructor from the Army Physical Training Corps (APTC).

The manpower of the Type 57 regiment – 44 officers and 539 men – is far in excess of that needed to man the unit's 57 main battle tanks. However, in the field, this strength is intended to provide the regiment with a degree of tactical and logistical autonomy unheard of in its Soviet counterpart. Each regiment therefore possesses its own reconnaissance troop, equipped with eight FV 101 Scorpion reconnaissance vehicles, and a guided weapons troop armed with Swingfire anti-tank missiles transported on FV 102 Striker carriers. To these can be added the Land Rovers, trucks, FV 432 armoured personnel carriers (APCs) and other support and maintenance vehicles within the regimental organisation. For example, the RHQ has a single Chieftain tank, three Sultan command vehicles, one FV 103 Spartan APC, three

Ferret scout cars and one Land Rover.

The headquarters squadron of a Type 57 regiment is essentially a supply and admin unit, possessing its own squadron headquarters (SHQ) and an admin troop equipped with sufficient vehicles to ensure that supplies are kept moving to armoured squadrons in the field.

Each of the four armoured squadrons has its own SHQ, comprising two Chieftains, a Ferret scout car and one Land Rover, and commands an admin troop, a contingent from the LAD and four armoured tank troops. The admin troop is equipped with an FV 432 ambulance and a variety of other vehicles, while the LAD has a Chieftain recovery vehicle (ARV), one FV 434 repair vehicle and an FV 432.

The Chieftain has guarded British forces stationed in Germany for almost 20 years

Ultimately, if the armoured regiments of 1 (BR) Corps clash with Warsaw Pact forces in a conventional tank battle, the outcome will depend heavily on the skill, determination and tactics of the crews of the three Chieftains within each armoured troop, each troop being capable of operating as an autonomous unit for a limited period. The armoured troop is usually a subaltern's command, though in most regiments a small number of troops are commanded by staff sergeants.

Generally acknowledged as one of the world's most powerful battle tanks, the Chieftain has guarded British forces stationed in Germany for almost 20 years. Each tank has a crew of four: commander, driver, gunner and loader, all of whom usually carry 9mm Sterling sub-machine guns as their personal armament. The tank itself is armed with a 120mm rifled gun, together with two 7.62mm machine guns – one co-axial with the main armament and the other located over the commander's hatch. Although in service since 1963, the 120mm L11A5 gun remains a formidable weapon and is capable of outshooting some of the more modern smooth-bore tank guns. The 1700kg barrel can fire a projectile to a maximum combat range of 3000m, and the various types of ammunition available include armour-piercing fin-stabilised discarding-sabot (APFSDS), armour-piercing discarding-sabot tracer (APDS-T) and high-explosive squash head (HESH). The one limitation on training in Germany is the lack of space to carry out any gunnery training other than the usual static and range-type practise shoots. To simulate 'live' battle runs, as preparation against an enemy

CHIEFTAIN MARK 5 MBT

Crew: 4

Dimensions: length 10.79m; width 3.66m; height 2.89m

Weight: Combat loaded 55,000kg

Engine: Leyland L60 Mk7A two-stroke multi-fuel six-cylinder engine developing 730bhp at 2250rpm

Performance: Maximum road speed 48km/h; range (road) 450km; vertical obstacle 0.91m; trench 3.15m; gradient 60 per cent; fording 1.07m

Armour: Conventional, 150mm maximum

Armament: One 120mm L11A5 gun; one 0.5in ranging machine gun (retrospectively being replaced by a laser rangefinder); two 7.62mm machine guns; two six-barrel smoke-grenade dischargers. one on each side of the turret.

offensive, the crews have to travel across the Atlantic to Suffield in Alberta where there is ample space for the live firing of ammunition of all types.

Because the Chieftain was designed to fulfil the three main priorities of firepower, protection and mobility – in that order – the tank weighs a hefty 55,000kg in combat, making it one of the heaviest tanks in service. Allied to a rather underpowered engine pack, generating only 750bhp, this means that the Chieftain is a relatively slow and ponderous fighting vehicle. Nevertheless, its considerable armour protection makes the interior of the Chieftain one of the safest places to be on the modern battlefield – a thick armoured carapace affords the crew virtual immunity from the effects of nuclear, biological, chemical (NBC) warfare, as well as from shellfire.

Although the layout of the Chieftain is conventional, the position of the driver is rather unusual. In an effort to keep the tank's silhouette as low as possible and secure minimum exposure to enemy guns, the driver sits in a reclined position, lying almost horizontal when driving with the hatch closed.

Chieftain crews are provided with one of the most envied pieces of equipment in NATO

Protected behind the well-sloped frontal armour of the turret are the three other crew members. In the right-hand side of the turret is the commander, who has a cupola that can be traversed through 360 degrees. Just in front of him is the gunner, with the loader sitting on the other side of the gun breech. The interior of the cast-steel turret is filled with a wide range of sophisticated equipment, but there remains enough room for the crew to be seated in relative comfort. This is just as well – in a conflict the crew could be expected to operate closed down for periods of up to 48 hours, using the Chieftain's three-stage NBC pack to provide air filtration (in a nuclear scenario) and ventilation. To ease this burden, the Chieftain crews are provided with one of the most envied pieces of equipment in NATO – a water boiler, for brewing the traditional cup of tea and making the compo rations more palatable.

When the time for daily maintenance comes around, all crew members muck in together, officers and men alike. While the Chieftain has been the subject of numerous modifications since its first public appearance in 1959, every day it requires routine attention of some kind. The crews are completely responsible for these tasks, and the REME are only called upon when major repairs such as engine pack replacements are required.

Although a large part of the crews' daily routines are associated with their tanks, they must also complete the normal day-to-day training that all soldiers in the British Army must undergo in order to hone their combat skills. The schedule begins with individual training and works up through small-unit exercises to at least one major exercise – possibly involving other NATO forces – every late summer or autumn.

Throughout the centuries, the most common British cavalry tactic has traditionally been the charge. Today, while the charge still has a place in modern armoured warfare, it appears well down on the list of possible tactical manoeuvres. No longer does cavalry operate in splendid isolation from all other service arms. Instead, the armoured regiment exists as part of a formation known as the battle group.

Within the NATO battle group, the armoured regiments are superbly equipped to counter the threat of a Soviet shock offensive. Mounted on FV 102 Striker carriers (top left), the Swingfire wire-guided anti-tank missile has a range of 4000m and its hollow-charge warhead is capable of defeating the armour of most main battle tanks. Centre left: The FV 107 Scimitar is a variant of the Scorpion series and is armed with a 30mm cannon. In combination with the Land Rovers (bottom left) and FV 101s of the armoured regiments, the Scimitars would perform an invaluable reconnaissance role on the battlefield. In areas where the terrain limits the use of heavy armour, a larger contingent of infantry would augment the battle group. Below: Troops deploy from FV 432 APCs.

There is no fixed establishment for the battle group, the emphasis being on flexibility in the field. The sophisticated weaponry of today's armed forces means that the survivability of 1 (BR) Corps' tank force relies heavily on close infantry, artillery and engineer support. The battle group is therefore best described as a grouping of various arms, including armour, infantry, artillery and engineers, that is raised to meet any local tactical situation. In order to meet this defensive requirement, the tidy organisa-tion of the armoured regiment is often broken up as various elements find themselves assigned to battle groups. For example, in the open plains to the north of the 1 (BR) Corps area, a battle group might possess a large tank complement and a Milan anti-tank guided missile force, with only a small force of supporting infantry. Alternatively, in the more broken terrain further south, the infantry element could possibly be increased with a corresponding drop in the strength of the tank force.

The tactical characteristics of the battle tank are firepower, protection and mobility

The offensive capability of the tank is reflected in the three main battle tasks of the modern armoured regiment: aggressive mobile action to engage and destroy enemy armour; close combat in conjunction with NATO infantry; and the use of 'shock' action against enemy forces. The latter is intended to exploit the primary tactical characteristics of the battle tank – firepower, protection and mobility. Linking these three tasks, and moulding them into a coherent tactical doctrine on the battlefield, is the concept of flexibility that permeates the British armoured units.

Each regimental commander is allowed a con-siderable amount of discretion as to the manner of executing his orders, along with a great deal of freedom when it comes to exploiting any local tactical advantage that might arise. The type of training given by the British Army instils in tank commanders the importance of initiative, with flex-ibility stressed as one of the primary considerations in combat. This ability to exploit opportunities as they arise is one of the armoured regiment's main assets, for the Chieftains and Challengers of the Royal Armoured Corps will almost inevitably be fighting against overwhelming numerical odds.

Tactics can only be pre-planned in very general terms, because the situation can alter dramatically once battle has been joined. However, the three battle tasks of the armoured regiment can be loosely sub-divided into nine spheres: defensive operations in both mobile and static situations; counter-attack

FROM CHIEFTAIN TO CHALLENGER

The Chieftain main battle tank (MBT) entered service in 1963 as a replacement for the ageing Centurion. After successful troop trials with the 1st and 5th Royal Tank Regiments in the British Army of the Rhine, the first production Chieftains began to equip the 11th Hussars in 1967.

Over 900 Chieftains were built for the British Army, together with a further 1000 destined for the export market. Some of the latter were known as Shir I and IIs, incorporating a new powerpack, and a hull and turret of Chobham armour. By 1975, however, British defence planners had recognised the need for a successor, and, when the Soviets introduced the T64/T72 series during the 1970s, this need acquired fresh urgency.

A project known as MBT-80 was abandoned in 1980 on the grounds that the new tank would not be operational by the mid-1980s, and the British Army settled for a less advanced though faster solution. It was decided to modify the Shir II for the European climate, and this tank became the basis for the FV4030/4 Challenger which made its first public appearance in 1982.

Powered by a 12-cylinder Rolls Royce engine, the Challenger MBT has a maximum speed of 60 kilometres per hour and weighs over 55 tonnes. Chobham armour affords a high degree of protection against all battlefield weapons, including those with HEAT warheads. The 120mm L11A5 gun has been retained, although work is currently under way to produce a weapon with improved fire control systems and greater muzzle velocity.

Initially, the Challenger will augment rather than replace the Chieftain, though the latter will inevitably be phased out of service as more Challengers emerge from the Vickers plant in Leeds.

and counter-penetration; exploiting situations during a limited nuclear scenario; covering force operations; advancing in contact with the enemy; the assault and destruction of the enemy; penetration, exploitation and pursuit; direct fire and other support of the infantry; and long-range anti-tank guided weapons fire.

Flexibility is not limited to the command level within the armoured regiment, and all members of a tank crew must demonstrate proficiency in each other's duties in case of an emergency. In addition, individual tank and platoon commanders are frequently given the opportunity to apply their skills at a higher level, and the progress of each officer is carefully scrutinised to allow the development of a cadre of potential leaders within the RAC.

Even as the new Challenger tank continues to re-equip the Royal Armoured Corps, one thing is certain to remain unaltered – the indefatigable spirit of the cavalry regiments themselves. The long tradition of high morale displayed by cavalrymen on the battlefield continues in the modern armoured regiments. Today, however, the tank crews possess an awesome firepower that the cavalry of the past could not have begun to contemplate.

THE AUTHOR Terry Gander is a freelance writer on military affairs and is the author of the *Encyclopedia of the Modern British Army*, now in its third edition.

Below: On manoeuvres. Bottom: The Royal Hussars put Britain's newest main battle tank – the Challenger – through its paces.

On Route 13, the massively outnumbered troopers of the US 4th Cavalry fought a bitter and bloody battle against the Viet Cong

WHEN THE M48A3 tanks and M113 armoured cavalry assault vehicles (ACAVs) of A Troop, 1st Squadron, 4th US Cavalry Regiment, rumbled out of their base at Phu Loi in the South Vietnamese province of Binh Duong on 8 June 1966, their crews could not know that by the end of the day they would have won one of the epic battles of the Vietnam War. Within a few hours of their departure, the men would have met and defeated the Viet Cong's (VC's) 272nd Regiment, part of the crack 9th Division that had inflicted humiliating defeats on the Army of the Republic of Vietnam (ARVN) in 1964 and 1965.

The build-up to A Troop's battle had begun in May, when a Special Forces team out of Loc Ninh found a map and battle plan on the body of an enemy officer that indicated the 9th Division was planning a campaign in the province of Binh Long for sometime in June. The 4th Cavalry's parent unit, the 1st Infantry Division, the 'Big Red One', sent infantry and artillery units to An Loc, the provincial capital, and other towns, but patrols revealed nothing and the troops were withdrawn. However, late in May, ARVN forces reported the presence of VC in Binh Long and US battalions returned in strength. After contact with the enemy near Loc Ninh and, in anticipation of a long, tough campaign, the decision was made to move more units into the area. The operation was known as El Paso. However, both the heavier artillery and the cavalry could only move by road and, thus, it fell to A Troop to lead the parade along Route 13, the main highway into Binh Long.

Captain Ralph Sturgis, commanding A Troop, and his men left Phu Loi and headed north for Lai Khe, the base of the 1st Division's 3rd Brigade. To avoid mines, Sturgis stayed away from the main roads, but his lead tank hit a mine some 10km out of Phu Loi and returned to base, escorted by an ACAV. Arriving at Lai Khe at 1100 hours, the rest of the troop stocked up on fuel, ate some combat rations and then waited for the order to move.

Once Sturgis had got his men on their way again, the 3rd Brigade's Air Liaison Officer, Captain Richard Wetzel, flew over the column in a Cessna 0-1 Bird Dog observation aircraft, acting as a Foward Air Controller (FAC). Wetzel was in constant communication with the Bien Hoa fighter base, the 4th Cavalry's 1st Squadron and A Troop. The squadron commander, Lieutenant-Colonel Lee Lewane, was also flying over Sturgis' troop, in an OH-13 helicopter, and ordered the column to move cross-country, on a track parallel to Route 13.

A TROOP, 4TH CAVALRY

On the eve of the battle of Ap Tau-O, A Troop, 4th US Cavalry Regiment, consisted of 41 armoured vehicles: nine M48 tanks, 29 M113 Armoured Cavalry Assault Vehicles (ACAVs), an ARV (Armoured Recovery Vehicle) and a pair of engineer dozer-tanks. Each of the troop's three platoons was equipped with a mix of three M48s and seven ACAVs. The remainder of the armour was split between the troop's HQ and trail party. Two of the ACAVs were fitted with radar and two others were fitted with flame-throwers. The ACAV, basically the standard M113 armoured personnel carrier fitted with heavy weapons, carried a 50-calibre machine gun, protected by an armoured shield, forward, and a shielded M60 on the left rear of the deck. Ammunition was plentiful: 2000 rounds for the 50-calibre and 7500 for the M60. The other weapon issued to the five-man crew was the 40mm M79 grenade-launcher, which was provided with 90 rounds.

A Troop's other main vehicle was the M48A3 medium tank which had a maximum speed of 48km/h. Armament comprised a 90mm main gun and two machine guns. A Troop was also equipped with specialist engineering vehicles – both based on the M48 chassis. The AVLB (Armoured Vehicle Launched Bridge) was fitted with a 19.2m-long scissors bridge and was deployed for obstacle crossing. The M88 ARV was fitted with a hydraulically operated dozer blade and a powerful A-frame winch that was capable of lifting up to 22,500kg. Above: The shoulder patch of the 1st Infantry Division.

ON THUNDER ROAD

It was the habit of the cavalry to ride on top of their vehicles whenever possible; the troopers feared mines more than enemy fire and the heat inside was nearly unbearable, anything up to 100°C. The column reached Chon Thanh at around 1300 hours, and from there it was necessary to move north along Route 13. Most of the large trees had been cut back from the road for a distance of 100ft or more, but secondary growth touched the roadside in many places. There were a few cleared areas scattered along the route, but the country was generally low and wet, with water in deep ditches along most of the road.

Lieutenant Joseph R. Lake, the commander of the troop's 3rd Platoon, later recalled that the whole atmosphere suddenly became tense and ominous: some of his scouts reported seeing figures lashed to the tree-tops; reports of furtive movement and brief sightings rippled over the troop's radio net. Lieutenant David Kinkead, CO of the 2nd Platoon, also remembered that there were reports of sniping and that one trooper was hit in the arm. The cavalrymen began to slip down behind their weapons.

Shortly after 1400 hours, as the 3rd Platoon's lead tank was approaching the railway crossing, a few kilometres north of the Ap Tau-O bridge, a mine exploded, taking off the M48A3's right track and sending up a column of black smoke. It was standard practice in the 4th Cavalry to 'herringbone' upon contact and alternate vehicles immediately faced outwards at 45-degree angles to give inter-locking fields of fire. Lake's lead tank reported the mine, adding that it was disabled and under heavy fire; his scouts reported heavy contact and the existence of a piece of cleared high ground on the east side of the highway. Lake, tearing off his armoured helmet with the earphones that had kept out the sounds of battle, immediately realised that his platoon was under intense fire from a variety of weapons. The 3rd Platoon began to jockey towards the cleared area, engaging the charging VC with every available weapon.

When the battle opened, Lake's 3rd Platoon had been stopped exactly where the enemy wanted them: in the first kilometre south of the railway crossing. Only the fact that his scouts reported the open area to the east saved Lake's platoon. Nonetheless, it was touch and go for the first 30 minutes: the lead tank could not move, and VC attempting to climb onto the vehicle were only shot off by the ACAV's moving to the nearby clearing. The tank fought the entire engagement in its exposed position and its commander, Sergeant Joseph Listle, quickly noticed the devastating effect of canister rounds on the VC. He reported this encouraging fact to Lake.

As the 3rd Platoon moved into the clearing, shooting VC off their companion vehicles, they acquired a little fighting room. However, the VC must have anticipated such a move, because the platoon was immediately hit by an intense 80mm mortar barrage. Lake's platoon sergeant, Richard Lanham, was firing his tank-mounted 50-calibre machine gun at the surging VC when the link-chute jammed. Private First Class (PFC) Avery G. Smith then went out on the rear deck with an M79 grenade-launcher to hold off the enemy, while Lanham leaned over the side to clear the chute. The intrepid Smith kept the VC away from his sergeant and then saved his life by shielding him from a mortar round which fell on the tank. Smith was awarded the DSC posthumously.

To add to his other difficulties, Lake's ACAV backed into a wet ditch and stuck there. The lieutenant, worried that he would be an ineffective platoon leader while stuck in the mud, ran to the nearest vehicle, which contained Sergeant Merle Slater's mortar squad. Lake climbed in and regained control.

While the 3rd Platoon was fighting for its life, Sturgis ordered Lieutenant David Kinkead's 2nd Platoon to move north and link up with Lake. The platoon moved rapidly, its vehicles hosing down the west side of the road with their machine guns as they moved. As he approached Lake's position, Kinkead saw some room on the east side of the clearing. Part of the 2nd Platoon went in on the east and other ACAVs intermingled with the 3rd Platoon where they clearly needed help. Within moments, Kinkead's troopers were also fully engaged.

As Saporito was settling into the driver's position, another 75mm round hit the command vehicle

Just after sending Kinkead forward, Sturgis' ACAV, accompanied by the vehicle of First Sergeant Pepe and one Zippo flame-thrower, was hit broadside by a 75mm recoilless-rifle round. One man, SP4 James Dempsey, was wounded while in the driver's seat, but when the ACAV came to a grinding halt, Sergeant Thomas Saporito quickly pulled Dempsey to the floor and took over the driving chores. As Saporito was settling into the driver's position,

A Troop's adversaries during the fight at Ap Tau-O on 8 June 1966 came from the three battalions of the Viet Cong (VC) 272nd Regiment, part of the 9th Division. This crack, battle-hardened division had already inflicted serious defeats on the Army of the Republic of South Vietnam (ARVN) in 1964 and 1965, and had then been reinforced by the 101st Regiment of the North Vietnamese Army.

In 1966, there were several large battles and innumerable skirmishes between the division and the 1st US Infantry Division; Ap Tau-O was to be the most hard-fought encounter. The VC commander placed his men along Route 13 with all the skill of a veteran of many battles. He also knew, thanks to friendly agents in the ARVN, the precise details of the US plans for the push up Route 13. Aided by this vital intelligence, he moved his regiment into position after dark on the 7th and then had his men dig their foxholes.

The foot and 'trigger' of the L-shaped ambush position was occupied by the regiment's reconnaissance company, and the long axis, running down the west side of Route 13, was covered by its three infantry battalions.

All told, the position extended for about three kilometres, from the Ap Tau-O bridge to the point where a disused railway crossed the highway. When the first US forces reached the recon company's front at the crossing, the trap was to be sprung.

The odds greatly favoured the VC, with the 135 members of A Troop being outnumbered by nine to one. However, by the end of the day the 272nd Regiment was shattered: its 1st Battalion had lost most of its strength and its commander, the 2nd suffered 50 per cent casualties and the 3rd was also badly mauled. So great were the losses that Hanoi Radio offered a bounty to any man who killed or captured a member of A Troop.

Ap Tau-O
A Troop, 1st Squadron, 4th US Cavalry Regiment

During May 1966 the Viet Cong's 9th Division prepared for a new campaign in the South Vietnamese province of Binh Long. Following encounters with the enemy in the Loc Ninh area, the US 1st Infantry Division decided to move more units into the area, and early on 8 June, A Troop, 1st Squadron, 4th Cavalry Regiment moved out from Phu Loi via Lai Khe and Chon Thanh. At 1415 the lead tank reached a position just south of a railway crossing near Ap Tau-O, and the Viet Cong 272nd Regiment sprang its ambush.

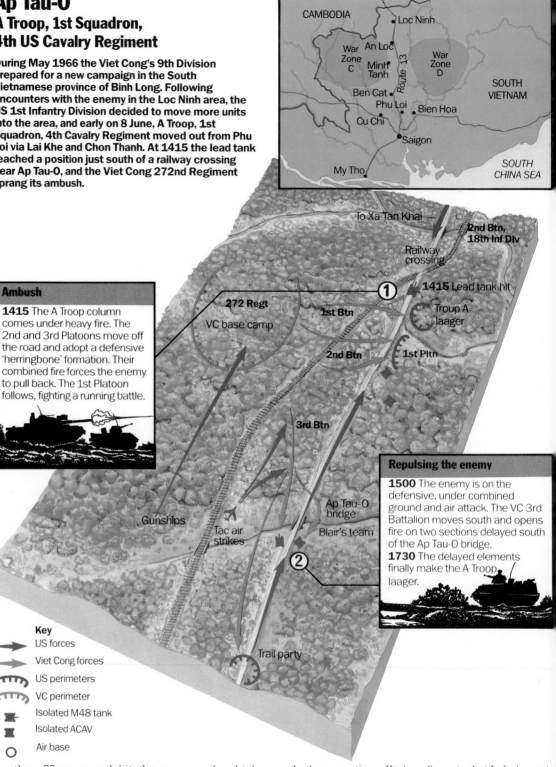

Ambush

1415 The A Troop column comes under heavy fire. The 2nd and 3rd Platoons move off the road and adopt a defensive 'herringbone' formation. Their combined fire forces the enemy to pull back. The 1st Platoon follows, fighting a running battle.

Repulsing the enemy

1500 The enemy is on the defensive, under combined ground and air attack. The VC 3rd Battalion moves south and opens fire on two sections delayed south of the Ap Tau-O bridge.
1730 The delayed elements finally make the A Troop laager.

Key
→ US forces
→ Viet Cong forces
⌒ US perimeters
⌒ VC perimeter
⬛ Isolated M48 tank
⬛ Isolated ACAV
○ Air base

another 75mm round hit the command vehicle. Sergeant First Class (SFC) Albert Armitage spotted the weapon and killed the crew with his 50-calibre. Jinking from right to left to avoid another hit, Saporito could not see another 75mm crew setting up to finish him off, but Armitage did, and he swung his machine gun around to engage the enemy. SFC Pearson Cole, following in a Zippo, also saw the VC. His driver gunned forward while Cole aligned his flame-thrower and, before the enemy could get off a round or Armitage could fire, the VC were consumed in a

In the meantime, Kinkead's arrival at Lake's position had proved timely: their platoons' combined firepower began to force the VC back to the west side of the road; Kinkead ordered his tanks to fire canister and aim low at the tree line. Just as Sturgis came up, Kinkead's second-in-command, Platoon Sergeant Robert A. Jackson, was gravely wounded by a mortar round and his machine gun was destroyed. Sturgis, not knowing all this, asked Kinkead to go back and help Pepe. Kinkead started back south, along Route 13, when he suddenly realised that his external radio might be hit, so he picked it up and placed it on the floor of the ACAV. As he bent down, a 75mm round hit exactly where his head had been. It

Advance from Phu Loi
8 June 1966

Loc Ninh

B I N H

L O N G

An Loc

2nd Btn 18th Inf Div

Minh Tanh road

Xa Tan Khai

Ap Tau-O

Chi Linh

1400

Minh Tanh

1300 Chon Thanh

Tp A, 4th Cav

B I N H

Phuoc Vinh

D U O N G

Route 13

Lai Khe **1100**

Ben Cat

SOUTH VIETNAM

Cu Chi

Phu Loi

Bien Hoa

Saigon

Below: Lieutenant Joseph R. Lake, CO of A Troop's 3rd Platoon, was first to taste the VC onslaught. He was soon supported by Lieutenant David Kinkead (centre), who brought his 2nd Platoon up to take on the attackers alongside the embattled Lake. Bottom: The cavalry 'herringbone'. When contact was made, the vehicles turned outwards at a 45-degree angle to engage the enemy with interlocking fields of fire.

gineer dozer-tank with the 1st Platoon pulled into the roadside ditch and stuck fast, and at about the same time on the southern approach to the bridge, an ACAV dropped out with mechanical trouble. Platoon Sergeant Eugene Blair, in a tank, radioed to Boualt that he would stay with the ACAV for security.

Shortly after Boualt's men had passed the bridge, the battle broke out up front. Boualt could hear the firing but could not raise Sturgis on the radio; he decided to move towards the sound of the guns. Sturgis was no doubt busy receiving 75mm recoil-less-rifle rounds from the VC. At this time, the 1st Platoon was moving across the front of the 272nd Regiment's 3rd Battalion. As it moved north with two tanks and six ACAVs, the platoon received fire from the west, to which it vigorously responded. Soon, however, Boualt was surprised to find large numbers of VC moving parallel to his course, 50 to 100m west of the highway.

Boualt's platoon was able to inflict some damage during this running battle, but its greatest contribution came as the stream of VC veered towards the road, hot on the tail of Kinkead's platoon, just then closing on 3rd Platoon's laager. The enemy presented a flank to Boualt, and he laced the VC with all of his weapons. This fire must have been galling to the

rocked the vehicle up on one track and knocked him to the floor. Recovering from the shock, Kinkead pulled up beside Pepe's disabled vehicle, and he and his medic, under fire, removed Pepe to their own vehicle, while a lightly wounded trooper also made it across under his own steam. They then returned to the laager.

The 1st Platoon, under Lieutenant Louis L. Boualt, was third in line, following Kinkead. About one kilometre south of the Ap Tau-O bridge, the en-

VC as they turned on the 1st Platoon.

As Boualt remembered the situation, he was some 500 to 800m south of the laager and hard pressed. One ACAV was hit and the crew evacuated; another was totally destroyed. The VC entered and drove off the first of these vehicles and then left it on the edge of the jungle. This left the platoon with four ACAVs and two tanks, one of which promptly received a mortar round inside the turret, leaving only the stunned driver alive and setting fire to the engine compartment. Boualt revived the driver and instructed him to back into a nearby stream to extinguish the fire.

Boualt described the configuration of the troop at that time as similar to a tadpole – he was the tail. His five surviving vehicles fought it out for the remainder of the battle in that position. Around 1730 hours, he finally closed on the southern sector of the laager.

By 1500, A Troop, minus the 1st Platoon, had coiled like a Texas rattler under attack. The VC were aware that they were facing a very dangerous adversary, but kept coming as their commanders called on the troops to try to wipe out the obstinate band of Americans.

During this long fight, Lewane in his helicopter and Sturgis on the ground combined with Wetzel to bring in tactical air strikes on the enemy. The road and railway provided excellent reference points for the F-4 Phantom and F-100 Super Sabre pilots, and within two hours, Wetzel had directed about 24 flights of 43 aircraft against the whole line of VC. Wetzel was a seasoned FAC and the Bien Hoa pilots were old hands; bombs, napalm and cluster bomblets blistered the area west of the road. A Troop was more than willing to share honours with the air force.

From the beginning of the engagement, D Troop of the 4th Cavalry kept relays of gunships working the flanks and rear of the enemy. The guns of the cavalry, combined with the fighters, drove the 1st and 2nd battalions of the 272nd Regiment back to the west. Lewane directed the 2nd Battalion, the 18th Infantry Regiment (a reaction force based at An Loc) to land to the north and sweep the west side of the highway, but the closest LZ (landing zone) was over four kilometres north and the battalion did not arrive until the show was over.

The VC were soon treated to a heavy dose of napalm and cluster bomblets and their fire dropped off

On two occasions in the heat of the battle, Lewane landed his fragile helicopter inside the laager under heavy fire. He wanted to 'eyeball' his troops and determine the state of their ammunition. He walked from vehicle to vehicle and found them full of fight with plenty to shoot. His presence in the thick of battle was just what the troopers expected of him.

In the meantime, the 272nd Regiment's 3rd Battalion, except for the fight with the 1st Platoon moving across its front, must have felt left out of the battle. However, this was about to change. SFC Eugene F. Blair, with his tank at the bridge, had repaired the ACAV and both crews were about to start north and join the noisy battle up the road, when elements of the enemy's 3rd Battalion slipped to their right and opened fire from the north of the bridge. Fortunately for Blair, he was separated from the VC by the stream and a wide stretch of swamp grass.

The VC opened fire from about 300m and began to work south, along Blair's west flank. He kept them under fire with his two machine guns and doses of canister from the tank, but it then occurred to him that some air support might come in handy. He called Sturgis, who sent Wetzel to help out, and the VC were soon treated to a heavy dose of napalm and cluster bomblets. The enemy's fire dropped off sharply, but just as Blair was feeling better about his situation, he spotted two VC setting up a 75mm recoilless rifle on Route 13. Then, two more appeared with some ammunition. Blair took a dim view of this development, called for canister, traversed his main gun to the right and fired. The VC were swept off the road. Not a bad performance for an infantry sergeant who had never fought in a tank before. When the VC finally broke contact, Blair had only one round of ammunition left.

Sturgis was also feeling better. The fight was still on, but he knew he had won it. His boss landed again and went to several fighting vehicles, checking the ammunition supply and the condition of the troopers. Still satisfied on both counts, he agreed with Sturgis that the trail party under Lieutenant Ronald Copes should move forward. Sturgis called Copes on the troop's radio net and told him to move up.

Copes had two ACAVs, two repaired tanks, and an M88 recovery vehicle. Just as he came up to the engineer dozer-tank, Lewane landed his OH-13

Weapons of the cavalry: M48 tanks (main picture), and an M88 ARV with a stranded M48 (bottom left).

ow: An ACAV (foreground)
ves off with an M48
ngside. Bottom: A Zippo
methrower in action against
'C gun position.

nearby. Copes and Lewane went to the dozer-tank, expecting to find the crew dead or missing, but to their astonishment, the hatch opened and out came four very happy engineers. Lewane recalled that he had an eerie feeling when he landed; it was too quiet. The engineers reinforced his concern when they said they had been fighting VC for over an hour. The M88 pulled the dozer out of the ditch and, as Lewane took off, Copes started north. Lewane circled one

time, saw the lead tank stop, saw smoke, heard a large explosion and realised that Copes had his own private war on.

The driver of Copes' lead tank, SP5 (Specialist, Grade 5) Hugh Oliver, was wounded by the mine explosion and was then thrown onto the road by the impact of a 75mm round, together with the tank commander, Sergeant Charles Norris. The remainder of the trail party then closed on the lead tank with all guns blazing. Norris was starting to pick himself up from the roadside, when he saw an automatic rifle lying nearby. He grabbed the weapon, only to find a VC on the other end. However, his hands had been badly burned and the VC won the tug of war. The enemy soldiers then broke for the jungle and Norris ran to Copes' ACAV. He climbed into what he thought would be a safe refuge, only to find a trooper inside loading M-16s and handing them up to the lieutenant, who was emptying them into the VC.

One very unfriendly VC then ran up to Copes' vehicle and flung a grenade through the hatch. Copes flung it back, and before it went off, put some bullets into the brave but impertinent Viet Cong as well as a nearby companion. The grenade then went off and cleared the enemy for some distance around. When the fighting subsided, Copes ordered his small army forward, leaving the lead tank smouldering on the road.

By then the battle was over. Many troopers had shed their flak jackets and some were stripped to the waist. Lake remembered that a dozen or so troopers were standing within the circle of vehicles, talking and cooling off, when two enemy soldiers, in North Vietnamese uniforms and holding rifles, popped out of a ditch, five metres away. Someone cut them down.

As evening began to fall, troopers at the laager saw a lone, battered and smoking tank drive up

A Troop had held the field of battle but the price was high; the platoons mourned their dead and evacuated their wounded. There was no exhilaration among the soldiers at the end of such a battle. Twelve troopers had been killed and 33 wounded. The supporting engineers lost two more killed and four wounded. On 9 June A Troop moved to An Loc under its own power, with 40 out of its original 41 armoured vehicles. For the battle on 8 June and two larger, but not tougher, battles with the 9th Division in June and July, the 1st Squadron, 4th Cavalry was awarded a Presidential Unit Citation. But one last event on 8 June tells us more about the 4th Cavalry than such an award could possibly convey.

Back at the scene of Copes' war, SP5 Hugh Oliver, the driver of the abandoned and smouldering tank, regained consciousness as he lay in the roadside ditch, sorely wounded and blinded in one eye. He heard VC talking all around him. He could see his tank three metres away. Incredibly, the engine was still running. Oliver crawled to the tank, climbed into the driver's compartment and drove away. As evening began to fall, troopers at the laager saw a lone, battered and smoking tank drive up Route 13 and into their lines with a bloody head sticking out of the driver's hatch. They let out a cheer and sent Oliver off in a medevac chopper.

THE AUTHOR General William E. De Puy served as a battalion commander in France and Germany during World War II and commanded the 1st Infantry Division at the time of the Ap Tau-O battle.

After the nightmare of Operation Goodwood, the Guards Armoured Division raced on towards a tumultuous reception in Brussels

OPERATION GOODWOOD was not the kind of military engagement armoured commanders would happily choose as an introduction to battle for their troops. In the words of General Sir Bernard Montgomery, commander of Allied ground forces in Normandy, Goodwood was designed 'to engage the German armour and to "write it down" to such an extent that it is of no further value as a basis of battle . . .'

By the end of D-day, the town of Caen, at the eastern end of the Normandy beachhead, was still in German hands. Attempts to take the town, on 10 June by the 7th Armoured and 51st Highland Divisions, and on 26 June by 15th Scottish, 43rd Wessex and the Yeomen and Hussars of 11th Armoured Divisions, had been repelled by the strong panzer reserves that Field Marshal Rommel had at his disposal. In an attempt to silence his critics, who were disappointed with the Second Army's slow progress, Montgomery launched a major attack designed to divert even more enemy reserves towards the eastern beachhead. Now regarding the capture of Caen as a subsidiary objective, Montgomery had designed his strategy in an attempt to allow a large-scale breakout across the foot of the Cotentin Peninsula by General Omar Bradley's US First Army. Scheduled for 18 July, Operation Goodwood was an exercise in attrition – the largest of its kind during World War II.

The plan was simple: VIII Corps, under Lieutenant-General Sir Richard O'Conner, and consisting of the 7th, 11th Armoured and Guards Armoured Divisions would cross the River Orne into the bridgehead taken and secured by the 6th Airborne. The force would then swing south and drive towards the area of Bourgebus, along a three-mile wide corridor to the east of Caen. Skirting along the wooded Troarn Ridge to the east, Guards Armoured would hold the left flank of the drive.

The huge 88mm barrel was still coming around when the Sherman smashed into the panzer amidships

Before any of the armour moved, however, the whole area of the advance was subjected to a pulverising air and artillery bombardment. A fierce concentration of fire was unleashed by a force of 1000 Lancasters, two Royal Navy cruisers, the 15in guns of HMS *Roberts* and the massed artillery of VIII Corps. This laid a bomb carpet that engulfed the known enemy gun and tank positions.

As a result of this terrifying bombardment, the initial advance of the armoured divisions encountered very little enemy opposition. An atmosphere of carefree superiority developed, as demoralised and shaken German soldiers were rounded up and directed to the rear. However, the battlefield changed dramatically once the armour moved beyond the range of their divisional artillery, and came up against German formations that had been given the opportunity to reorganise their defences.

By mid-morning, the men of the leading Guards battalion – 2nd (Armoured) Grenadiers – were only 2000yds short of Cagny when they ran into heavy anti-tank fire. The commanding officer ordered the line of advance to veer east towards Emieville, with

the intention of swinging around to take Cagny from the south. However, lurking in Emieville waited six panzers of the 503 Heavy Tank Battalion. As the Grenadiers came out of the shadow of broken ground, they were greeted by a bruising storm of fire. Within minutes, 12 Shermans had been set ablaze, their crews mostly jumping clear and racing to the rear under a hail of machine-gun bullets. The remaining Shermans quickly backed away.

However, the battle took an unexpected turn when Lieutenant J. R. Gorman of the 2nd (Armoured) Battalion, Irish Guards, discovered a vantage point overlooking the German positions. Coming up from behind, Gorman had followed a narrow route sandwiched between hedgerows to arrive at a hillock from where he was able to pinpoint the source of enemy fire – four German panzers, two of which were Tigers. With the enemy only 200yds away, Gorman's gunner loosed off a shot at them, but the lieutenant was dismayed to see it 'bounce off and go sizzling up into the air'. Ordering another shot, Gorman was further vexed by a voice emanating from the bowels of his Sherman: 'Gun's jammed sir.' A firm believer in the precept, 'When in doubt, advance,' Gorman's next order was simple: 'Driver. Ram!'

Thundering through open terrain, a Sherman tank throttles back, leaving a cloud of dust in its wake. The Shermans and Cromwells that equipped the Guards Armoured Division were vastly outgunned by the devastating 88mm firepower of German heavy tanks such as the Panther and Tiger. However, the Sherman's basic design did provide scope for innumerable modifications. The British variant – the Sherman VC Firefly – was equipped with a 17-pounder gun. By reducing the five-man crew to four, 42 rounds could be carried and, at the time of the Normandy landings, this was the only Anglo-American tank capable of piercing the formidable armour of the German panzers.

The design of the Tiger tank was such that its turret was severely underpowered, and the huge 88mm barrel was still coming around when the Sherman smashed into the panzer amidships. Both crews were forced to bale out and briefly share a ditch, to shelter from the artillery bombardment that was now being concentrated in the area. Undeterred, Gorman managed to commandeer a Sherman VC Firefly armed with a 17-pounder gun. Returning to the scene, the lieutenant proceeded to complete the destruction of the stranded Tiger and Sherman. Following this, Gorman destroyed the only other German tank still remaining in the area – an epic feat for which he received the first Military Cross won by the Guards Armoured Division.

Operation Goodwood lasted two days, and although Montgomery later declared himself satisfied with the results – American forces broke out across the Cotentin Peninsula not long afterwards – it has since become the subject of great controversy. The operation was flawed in many respects, particularly in the failure of intelligence to foresee the strength of German defences, resulting in heavy losses at the hands of enemy 88mm flak guns. In addition, the failure of the armoured divisions to keep pace with their supporting artillery, combined with the lack of tank-infantry co-ordinatión, made Goodwood a military disaster. In view of this, many historians now regard Montgomery's 'writing down' strategy as having been formulated retrospectively. They argue that his original aim was, in fact, the capture of Caen and that the idea of the Second Army acting as a focus for German reserves was constructed by Montgomery in the light of Operation Goodwood's ultimate failure.

The aftermath of Goodwood was also a miserable time for the armoured formations. The brigades of the Guards Armoured remained entrenched in the *bocage* country, tasked to clear out the remaining pockets of German resistance. It was difficult terrain

to traverse in search of the enemy, with innumerable 'blind spots' adding to the danger of ambush. It was a long and painful process – nudging cover aside in the hope of finding clearance, knowing that a blast from a waiting gun could end in holocaust.

However, with the breakout of General Bradley's army towards Cherbourg and the Atlantic coast, followed by General Patton's sweep across France towards the Seine and the massacre of the German divisions in the Falaise pocket, the pressures eased throughout Normandy. Formations of the 21st Army Group could now move eastwards to close up the Lower Seine. By the end of August, their tank losses made good and the bitter memories of the *bocage* fading, the Guards Armoured Division was deployed around Flers – awaiting orders to move across the Seine.

By the morning of 31 August, 5th Guards Armoured Brigade was streaming through Gisors

By this stage in the offensive, the division had been transferred to XXX Corps under the command of Lieutenant-General Sir Brian Horrocks. Guards Armoured were then cheered by the welcome news that their original Reconnaissance Regiment, 2nd Household Cavalry, was returning to them, thus releasing the Welsh Guards to go back to their intended role as an armoured battalion. The division was also reorganised into four regimental groups – Grenadier, Coldstream, Irish and Welsh.

Crossing the Seine at Vernon on 29 August, the tank crews found themselves in terrain ideal for the type of operation for which they had been trained – flat, clear of forest and serviced by good roads. A certain amount of agoraphobia lingered during the first few hours but, by the morning of 31 August, 5th Guards Armoured Brigade was streaming through Gisors on its way to Beauvais and Amiens. Relishing

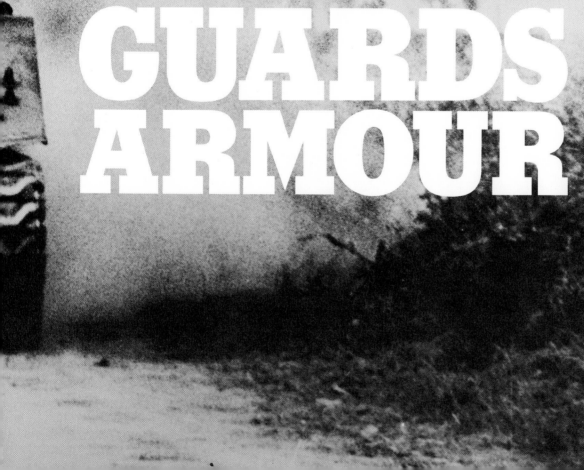

GUARDS ARMOUR

their new-found mobility, in stark contrast to conditions in the *bocage*, the tank crews set a hectic pace. Two abreast and head-to-tail through the streets, the Grenadiers began to catch up with the 2nd Household Cavalry who, in turn, were trying frantically to shake them off. As the various elements of the division passed through the small towns and villages on their route, they experienced the first signs of a phenomenon to which they would shortly become accustomed. Once the local inhabitants realised who they were, the liberators received a tumultuous welcome.

In front of the leading elements of 5th Brigade, the 2nd Household Cavalry now raced on ahead, tasked with three specific targets. The bridges over the Somme just east of Amiens had been given the codenames of Faith, Hope and Charity, and all three were required intact if XXX Corps was to attain its objective of breaking quickly into the Belgian Plain. Traffic jams in Beauvais delayed the Reconnaissance Regiment for a short time – it was forced to use the minor roads as the 11th Armoured Division, on its left, had the main access route to Amiens. However, once free of Beauvais, the tempo quickened. Villages began to slip by and French residents, recognising the different engine notes from those they had been used to hearing during the last four years, came out of their homes to cheer on the British tank crews. They reached the first of the bridges under the cover

Top left: The advance begins. Left: Horrors of the *bocage*. Infantry take up position beside a crippled panzer, on the alert for snipers. Above right: A Sherman's 75mm gun covers the entry of the Guards Armoured into Arras, while a Coldstream Guardsman (far left), armed with a Bren gun, provides additional support. Above left: Major-General Adair's triumphant arrival in Brussels.

From Caen to Brussels
Aug – Sept 1944

Key
- ---- Front line, 1 August
- --- Front line, 16 August
- —— Front line, 3 September
- → Allied forces

Labels on map: Calais, Dunkirk, Brussels, Boulogne, Lille, BELGIUM, Dieppe, Amiens, St Quentin, Cherbourg, le Havre, Rouen, F R A N C E, Seine, Oise, Caen, St Lô, Falaise, Paris, Avranches, Argentan

of darkness, with the Germans unaware of their approach. Engineers were deployed to defuse the demolition charges and all three bridges were captured before the enemy had time to open fire.

Although the Germans had been negligent in allowing the bridges to be captured so easily, once the defenders realised their predicament, they reacted with lightning speed and launched counter-attacks on all three bridges. Local French resistance groups sprang into action, not only supporting the Cavalry with rifle and Sten-gun fire, but also guiding them to cover when enemy attacks became too intense. By midnight, all the demolition charges had been dismantled. The action continued throughout the night, until finally, as dawn broke, the Shermans

CRUISER TANK, A27M CROMWELL

The Cromwell (below) was numerically the most important British-built tank of World War II, forming the main equipment of British armoured divisions in 1944-45 together with the American M4 Sherman. Built as the successor to the Crusader, the Cromwell was intended for service in 1942, but teething troubles delayed its appearance until 1944. Equipped with a 75mm gun, able to fire armour-piercing (AP) and high-explosive (HE) shot, the Cromwell's secondary armament comprised two Besa 7.92mm machine guns.

Designated the A27M, the Cromwell possessed a simple box shape and composite construction – an inner skin with an outer layer of 76mm-thick armour bolted on. Five crew members manned the tank: driver, co-driver/hull machine-gunner, commander, gunner and shell-loader/radio-operator.

Although the Cromwell's Rolls Royce Meteor engine made it the fastest and most powerful of all British tanks produced in this period, the tank's narrow width prevented it from being equipped with 17-pounder gun armament. Face-to-face, therefore, the Cromwell was no match for the greater firepower and armour of the German Tiger and Panther tanks.

A hedge-cutting device known as a 'prong' was included in some versions of the tank.

Operation Goodwood
July 1944

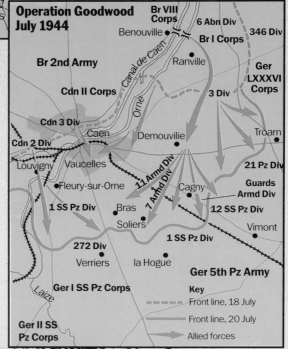

Labels on map: Br VIII Corps, 6 Abn Div, 346 Div, Benouville, Br I Corps, Br 2nd Army, Ranville, Canal de Caen, Ger LXXXVI Corps, Cdn II Corps, Orne, 3 Div, Cdn 3 Div, Caen, Demouvile, Troarn, Cdn 2 Div, 21 Pz Div, Louvigny, Vaucelles, 11 Armd Div, Cagny, Guards Armd Div, Fleury-sur-Orne, 7 Armd Div, 12 SS Pz Div, 1 SS Pz Div, Bras, Vimont, Soliers, 272 Div, 1 SS Pz Div, Verriers, la Hogue, Ger 5th Pz Army, Laize, **Key** ---- Front line, 18 July —— Front line, 20 July → Allied forces, Ger I SS Pz Corps, Ger II SS Pz Corps

Below: Victim of the *bocage*. Artist, designer and Welsh Guardsman, Rex Whistler.

After the breakout from Caen, although always outgunned by the enemy, the Shermans and Cromwells of the Guards Armoured were able to outflank the panzers by virtue of their greater speed and manoeuvrability. Below left: A camouflaged Sherman passes the remnants of a German column, destroyed by elements of the French Resistance.

of the armoured battalions arrived. They were soon pouring across the Seine, sweeping away the enemy strongpoints that lay ahead of them.

That same day, 1 September, the Welsh Guards reached Arras, 60 miles northeast of Amiens, with the rest of the division following closely behind. On the left flank, the 11th Armoured Division was racing towards Bethune. The territory which between 1914 and 1918 had taken many months to dominate, claiming countless lives, had fallen to the two armoured divisions within a matter of hours.

Compared with the rapid advance of the previous day, only a leisurely 15-mile jaunt to Lens and Douai was planned for 2 September; stop-lines had been agreed prior to an airborne assault that was scheduled for the following day. This respite afforded the division time to catch up on small maintenance duties. Thus, by the late afternoon, tanks were being serviced, brasses were being polished, webbing blancoed and trousers pressed. In the early evening, Generals Dempsey and Horrocks arrived to discuss strategy with Major-General Adair. This resulted in a change of plan for the division, as Adair explained to his battalion and squadron commanders later that same evening. 'My intention,' he declared, 'is to advance and liberate Brussels.'

A distance of 75 miles had to be covered in order to reach Brussels; on paper this was within a day's range for the Guards Armoured. However, this calculation did not take into account the enemy resistance that would almost certainly be encountered along the route. Accordingly, Adair proposed to raise the speed of the advance – as well as the excitement – by the simple expedient of turning it into a race. Dubbed 'The Great Swan', this novel competition was to take place along two lines of approach, thereby pitting the two brigades against each other. On the left flank, 5th Brigade, with the Grenadier Group leading, would advance along narrow. secondary roads which were likely to be

relatively undefended. The right flank, with the Welsh Guards leading 32nd Brigade, would use the main roads and could expect to encounter stiff German resistance from gun emplacements along the route. The 'winning post' was a road junction on the outskirts of Brussels.

At 1700 on 3 September, the armoured cars of the Household Cavalry crossed the Belgian frontier, followed one hour later by both armoured brigades on their separate routes. Enemy opposition was soon encountered by the 32nd Brigade at Pont-à-Marcq and Leuze. However, local resistance joined the battle immediately, picking off snipers and machine-gun posts and guiding the tanks in attacks against enemy rear and flank positions. The Germans were swept aside and, as the brigade raced on through narrow streets, their route became packed with Belgians, all thrusting forward food, drink, flowers and their prettiest daughters to encourage the tank crews. By noon they were well past the halfway mark. In the mid-afternoon, however, the Welsh Guards of the 32nd Brigade reached Enghien and became embroiled in a hard-fought action that delayed them for over an hour. Now behind schedule, the Welsh Guards obtained permission to race on at the full speed of their Cromwell tanks – 40mph. Travelling much faster than the Grenadiers, whose Shermans were only capable of 25mph, the 32nd Brigade won the race, crossing the road junction at 2200 hours. The Grenadiers arrived a few minutes later, having been held up by enemy fire only 10 miles short of their goal.

The car was swamped with jubilant Belgians, anxious to make their liberators as welcome as possible

Of course, not even the Welsh Cromwells had reached Brussels before the Household Cavalry's leading armoured cars. Lance Corporal of Horse, I. W. Dewar, and Trooper Ayles were among the first to enter the city, though their initial welcome was somewhat unexpected. Their arrival was looked upon with scorn by the local populace and they were warned to leave quickly, as 'les Anglais' were reputed to be close by! Corporal Dewar's French was adequate enough to put across the simple message 'Nous sommes les Anglais!' Immediately the car was swamped with jubilant Belgians, anxious to make their liberators as welcome as possible.

For the Guards Armoured Division, 3 September was a day of almost delirious celebration. As they drove through the streets towards the Château Royale, their route lined by people clamouring to catch a glimpse of the victorious Allied forces, one young officer felt as though he was:

'Floating on a sea of upturned faces ... Spontaneously they lined the streets and pavements 20 deep, and cheered and cheered and cheered. Veterans of the last war saluted, wives cried and laughed alternately, young women leapt on the vehicles embracing the dusty soldiers, and youths fired rifles into the air.'

It was the most memorable day of their lives, both for the Bruxellois and for the guardsmen. For the latter, there was also the satisfaction that they had been in the forefront of the longest opposed advance that any division, in any army, had completed in a single day.

THE AUTHOR Barrie Pitt is well known as a military historian and edited Purnell's *History of the Second World War* and *History of the First World War*.

Order of battle
Guards Armoured Division

Operation Goodwood, 18 July

Reconnaissance Regiment	— 2nd (Armoured) Battalion Welsh Guards
5th Guards Armoured Brigade	— 1st (Motor) Battalion Grenadier Guards 2nd (Armoured) Battalion Grenadier Guards 1st (Armoured) Battalion Coldstream Guards 2nd (Armoured) Battalion Irish Guards
32nd Guards Brigade	— 5th Battalion Coldstream Guards 3rd Battalion Irish Guards 1st Battalion Welsh Guards

Crossing the Seine, 29 August

Reconnaissance Regiment	— 2nd Household Cavalry Regiment	
5th Guards Armoured Brigade	— Grenadier Group	: 1st (Motor) Battalion 2nd (Armoured) Battalion
	— Coldstream Group:	1st (Armoured) Battalion 5th (Infantry) Battalion
32nd Guards Brigade	— Irish Group	: 2nd (Armoured) Battalion 3rd (Infantry) Battalion
	— Welsh Group	: 1st (Infantry) Battalion 2nd (Armoured) Battalion

PANZER ATTACK

Fanatical teenage Nazis – or hand-picked young men who were forged into a superb fighting formation during the heat of the Normandy battles of 1944? Whatever your viewpoint, the Hitlerjugend Division is still recognised as the deadliest opponent faced by the Allied armies in northwest Europe

THE DEAFENING ROAR of 300hp Maybach panzer engines and the sharp squeal of tank tracks filled the warm June evening as leading elements of the crack 12th SS Panzer Division 'Hitlerjugend' (Hitler Youth) poured west towards the Normandy town of Caen. Panzer grenadiers, hunched grimly in hastily-applied camouflage foliage, clung to their Mark IV tanks as motorcycle combinations and scout cars raced past. Bringing up the rear, convoys of trucks wound their way along the narrow French country roads ferrying more and more troops into the area in which some of the bitterest fighting in the Normandy campaign would soon take place.

On 5 June 1944, the 12th SS Panzer Division 'Hitlerjugend' had been deployed in an area west of Paris and south of Rouen, with its divisional headquarters at Acon. The divisional strength was slightly above establishment at 20,540 all ranks, although it lacked 144 officers of its authorised total of 664. The division incorporated one panzer regiment, consisting of two tank battalions, one equipped with Panthers and one with Mark IV tanks; an anti-tank battalion; two panzer grenadier regiments, each of three battalions; an artillery regiment, an anti-aircraft regiment, and various support units. At the time of D-Day the panzer regiment was lacking 36 of its establishment of 186 tanks.

The youth of the force can be shown by the fact that in the 1st Battalion, 25th SS Panzergrenadier Regiment, no less than 65 per cent of the personnel were under 18 years of age, and only three per cent, nearly all officers and NCOs, were over 25. The young soldiers hero-worshipped such tough and exciting leaders as Kurt Meyer (known as 'Panzermeyer') and Max Wünsche. The Hitlerjugend recruits were taught to be fighters, not soldiers, and the emphasis was placed on obedience, hardness, camaraderie and the belief that the word 'impossible' did not exist. As in other elite Waffen SS divisions, the tactic of the aggressive attack and counter-attack was cultivated. Even before its baptism of fire, the Hitlerjugend Division was already characterised by reckless determination combined with fanaticism and self-sacrifice.

Only after darkness had fallen did the fighter-bombers let up

On the morning of 6 June, the Hitlerjugend Division was transferred from the OKW reserve and placed at the disposal of Rommel's Army Group B. Its orders were to assemble east of Lisieux where it would be deployed by the Seventh Army. Like so many German reinforcements moving towards the Allied beachhead, the Hitlerjugend Division was unable to move as an entire division, but instead was divided up for transport. The first units which moved off at 1000 hours on 6 June were the 1st Battalion of the 12th SS Panzer Regiment along with the 26th SS Panzergrenadier Regiment, and the 2nd Battalion with the 25th SS Panzergrenadier Regiment.

Elements of the Hitlerjugend Division arrived in the area of Lisieux at 1500, but were then ordered to regroup west of Caen to participate in a counter-attack against the Canadians. The various units of the Hitlerjugend Division straggled into the deployment area over the next 24 hours. With no air cover to speak of, the assembling German forces were subjected to furious low-level rocket and cannon attacks by RAF Hawker Typhoons, stretching the tough discipline and combat training of the young soldiers to the limit. Only after darkness had fallen did the fighter-bombers let up. Hard information on enemy movements was scarce and rumours ran like wildfire through the massing battalions, but morale held. Panzer grenadier companies dashed into position, digging trenches and dugouts, while anti-tank gun crews hauled their heavy weapons into line. Camouflage netting went up and finally, in the early hours of the morning, the exhausted troops were able to catch a few hours sleep.

The 2nd Battalion of the 12th SS Panzer Regiment

Clockwise from top: Hitlerjugend commanders Kurt Meyer (left) and Fritz Witt (centre) confer with Field Marshal von Rundstedt, German C-in-C West; a PzKpfw IV Ausf H with the long-barrelled 75mm L/48 gun; hit by a German shell, an ammunition lorry explodes just by a US Army Sherman; and a Hitlerjugend 75mm anti-tank emplacement – such units in ambush positions devastated the advancing Allied armour. Far left: Steadying the swinging ammunition belt of his 7.62mm MG42 a Hitlerjugend trooper runs at a crouch into position.

12th SS PANZER DIVISION 'HITLERJUGEND'

The Waffen ('fighting') SS was formed early in World War II, based upon the para-military SS (Schutzstaffel, or Protection Squads) organisations already in existence, and rapidly grew in size. On 20 July 1943 at Antwerp, cadres of the 1st SS Panzer Division Leibstandarte Adolf Hitler (Adolf Hitler's Life Guards) were brought together with personnel of the Hitlerjugend (Hitler Youth) leadership schools in a new panzer grenadier division that was, along with additional Leibstandarte forces, to form 1 SS Panzer Corps. On 21 October Hitler ordered that the corps should consist of two panzer divisions, not one, and the following day the new division was redesignated 12th SS Panzer Division 'Hitlerjugend'.

The 12th SS Panzer Division had no precedent in the German Army. Most of the officers and NCOs were picked from able veterans of the Leibstandarte on the Eastern Front and these seasoned men were given the responsibility of training the young recruits. Their methods were unorthodox. In order to prepare them for immediate battle the youths were subjected to hunger, deprivation, and exposure to live bullet and shell attacks. Inevitably there were casualties, yet the troops came to war fully hardened and eager to fight. The division's rank and file constituted the new blood of Nazism. Boys in the Hitler Youth were introduced to the doctrine and embraced it totally. Imbued with the romance of the Germanic warrior, the soldiers of the Hitlerjugend were given the chance of ultimate glory – death in defence of the Fatherland.

only arrived on the morning of 7 June, and with only 50 tanks. The Panther tanks of the 1st Battalion were stranded on the east bank of the Orne river due to lack of petrol. Thus, Army Group B, instead of being able to deploy the whole of the Hitlerjugend Division for a counter-attack, was only able to muster a Kampfgruppe (battle group) under the command of Panzermeyer. Despite the losses of men and material in the air attacks, the Hitlerjugend units, together with the 21st Panzer Division, were the only force capable of making a counter-attack west of Caen.

The Canadians reeled back under the sheer fury of their attack

The divisional orders of the Hitlerjugend for the morning of 7 June stated that the division would attack the enemy and throw him into the sea, the final objective being the beaches. In fact, Panzermeyer's own orders were much more realistic, and he appears to have decided to take up a covering position protecting Caen pending the arrival of reinforcements. He put all three panzer grenadier battalions into the line, with two companies of tanks behind each flank, and deployed his artillery support well to the rear, preparing an ambush for the Canadian forces pushing out from the Allied beachheads. Then Meyer positioned himself in the tower of Ardenne Abbey, in order to view the whole area.

Panzermeyer watched the Canadian advance unfold, and listened to the radio reports of Allied tank movements, his gaunt features lined with concentration and fatigue. Sinister in their black leather clothing, the tank crews mounted their panzers. Unsuppressed excitement and anticipation of the battle to come showed on their faces as they lowered themselves into the turrets they had daubed with the names of their girlfriends. And then they waited. Months of training had pushed home the crucial need to hold their fire until they could engage the oncoming armour decisively and at close quarters.

Grenadier, Hitlerjugend Division, Normandy 1944

As a consequence of the shortage of uniforms in Nazi Germany large numbers of Hitlerjugend troops were equipped with uniforms made from Italian camouflage material, requisitioned from the Italians following their surrender in 1943. Besides his Italian camouflage uniform this grenadier has a helmet cover of the same material. By the summer of 1944 the old German jackboots had virtually disappeared from the armed forces and had been replaced by the ankle boots worn here. He is armed with a 7.92mm MG42 machine gun and consequently carries a leather box containing spares and cleaning materials. The MG42 was greatly respected by Allied troops but was a difficult weapon to use as its very high rate of fire (up to 1200rpm) demanded the highest fire-control qualities from the machine gunner. Nevertheless the MG42 was the first modern general-purpose machine gun, as it could be used in a light-machine gun role – when bipod mounted – or was capable of sustained long-range fire when tripod mounted.

Above far left: Members of the Hitlerjugend Division relax around a half-track transport vehicle. Most are wearing the distinctive fighting gear of the Hitlerjugend, the black leather jacket and trousers of U-Boat crews. Above left: Hitlerjugend recruits swear allegiance to Adolf Hitler over a weapon of their unit, a 75mm Pak anti-tank gun. Their commander, Panzermeyer, stands directly behind the gun. Above: Max Wünsche, commander of the Hitlerjugend tank regiment. Wünsche was one of the select group of brilliant and charismatic Hitlerjugend commanders who inspired adulation and absolute loyalty in young recruits arriving fresh from the Hitler Youth leadership schools in Germany. Standing in the turret of a Panther of the 1st Battalion of the 12th SS Panzer Regiment, he is wearing the Italian DPM jacket common in the division, and wears his Knight's Cross at his throat.

In the tower of the abbey, Meyer calculated the best moment to attack. The Canadians pushed through the tiny village of Franqueville heading for the airfield at Caen and then, when only 80m separated the leading tanks and the German ambush, he gave the signal to go. Panzer Mark IVs and infantry burst from their concealed positions and stormed over the small ridge, cutting deep into the Canadian flank while at point-blank range the well-hidden anti-tank crews poured round after lethal round into the oncoming Stuart tanks. The teenage troops of the Hitlerjugend fought ferociously and the Canadians reeled back under the sheer fury of their attack. Within hours the villages of Authie and Franqueville were retaken. The Hitlerjugend attack was well co-ordinated, with panzers, panzer grenadiers and the artillery all working together, and the Canadians found it very difficult to stop the Mark IV tanks. But although Panzermeyer was later to claim that his 'push to the sea' was eventually stopped by shortages of fuel and ammunition, it was actually halted by a heavy artillery barrage from Allied guns and determined Canadian resistance.

The panzers moved in a wedge formation with the panzer grenadiers clinging on the turrets

Although the Hitlerjugend counter-attack had failed to reach the beach, it had prevented the Canadians from reaching the important airfield at Carpiquet. The Canadians suffered over 300 casualties and lost nearly 30 tanks, while the Hitlerjugend had lost six tanks and sustained about 200 casualties. In its first battle the Hitlerjugend Division had fought with a bravery and determination that deeply impressed

the Canadians. It had also suffered heavy casualties, the hallmark of an elite Waffen SS division. Emil Werner, of the 25th Panzergrenadier Regiment, described the bitter fighting of 7 June:

'Until Cambes, everything went well. So far as we were concerned, the village looked fine. But on the outskirts we came under infantry fire and then all hell broke loose. We stormed a church where snipers had taken up positions. Here I saw the first dead man from our company; it was Grenadier Ruehl from headquarters platoon. I turned his body over myself – he'd been shot through the head. He was the second member of our company to die. Dead comrades already, and we still hadn't seen any Englishmen. Then the situation became critical. My section commander was wounded in the arm and had to go to the rear. Grenadier Grosse from Hamburg leapt past me towards a clump of bushes with his sub-machine gun at the ready, screaming "Hands up! Hands up!" Two Englishmen emerged with their hands held high. As far as I know, Grosse got the Iron Cross, second class, for this.'

On 8 June a company of Panther tanks from the 1st Battalion finally arrived, and these, with some panzer grenadiers, made a night attack along the Caen–Bayeux road. The panzers moved in a wedge formation with the panzer grenadiers clinging on behind the turrets. As usual, Panzermeyer was leading the advance of the reconnaissance company on his motorcycle. At midnight they reached the village of Rots and after several hours of confused fighting, in which the Hitlerjugend lost six tanks, Meyer withdrew his force. Although this attack was pressed home with courage and determination, there appeared to be little tactical control, and Canadian observers commented that the Hitlerjugend had attacked piecemeal and had failed to exploit the weakness of their opponent's position.

Although the Germans had planned to launch a major offensive to reach the coast on 10 June, one that would have included the Hitlerjugend, it never took place because the Allies seized the initiative on the left flank against the Panzer Lehr Division. On 16 June the Hitlerjugend divisional headquarters, which was positioned some 27km southwest of Caen, came under heavy and accurate Allied naval shell-fire, and SS Brigadeführer (Major-General) Fritz Witt, the divisional commander, was killed along with several other officers. He was replaced by Panzermeyer. The Hitlerjugend Division had been deployed piecemeal to the north and west of Caen and had already suffered heavy casualties, and there were shortages of petrol, ammunition and equipment. North of Caen the panzers of the Hitlerjugend were supporting shaky units such as the 16th Luftwaffe Field Division. Carpiquet airfield was held by a flak battery of the Hitlerjugend, elements of the 1st Battalion of the 26th SS Panzergrenadier Regiment and some 15 tanks.

On 4 July the Canadians launched an attack with their 3rd Division to capture Carpiquet village and the airfield. A German artillery barrage caused heavy casualties amongst the first wave of attacking Canadians, and there was a bitter fight between two battalions of Canadian infantry and some 50 panzer grenadiers defending Carpiquet village. By evening the Canadians had captured the village and the northern end of the airfield, but the Germans still held the southern end. The men of the Hitlerjugend were exhausted but only the lack of infantry prevented them from making further counter-attacks

Between 4 and 9 July the Hitlerjugend Division was one of the corner-stones of the German defence of Caen against the attack of the British I Corps. A heavy Allied air attack on Caen caused relatively few German casualties, but for the ordinary SS soldier in the Hitlerjugend it meant shortages of food, ammunition and petrol. Under Panzermeyer's personal leadership the Hitlerjugend Division bitterly contested the remorseless British advance. Panzermeyer attempted to prevent the Canadians from capturing the village of Buron to the north of Caen, but after fighting them to a standstill with a few tanks and panzer grenadiers, he was forced to withdraw. By 9 July the Allies held most of Caen, although the suburbs to the south remained in German hands.

After 9 July the Hitlerjugend Division was a shadow of its original strength. The division's total infantry strength equalled that of only one battalion, and there were only 65 of the original 150 tanks. Total casualties for the division since D-Day had been 60 per cent of the original strength, with 20 per cent dead and 40 per cent wounded. Replacements were only a few hundred, and the schoolboys of 6 June had become hardened veterans.

Smeared with blood, covered with dust, gasping and fighting

The nature of the fighting at Caen for the Hitlerjugend Division during this period can be seen in the rather excited prose of an SS war reporter writing for the periodical *SS Leitheft*:

'Thousands of aircraft, rolling barrages of the batteries, massed tank attacks hammered them in with bombs and shells. The earth heaved thunderously. An inferno was unleashed. But faith was the strongest support of courage. Smeared with blood, covered with dust, gasping and fighting, doggedly dug into the earth, these youths brought the Anglo-Americans to a halt.'

Further to the west of Caen there had been a bloody attritional battle between the British and Germans for the key position of Hill 112, known by the Canadians as the Hill of Calvary. Elements of the Hitlerjugend were involved in the defence of Hill 112, and Private Zimmer, a panzer grenadier, noted in his diary what it was like to face the British attack of 10 July:

'From 6.30 to 8.00 am, again heavy machine-gun fire. Then Tommy attacks with great masses of infantry and many tanks. We fight as long as possible but we realise we are in a losing position. By the time the survivors try to pull back, we realise that we are surrounded.'

On 11 July the Hitlerjugend Division was withdrawn from the line and sent to the Potigny area 30km north of Falaise for a rest and refit. But on 18 July the division was recalled to the front to help stop the British Operation Goodwood from breaking through the German position at Caen. The Hitlerjugend Division was now divided into two battle groups, Kampfgruppe Krause and Kampfgruppe Waldmüller, with a combined strength of some 50 armoured vehicles. Over the next three weeks the Hitlerjugend Division continued to act as the backbone of the German position south of Caen.

The whole German position in Normandy was coming apart, however, under successive Allied attacks. On 25 July Bradley's First US Army launched Operation Cobra from the direction of St Lô into the German left flank, an attack that would eventually roll up the German position in western Normandy.

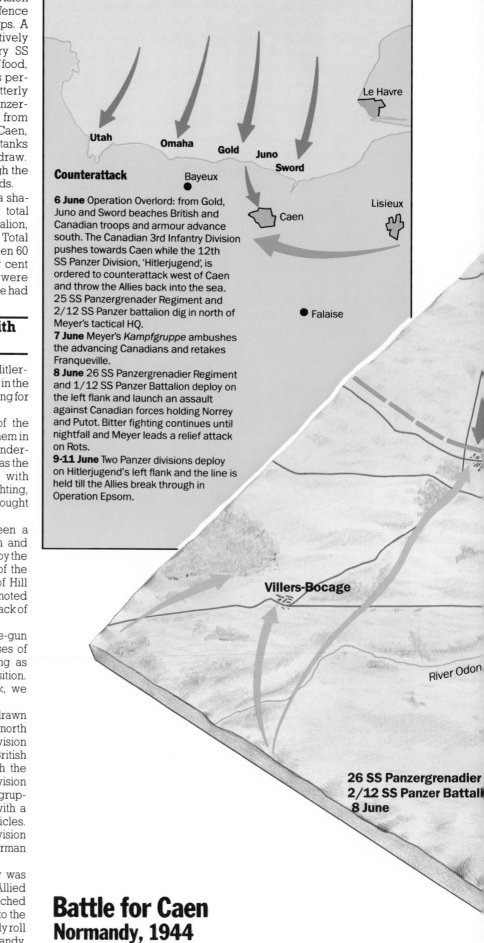

Counterattack

6 June Operation Overlord: from Gold, Juno and Sword beaches British and Canadian troops and armour advance south. The Canadian 3rd Infantry Division pushes towards Caen while the 12th SS Panzer Division, 'Hitlerjugend', is ordered to counterattack west of Caen and throw the Allies back into the sea. 25 SS Panzergrenadier Regiment and 2/12 SS Panzer battalion dig in north of Meyer's tactical HQ.

7 June Meyer's *Kampfgruppe* ambushes the advancing Canadians and retakes Franqueville.

8 June 26 SS Panzergrenadier Regiment and 1/12 SS Panzer Battalion deploy on the left flank and launch an assault against Canadian forces holding Norrey and Putot. Bitter fighting continues until nightfall and Meyer leads a relief attack on Rots.

9-11 June Two Panzer divisions deploy on Hitlerjugend's left flank and the line is held till the Allies break through in Operation Epsom.

26 SS Panzergrenadier
2/12 SS Panzer Battali[on]
8 June

Battle for Caen
Normandy, 1944

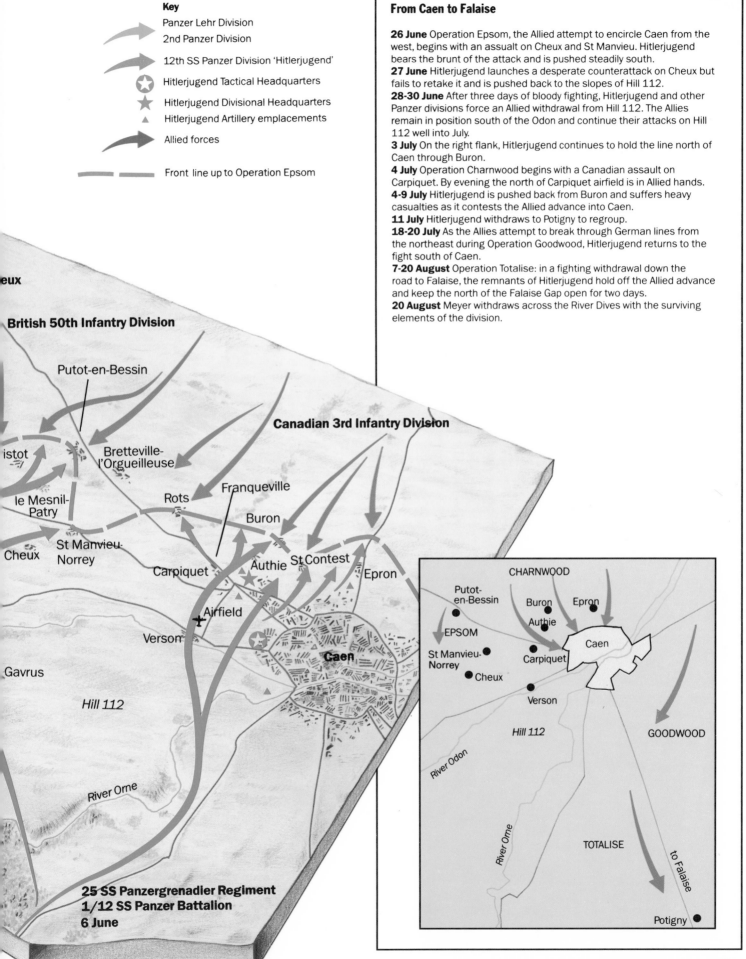

Key

- Panzer Lehr Division
- 2nd Panzer Division
- 12th SS Panzer Division 'Hitlerjugend'
- Hitlerjugend Tactical Headquarters
- Hitlerjugend Divisional Headquarters
- Hitlerjugend Artillery emplacements
- Allied forces
- Front line up to Operation Epsom

From Caen to Falaise

26 June Operation Epsom, the Allied attempt to encircle Caen from the west, begins with an assualt on Cheux and St Manvieu. Hitlerjugend bears the brunt of the attack and is pushed steadily south.

27 June Hitlerjugend launches a desperate counterattack on Cheux but fails to retake it and is pushed back to the slopes of Hill 112.

28-30 June After three days of bloody fighting, Hitlerjugend and other Panzer divisions force an Allied withdrawal from Hill 112. The Allies remain in position south of the Odon and continue their attacks on Hill 112 well into July.

3 July On the right flank, Hitlerjugend continues to hold the line north of Caen through Buron.

4 July Operation Charnwood begins with a Canadian assault on Carpiquet. By evening the north of Carpiquet airfield is in Allied hands.

4-9 July Hitlerjugend is pushed back from Buron and suffers heavy casualties as it contests the Allied advance into Caen.

11 July Hitlerjugend withdraws to Potigny to regroup.

18-20 July As the Allies attempt to break through German lines from the northeast during Operation Goodwood, Hitlerjugend returns to the fight south of Caen.

7-20 August Operation Totalise: in a fighting withdrawal down the road to Falaise, the remnants of Hitlerjugend hold off the Allied advance and keep the north of the Falaise Gap open for two days.

20 August Meyer withdraws across the River Dives with the surviving elements of the division.

British 50th Infantry Division

Putot-en-Bessin

eux

istot

Bretteville-l'Orgueilleuse

le Mesnil-Patry

Rots

Franqueville

Canadian 3rd Infantry Division

Cheux

St Manvieu-Norrey

Carpiquet

Buron

Authie

St Contest

Epron

Airfield

Verson

Caen

Gavrus

Hill 112

River Orne

**25 SS Panzergrenadier Regiment
1/12 SS Panzer Battalion
6 June**

CHARNWOOD

Putot-en-Bessin

Buron

Epron

EPSOM

Authie

St Manvieu-Norrey

Carpiquet

Caen

Cheux

Verson

GOODWOOD

Hill 112

River Odon

River Orne

TOTALISE

to Falaise

Potigny

On 30 July Lieutenant-General Sir Miles Dempsey's Second British Army attacked the German Seventh Army in Operation Bluecoat. The Hitlerjugend Division was deployed north of Falaise when on 7 August the First Canadian Army launched Operation Totalise, intended to break the German front south of Caen. This attack was carried out with an estimated 600 tanks against the 50 assorted armoured vehicles of the Hitlerjugend.

There is no doubt that the formidable tenacity and fighting ability of the soldiers of the Hitlerjugend Division, combined with the forceful personality and aggressive leadership of Panzermeyer, was responsible for the failure of the Allies to break through the German position. The Canadian attack was preceded by a massive air attack which destroyed the morale of the two supporting German infantry divisions. Panzermeyer discovered while reconnoitering behind the front that:

'Before me, making their way down the Caen-Falaise Road in a disorderly rabble were the panic-stricken troops of the 89th Infantry Division. I realised that something had to be done to send them back into the line and fight. I lit a cigar, stood in the middle of the road and in a loud voice asked them if they were going to leave me alone to cope with the enemy. Having a divisional commander address them in this way, they stopped, hesitated, and then returned to their positions.'

The stubbornness of the soldiers of the Hitlerjugend and the defensive firepower of the German 75mm and 88mm anti-tank guns meant that the Canadians only advanced 5km in the first 24 hours. But the losses of the Hitlerjugend were such that it could no longer assemble even one offensive Kampfgruppe. When the Allies tried to bomb the Hitlerjugend Division out of the way, Panzermeyer had already anticipated the move and had withdrawn his men and vehicles from their defensive positions in the villages before the attack began. For two days, from 14 August, Panzermeyer held Hill 159 to the northeast of Falaise, against elements of the 3rd Canadian Division, with only 500 men. After the position had been attacked continuously and bombarded by artillery fire and ground support aircraft, Panzermeyer was forced to withdraw over the Ante river. By this time the strength of the Hitlerjugend Division had been reduced to 15 tanks and a few hundred men.

On 16 August the 2nd Canadian Division entered Falaise and fought a house-to-house battle with a small detachment of the Hitlerjugend. About 60 men from the Hitlerjugend held out for three days in the *école superieure* and only four survived to be taken prisoner. With the loss of Falaise, the gap between the British and American forces had narrowed to 20km. In what had become the Argentan-Falaise pocket were trapped some 19 German divisions under incessant Allied artillery and air bombardment. The battered remnants of the Hitlerjugend Division were ordered to help hold open the northern side of the pocket to let as many German units escape as possible. Less than half the trapped German units were able to get away, but the fact that any of them did was largely due to the efforts of the Hitlerjugend Division, which held their side of the gap for two days. Panzermeyer himself escaped across the Dives river with some 200 men on the morning of 20 August, having 'persuaded' a French peasant to guide them. On 22 August, Army Group B reported that the 12th SS Panzer Division 'Hitlerjugend' had a strength of 300 men. 10 tanks and no artillery. It had destroyed itself in Normandy.

Seriously wounded, Durr attacked a Canadian flame-throwing tank which had pinned down his men

Many of the military characteristics of the Hitlerjugend Division were common to other units of the Waffen SS and the German Army in Normandy in 1944. Divisions like the Leibstandarte and Panzer Lehr fought just as well and suffered equally heavy casualties. The Hitlerjugend as a panzer division was not better armed and equipped than its equivalent divisions, and in some respects it was less well provided for. Like many other German divisions it fought for most of the Normandy campaign divided up into separate battle groups (Kampfgruppen) with gunners, engineers, clerks and cooks all being used as panzer grenadiers. The difference between the Hitlerjugend Division and other German units lay in its absolute acceptance of the necessity for self-sacrifice and death in battle. Not all of these young boys had been volunteers and the fact that they too accepted the ethos of the division was largely a result of the influence of their charismatic leaders.

Given the shortage of officers and the fact that during the Normandy campaign the division oper-

Left: Troops from the Hitlerjugend panzer regiment pose for the camera during a break in the fighting for the notorious Hill 112. An interesting range of uniforms is worn by this group, including the U-boat leather jacket worn by Herbert Walther (standing, fourth from right). Right: Following rumours of the killing of Canadian prisoners, Hitlerjugend captives received rough treatment from the Allies, and this grenadier, bloody but unbowed, bears all the hallmarks of having been beaten up by his captors – a far cry from the enthusiasm and optimism of the Hitler Youth training corps (above right).

ated in small units, leadership in the battle groups devolved down to the NCOs, and they played a very important part in maintaining a high degree of determined fanaticism amongst the young soldiers. One example was SS Unterscharführer (Corporal) Emil Durr of the 26th SS Panzergrenadier Regiment, who was awarded the Knight's Cross posthumously for his leadership and bravery near Caen on 27 June 1944. Although seriously wounded, Durr attacked a Canadian flame-throwing tank which had pinned down some of his men. He finally succeeded in destroying the tank after three attempts, but was killed in the process. This kind of bravery characterised the whole division.

The tenacity, personal hardness and willingness for self sacrifice also resulted in a sometimes brutal attitude towards prisoners and civilians. Throughout the Normandy campaign there were frequent instances of prisoners being shot by both sides, but the Hitlerjugend gained a fearsome reputation, particularly amongst the Canadians, for shooting prisoners. In the 10 day period between 7 and 16 June the Hitlerjugend was responsible for shooting 64 British and Canadian prisoners. After the war, Panzermeyer and other officers of the Hitlerjugend were tried by the British and Canadians for war crimes. Panzermeyer was held responsible and sentenced to death, but this was later commuted to life imprisonment, and he was actually released in 1954.

Two things stand out from any study of the Hitlerjugend Division in Normandy. The first is the overall fanaticism of the young Hitler Youth boys and their willingness to sacrifice their lives, and the second is the aggressive fighting leadership of the senior officers, especially Panzermeyer. Sometimes, this fanaticism, self-sacrifice and aggressive leadership became a substitute for tactics and firepower: a high level of casualties does not necessarily indicate good soldiering. One British tank commander recalled how the Hitlerjugend had sprung at Allied tanks 'like young wolves, until we were forced to kill them against our will.' But that readiness to sacrifice their lives, and ability to endure fierce attritional battles beyond the endurance of ordinary German soldiers, raised the Hitlerjugend to an elite force. In the words of Max Hastings in his book, *Overlord*, 'No formation caused the Allies such deep trouble in Normandy until the end as 12th SS Panzer.'

THE AUTHOR Keith Simpson is senior lecturer in War Studies and International Affairs at Sandhurst. A member of the Royal United Services Institute and the International Institute for Strategic Studies, he has a special interest in modern warfare and is currently writing a book on the German Army.

POLISH BLITZKRIEG

As formulated, the German plan for the invasion of Poland in September 1939 called for a two-pronged advance on Warsaw. From the northern sector of the border, Army Group North, some 630,000 men under Colonel-General von Bock, was to thrust into the Danzig corridor, strike out for the Bug river and drive on to the Polish capital, where it would link up with Army Group South consisting of 680,000 troops led by Colonel-General von Rundstedt. To ensure mastery of the air, the most essential element of Blitzkrieg, almost 2000 aircraft were available to support the Wehrmacht's pincer movements.

Although the bulk of the 55 divisions deployed against Poland consisted of infantry, nine were panzer divisions.

The 4th Panzer Division, part of Army Group South, was made up of the 35th and 36th Panzer Regiments, the 12th Schutzen Regiment, the 103rd Artillery Regiment, the 7th Reconnaissance Battalion, the 49th Anti-tank Battalion and the usual support services.

On paper, the Polish High Command could put 45 divisions into the field, but on closer analysis, they were ill-prepared to meet the German onslaught. Many of the divisions were unable to meet the demands of modern warfare and much of their equipment was obsolete. To make matters worse, these divisions, many of which were still mobilising when the Blitzkrieg began, had to defend a frontier that ran for some 1750 miles across terrain that offered little in the way of defensive possibilities.

When the storm finally broke, the Poles fought with grim, often suicidal ferocity and did, on occasion, inflict damage on the Germans, but their bravery could not overcome armies trained for lightning battle.
Above: The 4th Panzer Division's insignia.

THE MAILED FIST

Tasked with the capture of Warsaw, the tanks and infantry of the 4th Panzer Division fought one of the bloodiest battles of the Polish campaign

FOR THE Wehrmacht's campaign in Poland during September 1939 the 4th Panzer Division was one of the two armoured formations under the XVIth Army Corps (Army Group South) which formed one arm of a vast encircling movement to the west of Warsaw. The first part of the German battle plan, following the initial attacks on the 1st, succeeded brilliantly, and by the end of the first week of the campaign, the 4th Panzer Division, led by Georg-Hans Reinhardt, was threatening the Polish capital. German confidence was high and XVI Corps' Order for 8 September directed the division to advance upon Warsaw along two main highways and to enter what was thought to be an open city. However, the panzer columns did not find an open city but one determined to resist. Barricades had been erected, anti-tank guns positioned, artillery deployed in parks and open spaces, and even the civilian population was willing to fight the invaders.

However, the deployment of Reinhardt's 4th Panzer Division was changed when, late in the afternoon of the 9th, a liaison aircraft dropped a message that told of massed Polish troops and heavy equipment advancing along the east-west highway between Sochaczev and Warsaw towards the Bzura river. What the message did not state – because it was not known at that time – was that the enemy force consisted of the mighty Poznan Army. What was quickly understood was that the only obstacle between the Poznan Army and Warsaw, was the 4th Panzer Division, isolated from the bulk of the German forces in Poland and with its units deployed facing eastwards.

The swift advances of the two armoured divisions of XVI Corps had created a long and narrow salient: the 1st Panzer Division stood to the southeast of Warsaw; the 4th Division was to the west of the city. Neither division was in physical contact with the other. To meet the developing threat, the energetic Reinhardt, one of Germany's foremost exponents of Blitzkrieg, then deployed the 4th so that it faced two ways, east and west, and then sent out a call to corps asking for more infantry.

Back on the main highway, the threat to the 4th Panzer Division was growing. On the western flank its 7th Reconnaissance Battalion had been swept aside by the advance guard of the Poznan Army. To meet this thrust, Reinhardt put in a battlegroup made up of the SS motorised infantry regiment Leibstandarte Adolf Hitler, which corps had rushed forward in response to his plea, the 2nd Battalion of the 103rd Artillery Regiment and the regrouped survivors of the reconnaissance battalion. Facing Warsaw, there was a mixed infantry, artillery and anti-tank battlegroup, while in reserve were his two panzer regiments and the 12th Schutzen Regiment. However, the division's situation deteriorated and became critical. There were shortages of fuel and ammunition. Its supply dumps, together with the main workshops,

Left: A column of Panzer IIs, led by a Panzer I, waits to crush Poland in September 1939. The distinctive white crosses, used as an aiming mark by the enemy's anti-tank gunners, proved a liability and were later replaced. Far left: Armed with a 98K rifle, a storm-trooper prepares to lob a 'potato-masher' grenade.

were at Petrikau, some 125km distant. Between the depots and the fighting echelons lay vast tracts of country across which roamed aggressive and un-shaken enemy units, all striking out to reach the capital from the direction of the Bzura.

The story of the battle for the Bzura is one of storming attack and dogged defence against in-numerable enemy counter-attacks, for the Poles did not consider themselves beaten even though there was no longer a central command to direct the operations of their field armies. The Poles in the pocket would never accept that they were defeated, and even on the last day, their charges were filled with great elan and fury.

During 10 September the enemy's Warsaw garri-son became more than usually active and bom-barded the units of the 4th Panzer Division. Simul-taneously, there were reports of massed Polish forces slipping past the open flank of the division, moving along the Vistula. With every unit of his division already stretched to the limit, Reinhardt could only respond to the Polish challenges with artillery fire. Many troops saw the bizarre sight of some batteries firing at targets to the west, while other batteries of the same artillery battalion en-gaged targets in Warsaw to the east.

The Polish assault came in upon men who had been in unceasing action for more than a week

Reinhardt's response to the aggression at his back was to launch the SS in an infantry attack on the western sector and for his panzer regiment to strike northwards to cut the Modlin-Warsaw road. One swift probe by the panzers into the northwest sub-urbs of the capital showed these arms to be strongly barricaded and, as a counter to the German recce thrust, the enemy put in a spirited tank attack of their own that went in under a strong artillery barrage. These actions were the prelude to waves of Polish counter-attacks against the thin German line. A description of the attack against the SS was written by an NCO of the 1st Battalion:

'Through the trodden-down vegetation they stormed; across the bodies of their fallen com-rades. They did not come forward with their heads bowed like men in heavy rain – and mostly storm-ing infantry do come on like that – but they came with their heads held high, as if they were swim-mers breasting the waves.'

Throughout the 11th, the furious Polish assaults came in upon men who had been in unceasing action for more than a week. At the end of each counter-attack, when the mass of brown-coated soldiers flooded back into the vast and gloomy forests out of which they had erupted, the German infantrymen, gunners and panzercrews fell to the ground in total exhaus-tion. When the alarm sounded again, they saw in despair the long lines of the enemy come into view and heard again the bellowing hurrahs as the Polish assault swept towards them.

Although the panzers had few enemy tanks to engage, they were constantly in action and were used as assault artillery to support the hard-pressed infantry, or for leading assaults to recapture lost ground. Small wonder then that by the end of the 11th, a day of ceaseless fighting, more than a half of the panzers were out of action. The fury of the battle rose to fresh heights during the early hours of 12 September, when a Polish night attack at Mokotov went in supported by 20 tanks. The enemy's armour did not have the firepower of the division's Panzer IIIs and IVs, but they were handled capably and forced the German line back.

On the western sector, the Poles, skilled at night-fighting, drove the SS from their positions, forcing Reinhardt to commit his last reserves before the situation was restored. Some enemy tanks broke through and in the confused fighting the infantry of the 33rd Regiment knocked out six of the 18 tanks that were destroyed that night. Most of the others fell victim to the 35th Panzer Regiment. Throughout the night and for much of the following day, Polish attacks produced German counter-attacks, but battle at such a pitch could not last and the fighting waned.

By the afternoon of the 14th, the division had regained contact with the units to the south, although the Vistula flank still lay open. A line, thin but still a line, of German units was now being cast round the enemy, seeking to break out eastwards. With this increase in strength, Reinhardt redeployed his divi-sion and set the SS in yet another assault to clear the western flank. The ground to the north of the main highway was good panzer country and their crews, liberated at last from days of restricted movement, began to thrust across the heathland with the SS clinging to the sides of their vehicles.

Below: Germans advance through the outskirts of Warsaw. After bitter street street fighting, the Polish capital fell on 28 September Bottom left: Crossing the Bzura. Tanks of the 4th Pan Division, under the comma of Georg-Hans Reinhardt (bottom), prepare to take o the Poles.

THE PZKPFW II

In the mid-1930s, a period of rapid expansion in the strength of the Wehrmacht, it was decreed that Hitler's newly created panzer divisions should be equipped with two types of tank: one capable of fighting in tank-versus-tank battles and one able to use high explosive rounds against 'soft' targets. However, delays in producing these heavy tanks led to the construction of an interim model.

This tank, the PzKpfw II, was ordered in 1935 and the first models were in service by the following year. Made by MAN of Nuremburg, it was powered by a water-cooled engine and had a top speed of 35km/h. The tank's three-man crew worked in a fairly cramped fighting compartment, protected by armour that varied in thickness from 10 to 30mm Armament consisted of a single 20mm Kwk 38 automatic gun and one 7.92mm machine gun. Both weapons were mounted in the turret.

The PzKpfw II served as the backbone of the Wehrmacht's armoured divisions during the early campaigns of World War II, with some 1000 taking part in the invasion of Poland in September 1939, and even as late as 1942, 800 were still on the establishment. The tank, although successively modified, was soon out-classed and was increasingly relegated to a training role.

However, the basic design was sound and the tank's chassis was used as the basis for other armoured fighting vehicles such as the Wespe and Marder self-propelled guns. Designed as a stop-gap tank, the PzKpfw II, in its various guises, saw action throughout the war.

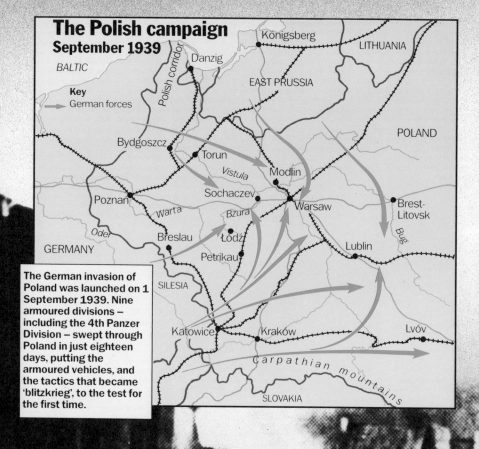

The Polish campaign
September 1939

BALTIC

Key
→ German forces

Königsberg
LITHUANIA
Danzig
Polish corridor
EAST PRUSSIA
POLAND
Bydgoszcz
Torun
Vistula
Modlin
Poznan
Sochaczev
Warsaw
Warta
Bzura
Brest-Litovsk
Oder
Breslau
Łódż
Bug
GERMANY
Petrikau
Lublin
SILESIA
Katowice
Kraków
Lvóv
Carpathian mountains
SLOVAKIA

The German invasion of Poland was launched on 1 September 1939. Nine armoured divisions – including the 4th Panzer Division – swept through Poland in just eighteen days, putting the armoured vehicles, and the tactics that became 'blitzkrieg', to the test for the first time.

The advance carried the German troops over ground that had been fought over for days. The earth was pock-marked with bomb craters and the dead lay in heaps, corrupting in the autumn sun. It was not an uncontested advance for the tanks and the SS. Shell barrages, snipers and anti-tank fire took their toll. After receiving new orders from XVI Corps headquarters, Reinhardt halted the attack. The instructions were that the division was to gain the line of the Bzura and comb the great woods that lay on the southern bank of the Vistula. The 4th Panzer Division, having borne the brunt of the defensive battle for long days and nights, was now to form the cutting edge of the German spearhead that was to be thrust into the vitals of the Poznan and Pomorsze Armies.

The Bzura was finally reached and the ground prepared in anticipation of the inevitable Polish reaction: savage counter-attacks. These were not long in coming, and were of a size and fury not previously encountered. The Polish infantry and cavalry flooded forward, overrunning some units and surrounding others. The air was filled with calls for help from German units suddenly isolated and fighting for their lives. However, the line was held.

Below left: Advancing behind an eight-wheeled Sd Kfz 232 armoured car, fitted with radio aerials, German infantry skirmish through the shell-blasted ruins of a Polish town, keeping watch for enemy snipers. Below: Although their weapons were, in general, inferior to the Wehrmacht's equipment, the Poles fought doggedly. Here, an anti-tank crew prepares to go into action against German armour during the Bzura battle. Bottom: Considered an elite, Poland's cavalry divisions suffered appalling casualties during the campaign, proving that bravery and horseflesh were no match for armour and the weapons of modern warfare.

But Reinhardt's expectation that his unit would continue to hold defensive positions along the eastern bank of the Bzura was dashed, when reports came in of large concentrations of Polish troops along the western bend of the river. Orders from Army Group South called for a general advance to destroy the enemy forces. In view of his division's weak state and the exhaustion of his men, Reinhardt questioned the sense of the order but was told, 'the decisive battle will be fought on the western bank.'

The division was formed into two columns for the attack. The left hand one, with the 12th Schutzen Regiment, the second battalion of the 35th Panzer Regiment and elements from the 49th Anti-tank Regiment, was ordered to attack Ruszki. The right hand column, made up of the other battalions of the 35th Panzer Regiment, the SS and the remaining detachments of the anti-tank regiment, was ordered to seize the road junction to the north of the town.

At 0700 hours on the 16th, the advance was launched across the shallow Bzura and the first objectives taken within 90 minutes. Bridges were constructed by 1045 and traffic began to flow across to the west. But the pace of the advance was slowing. Late in the afternoon, the expected enemy counter-attacks struck the division. These assaults were made by two fresh enemy divisions, and their thrusts overran some German infantry and, at one place, reached as far as the artillery lines before they were halted. Reinhardt reported to corps that the day's fighting had cost his 35th Panzer Regiment no fewer than 23 vehicles and that the unit had only 65

'runners'. His division could do little more.

Unknown to the anxious Reinhardt or to the German High Command, the previous day's thrust by the division had struck the Poles as they were about to launch an offensive and the German attack had destroyed what little cohesion still remained among their units. A process of slow disintegration set in. However furious the enemy infantry assaults, however spirited the cavalry charges, however accurate the Polish anti-tank gunners, their efforts were the death agonies of a disintegrating army.

But even death struggles can be violent, and as the 4th Division thrust northwards, driving up the eastern bank of the Bzura, the Poles made their last furious attempts to reach Warsaw. For their final effort, the fighting troops abandoned their heavy equipment and their ration trains in the deep woods. Armed only with smallarms and carrying ammunition, they charged into action, isolating some German units, driving others back. In the 4th Division's sector, during the early evening of the 18th, they overran the 2nd Battalion of the 12th Schutzen Regiment, cut off groups of anti-tank gunners and surrounded the 1st Battalion of the SS. From the bushes covering the ground on the western bank of the Bzura, Polish soldiers, who had lain concealed all day, rose up and stormed through the shallow river.

To his men, surrounded and cut off, Reinhardt could only repeat his order to 'hold on'

The berserker fury with which they attacked, tore open the left flank of Reinhardt's division and the Poles poured through the battery positions of the heavy artillery. The gunners, firing over open sights, destroyed whole groups of men, but as fast as those charging men fell, others came to take their place. In the confusion of the fighting, senior officers of both sides fired rifles like common soldiers and General Skotnicki, a Polish cavalry commander, led one bayonet charge with a pistol in his hand, cheering his men on until he fell mortally wounded.

To his men, surrounded and cut off, Reinhardt could only repeat his order to 'hold on'. The last major Polish attack came in at 0400 hours, but it was weak and easily repulsed. At first light on the 19th, two battalions of SS troops and the 35th Panzer Regiment fought their way through scattered Polish resistance and reached the units that had been cut off.

At 1100 hours on the 19th, the Poles began to surrender en masse, until 170,000 of them had been taken. The exhausted men of the 4th Panzer Division moved through the killing grounds, horrified at the results of the 10-day battle. Both banks of the Bzura were covered with the sprawling dead. On the southern bank of the Vistula the dead lay piled up, four or five deep in places. The Poles, seeking to escape to the northern bank, had not known that the German II Corps was waiting for them to make the break-out attempt. Between these two principal places of slaughter lay the dead and wounded in their thousands. In the bend of the Bzura died the hopes of the Poznan Army and the unit whose fighting ability had held those Polish thrusts, the 4th Panzer Division, stood exhausted on the battlefield and shaken by the scale of the losses.

THE AUTHOR James Lucas served with the Queen's Own Royal West Kent Regiment during World War II and was Deputy Head of the Department of Photographs at the Imperial War Museum, London.

Outgunned by powerful Tiger tanks at Kursk in 1943, the Soviet 5th Guards Tank Army improved the odds by fighting at point-blank range

THE GREAT PLAINS of European Russia are scattered with a number of large towns that are like their counterparts all over the world – too small to be important, too big to be charming. The most remarkable fact one can normally relate about one of these towns, Kursk, is connected with magnetism: the town is built over large deposits of magnetite. This mineral renders compasses useless and is responsible for an effect known as the 'Kursk magnetic anomaly'. However, the summer of 1943 was not a normal time for the Soviet Union; and the sort of metal pulled toward Kursk was of a different kind. Since the beginning of spring, thousands of men and tanks, artillery and aeroplanes had been arriving in its vicinity. They belonged to the German Wehrmacht

and the Workers' and Peasants' Red Army of the Soviet Union. Both armies were preparing to lock horns for the third successive year.

The influx of men and arms was of a scale unseen in any previous summer campaign on the Eastern Front. Both sides knew that an attack on the Kursk salient was inevitable, and for the Red Army the question was how best to counter a German offensive. A defensive strategy was chosen and a powerful network of entrenchments was constructed with the help of the citizens of the Kursk district. To top it off, extensive minefields were laid all along the front, on average 1700 anti-personnel and 1500 anti-tank mines per kilometre. This time the Germans would not meet an unprepared or battle-weakened foe.

At the beginning of July, the Soviet soldiers knew that the attack was imminent. German aerial bombardments had increased in intensity and an order arrived from STAVKA (the Soviet Supreme Command) warning that the attack would take place between 3 and 6 July. It actually began on 5 July, with a heavy bombardment of the Red Army's positions at

Below: Viewed from a Soviet tank-driver's slit, a T-34 advances into the inferno of the Kursk battlefield. Right: Lieutenant N.P. Borozdnov, whose tank was the first to break into Orel. Far right: A member of a Soviet reconnaissance team. Below right: General Apanasenko, deputy commander of the Voronezh Front (left), with Major-General Rodimtsev (centre) and Lieutenant-General Rodmistrov, commander of the 5th Guards Tank Army.

BLOOD AND STEEL

5TH GUARDS TANK ARMY

The Soviet tank arm in World War II was unique among the armies of the major combatants for one significant reason: it was the only one to undergo a complete reorganisation in the middle of the war. Soviet armoured doctrine had been totally discredited by the defeats during the German invasion in 1941 and the battles of spring and summer 1942. By the beginning of 1943, however, a new generation of tank commanders had come to the fore. They managed to institute a new organisation, based on five (later six) tank armies.

One of these new formations was the 5th Guards Tank Army. Its first operations, under the command of Lieutenant-General Pavel Rotmistrov, began on 29 January 1943, when it attacked near Voroshilovgrad as part of the Southwestern Front's offensive in the important Donbass region. This was a successful campaign, marred only by the Soviet failure to retake Kharkov. The 5th Guards Tank Army was then moved north to join the Steppe Front, and was then reorganised for the defence of Kursk. After the 5th Guards Tank Army's important role in the Kursk battles, the formation received reinforcements and then took part in the Soviet counterblow that drove the Germans back from Belgorod and Kharkov, and eventually led to the recapture of Kiev. Again, during these attacks, the 5th Guards Tank Army was in the forefront of the fighting and suffered heavy casualties. It was pulled out of the line and placed in reserve for rest and re-equipment.

The army returned to action in October 1943 as the fierce battles for the liberation of the western Ukraine began. After service on this front, the 5th Guards Tank Army was again moved north. Participating in the autumn campaign of 1944, clearing the Germans from the Baltic states, the 5th Guards Tank Army had reached a position just west of Stettin by the end of the war.

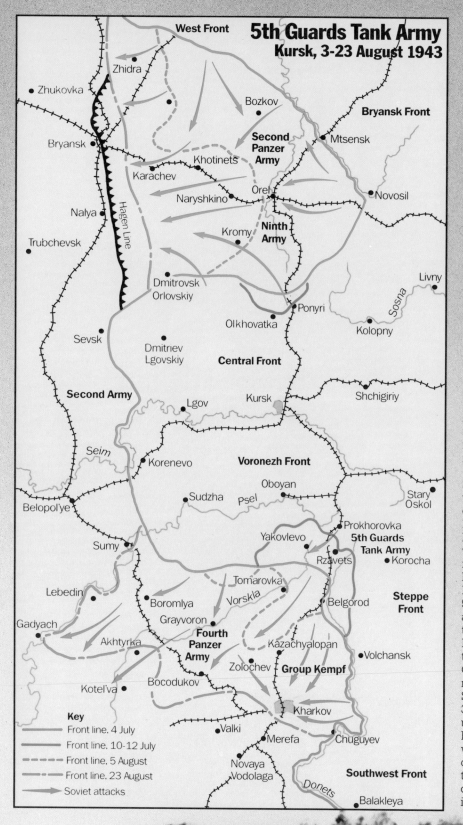

5th Guards Tank Army
Kursk, 3-23 August 1943

Key
— Front line, 4 July
— Front line, 10-12 July
-- Front line, 5 August
-·- Front line, 23 August
→ Soviet attacks

0430 hours. Two *schwerpunkts* were identifiable: in the north, a 25-mile sector between Krasnaya Slobodka and Izmailovo, and in the south, at the corner of the salient, northeast of Belgorod. The fighting was fierce as the German tank and infantry forces battered slowly through the Soviet defences. The Soviet commanders began to move their tank armies into positions where they could launch their own counter-attacks to blunt the enemy thrusts. In the north, in the Central Front's area, the Germans made some gains until they ran up against the Sredne-Russkie heights near Olkhovatka. There they hurled themselves against the Soviets, but were driven off as the commanding ground gave the Red Army a decisive advantage.

They sent a message to Moscow asking for urgent reinforcement before the front gave way

In the south, on the Voronezh Front, the situation was more critical. The Germans were developing two thrusts, one by Abteilung (Operational Group) Kempf and one by the Fourth Panzer Army. The latter's thrust in the direction of the town of Oboyan was the more dangerous, especially after II SS Panzer Corps had established a bridgehead over the Psel river. By 8 July the situation worried Lieutenant-General N.F. Vatutin, commander of the Voronezh Front, and the Central Committee's representative, Nikita Krushchev, to such an extent that they sent a message to Moscow asking for urgent reinforcement before the front gave way and the road to Kursk was opened.

The 5th Guards Tank Army was a part of the Steppe Front, a reserve formation of armies which was being slowly broken up and fed into the battle. In command of the 5th Army was Lieutenant-General Pavel Rotmistrov, one of the Soviet armoured force's leading officers. He had a scholarly appearance, with no resemblance to the heroic and romantic image of the German panzer commanders. Indeed, he had been a lecturer at the Stalin Academy of Mechanisation and Motorisation before the war. On 9 July Rotmistrov received his orders to move his army from its billets around the town of Ostrogozhsk to new positions 360km away, to the northwest of Prokhorovka. His force comprised two tank corps, the 18th and 29th, and the 5th Guards Mechanised Corps. He had his full complement of over 500 medium T-34 tanks, and was well provided with SU-85 tank destroyers, but his only heavy tanks were 35 British lend-lease Churchills, a model extremely unpopular with the Soviet tankmen. His force moved by night to Prokhorovka, via Stary Oskal. The long winding columns of tanks, their single headlamps dimly lighting the roads, reached their concentration point on 11 July. Rotmistrov began to prepare a counter-attack that would halt II SS Panzer Corps in its tracks. The situation was desperate. The Germans were across the Psel and nearly in possession of Prokhorovka, and the 5th Guards Tank Army was the only rested formation standing between the SS and the rear of the Kursk salient. Rotmistrov was fully aware of the dangers and he proposed to go ahead with his plan of attack in the hope of bringing on a meeting engagement with the German panzers. The date for the attack was set for 12 July.

His tanks were to drive full-pelt down the hill directly into the advancing Germans!

At 0830 on the 12th, the Voronezh Front's guns and mortars opened up a tremendous 15-minute barrage on II SS Panzer Corps' positions. Their tanks were in their night leaguers, but preparing to move off. At the same time, the Soviet tanks began advancing in the direction of the enemy. In the sky the first aerial engagements of the day were already taking place. Throughout 12 July, streams of aeroplanes battled it out for aerial superiority over the fields of Prokhorovka; but neither side gained it and for once a major battle would be settled solely on the ground.

Rotmistrov had set up his headquarters on a hill overlooking Prokhorovka. He waited patiently yet nervously for the first reports from his leading elements to come in. The terrain around Prokhorovka is rolling farmland, cut up by gullies. Between the German and Soviet lines there was another hill. As the Soviet tanks reached the position they reported sighting II SS Panzer Corps on the move before them – over 400 tanks, Tigers, Panthers and Mark IVs, with tough, battle-hardened crews. They were advancing on a narrow front between the Psel and a railroad embankment. Rotmistrov knew that the newer German tanks were thickly armoured and that their guns outranged the T-34's 76.2mm weapon. In order to counter the German advantages, he now issued a daring order: his tanks were to drive full-pelt down the hill directly into the advancing Germans!

The Soviet battalion and company commanders must have been shocked by such orders. The terrain meant that at close quarters each tank would be on its own, with no possibility of organised tactics. However, they did as they were ordered. They 'buttoned-up' their tanks, sealing themselves in metal, their only view of the outside world provided by narrow slits. A German tank commander recalled the Soviet onslaught:

Below: Laden with infantrymen, T-34s of the 5th Guards Tank Army pour westwards for the great clash at Prokhorovka on 12 June 1943. Top right: Massed Soviet forces race to join battle. Above right: A PTRD anti-tank rifle team establishes a sniping position. Right: A terrible death for one T-34 crew.

THE BATTLE OF KURSK

Kursk was arguably *the* decisive battle on the Eastern Front during World War II. Indeed, since the middle 1960s, Soviet military historians have been inclined to place increased emphasis on this battle, at the expense of the Stalingrad campaign. The latter, it is true, was a catastrophe for the Wehrmacht, but it remained a formidable instrument. Hitler was confident that a new victory would restore Germany's strategic situation on the Eastern Front. It was apparent, however, that the German Army could no longer mount a single massive operation. Instead, it would be necessary to maintain a steady succession of limited offensives which would always keep the Red Army off balance. The Kursk salient was chosen because it was an easy place to recreate the vast encirclements that had marked Germany's first campaign against the Soviet Union.

This strategic option was also recognised by the Soviet commanders. Their analysis of the situation was confirmed by information from intelligence sources, including the famous agent 'Lucy' (Rudolf Rossler), and the Red Army devoted all its efforts to strengthening the Kursk salient. Some 40 per cent of its entire complement of rifle divisions and every tank army was deployed in or around the town. The key to the Soviet plan of defence was timing – to know when to go over to the attack. On 12 July it was plain that the German offensive had run out of steam, so the Soviet forces struck at the Orel salient in the German lines. This was followed three weeks later by an attack in the south which eventually achieved the liberation of the important eastern Ukrainian city of Kharkov. Kursk ruined the German Army in the East. Soviet superiority was never again threatened by German military might. In that sense, it was truly the decisive battle of the war.

'We had been warned to expect resistance from the pakfronts [anti-tank defences] and some tanks in static positions, also the possibility of a few independent brigades of the slow KV type. In fact we found ourselves taking on a seemingly inexhaustible mass of enemy armour – never have I received such an overwhelming impression of Russian strength and numbers as on that day. The clouds of dust made it difficult to get help from the Luftwaffe, and soon many of the T-34s had broken past our screen and were streaming like rats all over the battlefield.'

Rotmistrov moved to a more forward position as the battle was fought and later remembered the scene: 'The Soviet tanks thrust into the German lead elements and penetrated the German tank screen. At extremely close range, the T-34s were knocking out the Tigers, since their powerful guns and massive armour no longer afforded them an advantage in close combat... There was neither time nor room to disengage from the enemy and reform in battle order, or to operate in motion. The shells fired at extremely close ranges not only penetrated the combat vehicles' side armour, but also their frontal armour. At such ranges, there was no armoured protection, and gun barrel lengths were no longer decisive. Often when a tank was hit, its fuel blew up, and torn-off turrets were flung through the air over dozens of metres.'

The fierceness of the combat, and its close nature, was characteristic of the fighting that took place between SS and Red Army units. Infantrymen would fight hand-to-hand with bayonets, gun butts and entrenching tools. For the men in the tanks, the equivalent was to blast the opponent at ranges of under 200m.

A famous incident in the fighting involved the tank of a battalion commander, Captain Skripkin, who led his force directly into a Tiger tank formation. His tank knocked out one Tiger before any of the Germans

Below: Soviet tankies look over a knocked-out PzKpfw V Panther, while (bottom) a shell-shocked Nazi awaits his fate.

even had time to react. Another three rounds fired from his gun destroyed a further Tiger, but the Germans were now reacting. An 88mm shell struck the side armour or Skripkin's T-34 while another smashed the turret. Skripkin was wounded but he was hauled from the wreck by his driver, Aleksadr Nikolaev, and the radio operator. They hid in a shell hole, but one of the enemy tanks had spotted their flight and moved towards them to finish them off. Nikolaev jumped up and ran to his old vehicle and restarted it. It was already on fire but he drove it into the approaching German tank. The two tanks exploded in a ball of fire.

There were other instances of battlefield valour. Major G.A. Miusnikov's battalion of the 25th Tank Brigade, 29th Tank Corps, destroyed 11 enemy tanks (three of them Tigers), three assault guns and 15 anti-tank guns. Finally, in bitter fighting around the 'Krasnaya Oktiabr' (Red October) collective farm, Guards Sergeant Danilov and his anti-tank gun crew beat off an attack by 15 Tigers, destroying six of the German tanks. For this exploit, Danilov was awarded the medal of Hero of the Soviet Union.

The battle around Prokhorovka was an extremely fluid affair, as villages and collective farms repeatedly changed hands. However, by mid-day on the 12th, it was apparent that the Germans had lost their offensive momentum. Rotmistrov despatched the 2nd Tank Corps, which had been attached to his command from another army, to attack the right flank of II SS Panzer Corps. A gap had formed here as German forces of Operational Group Kempf had been unable to maintain the same rate of advance as their SS comrades in the Fourth Panzer Army. Now it was the Germans who launched desperate counter-attacks in order to blunt the enemy's armoured thrusts. The battle went on throughout the day and ended in a stalemate. At 2100 hours, both sides assumed defensive positions.

In the north, the Soviets now launched their own offensive to eliminate the Orel salient, a mirror-image of Kursk. In the south, the offensive potential of the Fourth Panzer Army and Operational Group Kempf was gone. In all, 208 German tanks littered the fields around Prokhorovka and another 100 had been destroyed in a battle fought around Rzavets, just to the south. The 5th Guards Tank Army had lost 420 tanks. These burnt-out wrecks marked the resting place of many brave men. There were still some local thrusts by the Germans as they sought a weak point in the Soviet lines around Prokhorovka, but they found none. The Germans did not have the strength to punch a hole in the Red Army's line. The 5th Guards Tank Army had seen to that.

THE AUTHOR Paul Szuscikiewicz is an American writer, based in London, who has published several articles on naval and military affairs.

Left: Heroes of the Battle of Prokhorovka. This T-34 crew destroyed two PzKpfw VI Tigers and four medium tanks. Below: Soviet tankies discuss the holes drilled by armour-piercing rounds into the turret of a Tiger.

Lieutenant of Armoured Troops, Red Army 1943

This officer is wearing a khaki tunic, worn outside the trousers, with the prestigious red piping of the armoured troops. He has the tankman's padded leather helmet and high boots and the Sam Browne belt and cross strap of an officer. The insignia on his tunic include the chevrons and black collar patches of a Red Army lieutenant, and on his right breast is a red wound stripe, the Order of the Patriotic War and (nearest his shoulder) the badge of the Guards.

The men of Israel's 7th Armoured Brigade, vastly outnumbered, fought a desperate battle against the Syrian Army during the Yom Kippur War of 1973. Rafael Eitan, an Israeli commander on the northern front, recounts their story

MY ASSOCIATION with the 7th Armoured Brigade of the Israeli Defence Forces (IDF) began in the early 1960s. I was in charge of a brigade of paratroopers in Major-General Israel Tal's division, and the 7th Brigade was the force's armoured spearhead. We first saw action together in the Six-Day War of 1967.

During the battles of the first two days our paths separated. The 7th Brigade, commanded by General Schmuel Gonen, turned south, and we moved north to clear the Gaza Strip. However, I was soon reunited with my friends in the brigade. On the morning of the third day of the war, we saw two tanks approaching us of the type, and carrying the markings, that we identified with the 7th Brigade. They halted in front of our headquarters, and a young officer climbed down from the tank. After presenting himself, he said: 'I am the officer in charge of these two tanks, and because of breakdowns we got separated from the brigade. I'm looking for a war.'

'Okay,' I answered, 'let's give you a little test, and then decide whether or not you can get into the paratroopers. The water tower of Khan Yunis is 4000 metres away. Each tank will be allowed to shoot one shell at the cement line running around the base of the tower. Whoever hits it, joins us. Whoever misses will have to look elsewhere for a war.'

The officer returned to his tanks to brief the crews, and I heard him say, 'Guys, now the honour of the 7th Brigade is on the line. Either we hit the target as ordered or we do not belong to the 7th Brigade.' They took aim and hit it. The two tanks accompanied us until the end of the war, without sustaining any damage, serving honourably and bravely. After our victory in the Six-Day War the 7th Brigade and I went our separate ways – but we were destined to meet again in 1973.

I was commander of the armoured forces guarding the Golan Heights, the frontier with Syria in 1973, and by the end of September tension was high. On 5 October, the eve of the Jewish holiday of Yom Kippur, general headquarters decided to move the 7th Brigade from its permanent base in the south to reinforce the armoured forces stationed along the Syrian border. Because of the pressing timetable only the crews had time to get to us; their tanks were left behind in the south. Our orders were to equip the crews with tanks from our division, and get them armed and ready for battle. The division's commanders and the brigade officers gathered in my office that evening, and I proposed a toast wishing them: 'Victory in tomorrow's war.'

Our border on the Golan Heights had no natural obstacles to hinder an assault by the Syrians, but we had constructed 17 strongpoints, each holding about 20 men and three tanks, extensive minefields and a deep, four-metre wide anti-tank ditch, partly filled with water. The latter ran from the lower slopes of Mount Hermon in the north some 20km south to Rafid. The 7th Brigade manned the northern half of the line, while the Barak (188th) Brigade with 75 tanks held the southern sector. We hoped that the Syrian attack would be blunted by these defences, which would have to be crossed in the face of accurate fire from our tanks sited behind earth ramparts or in hull-down positions. If we could slow the enemy offensive our reserves would have time to get into position. In the

Below: One of the 7th Armoured Brigade's Centurions dug in facing the Syrian border. Well sited emplacements gave the Israeli tanks extensive fields of fire that they used to devastating effect during the desperate first few days of the Yom Kippur War. There were few natural obstacles to the Syrian advance, but a ditch 4m wide had been dug in front of the Israeli lines, and minefields would direct the Syrians into chosen killing grounds. There were also 17 fortified observation posts along the front, but these could be little more than a supplement to the armoured vehicles used in a defensive, hull-down capacity.

VALLEY OF TEARS

ARMOUR IN ACTION

The origin of Israel's 'mailed fist' dates back to the War of Independence in 1948, when a handful of tanks, 'liberated' from their British owners, were used against the invading Arabs. From these humble beginnings, growth has been rapid; in the 1950s the Israelis purchased AMX13 light tanks from France, then Centurions from Britain and later, M48s and M60s from America. By the early 1980s, frontline strength stood at 2700 vehicles, deployed in 20 brigades.

Like other Israeli tank units, the 7th Brigade's armoured core during the Yom Kippur War consisted of 72 Centurions organised in two battalions. These were supported by a further 20 tanks and armoured personnel carriers (APCs) of the brigade's reconnaissance company, and an artillery battery of 16 self-propelled guns (SPGs).

Four bulldozers were available to build defensive positions or clear battlefield debris. Repair, logistics and signal companies provided vital back-up facilities.

The brigade also had its own mechanised infantry battalion. Transport for its three companies was provided by 36 American-built M113 APCs and half-tracks, while a heavy weapons company armed with mortars, heavy machine guns and anti-tank weapons was available for close support.

Neither the organisation nor the equipment of the 7th Brigade marked the unit as an elite, yet during the running battles along the Syrian border its soldiers proved that they were of outstanding quality.

meantime, I decided to set up my headquarters at the Nafekh camp in the centre of the battle zone – I was determined to have a good view of my troops as they went into action against a vastly more numerous foe.

We weaved through heavy fire and, miraculously, made it to the new position without a scratch

The Syrian army that we faced consisted of five divisions with over 1700 tanks, including the latest models of the powerful Russian-built T62 which mounted a 115mm gun. Backed by an abundance of artillery and anti-aircraft batteries, the Syrians planned a three-echelon attack on our positions. From north to south, the 7th, 9th and 5th Infantry Divisions, backed by almost 1000 tanks, were detailed to smash through our defences to open the way for two armoured divisions, the 1st and 3rd, to drive into the rear of our line. Before their onslaught, a firestorm from over 1000 guns would be brought down on our forward defences.

On 6 October at 1400 hours, the shooting began in earnest. Two hours later I took my headquarters onto the Golan Heights and at midnight Major-General Yitzhak Hofi, the GOC Northern Command, gave my division the responsibility for the defence of the Golan Heights. I was put in overall charge of all the forces deployed in the area. On Sunday morning (the 7th) we began to get a better picture of the situation, but with Syrian tanks threatening to overrun my headquarters, I decided to leave Nafekh camp, which had already been under heavy bombardment since midnight, and move northwards to find a less dangerous position. However, there was a grave problem. We only had a few half tracks and one jeep. Who would drive the jeep which, unlike our other vehicles, had no armoured protection? Eventually, I took the jeep myself, and ordered the others to follow me. We weaved through very heavy fire and, miraculously, made it to the new position without a scratch. As we left, I saw a herd of cows huddled together at the side of the road, waiting silently for their fate – their heads were turned away, as if trying to hide from the shooting and shelling. As a farmer's boy who still lived in the country, I was very worried about the lot of those quiet, beautiful cows.

Finally, we set up new positions and carried on the

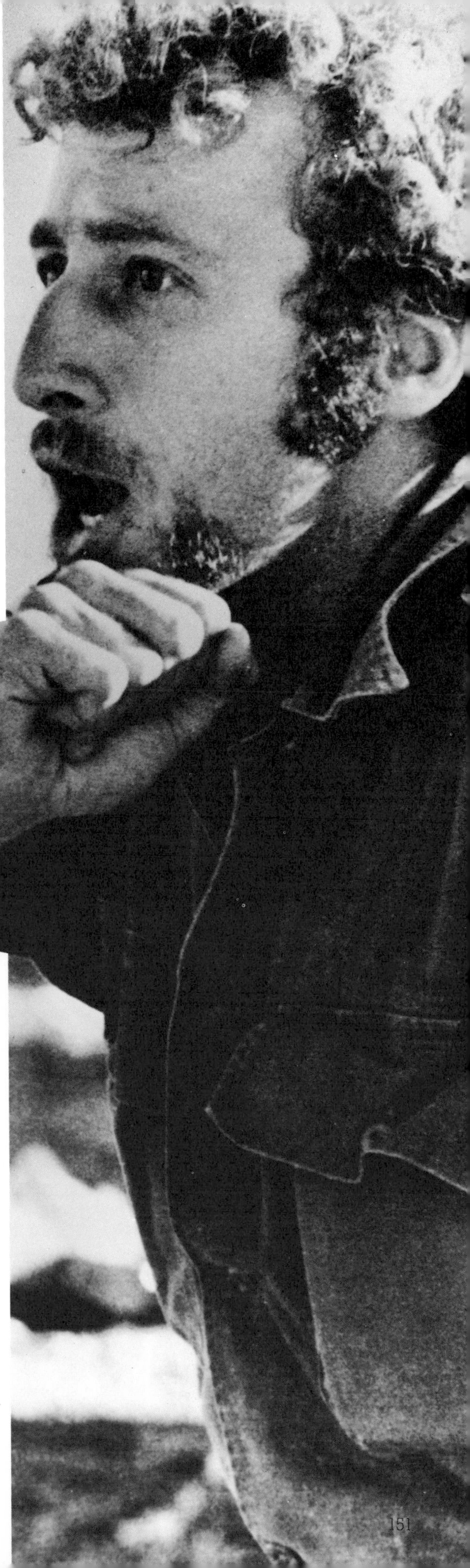

Below: Jeep-borne members
7th Armoured advance
wards the front. The ability
react quickly to a
ccession of threats and the
exibility that enabled the
igade to turn desperate
efence into counter-attack
ere the great strengths of
h Armoured during the Yom
ppur War. Right: A member
the brigade reacts
thusiastically to orders for
e offensive against Syrian
ositions, given on 11th
ctober.

THE CENTURION

Despite a first-rate reputation, the Centurion tank's entry into service with the IDF in 1960 was greeted with little enthusiasm by Israeli tank crews. The Centurion performed badly in the desert; radiators clogged up with dust, causing the engine to overheat or seize up. As a result, over the next three years, the Centurion was up-rated with a more powerful engine, a simplified gear-box, an improved cooling mechanism and an advanced steering system. The most important change, however, was the introduction of the British 105mm L7 gun. The 'upgraded' Centurion had double the operational range of the Mark 5, on which it was based, as well as a superior maximum road speed of 43km/h and greater battlefield punch.

The Israelis' work on the Centurion paid dividends in the Yom Kippur War. Although outnumbered 15 to one, the efficient gunnery of the highly trained Centurion crews coupled with the deadly 105mm gun proved more than a match for the Syrian armour. Hundreds of Syrian T55s and T62s were knocked out. Israeli tank losses were also heavy, but many of their disabled Centurions were repaired under combat conditions and returned to battle. This ability to absorb punishment, and its superb combat performance, made the Centurion a formidable fighting machine.

Below: A young member of 7th Armoured Brigade mans the 0.3in anti-aircraft armament of his Centurion tank.

fight. I looked around me and said: 'This will be a decisive, fateful battle. Whatever happens to me personally, I will not cross the Jordan to the west as long as I am alive.' By Sunday afternoon, the Golan Heights had been divided into two divisional sectors. The northern sector was held by my division with the 7th Brigade and its 90 Centurion Mark 5 tanks in support.

The initial Syrian offensive, however, was directed at the southern and central border areas. Our forces were able to contain these early attacks. On the night of 6/7 October, one company of the 7th Brigade, a unit numbering eight tanks under the command of Captain Meir Zamir, was directed to assist a neighbouring reserve brigade, south of the town of Kuneitra. The commander of the company arranged the vehicles in such a way as to close the main artery along which the Syrian 43rd Armoured Brigade was travelling. In a night battle, at medium and close ranges, the company succeeded in halting and destroying the enemy brigade, without suffering any losses. Their action prevented the collapse of the central sector of the Golan Heights. It was a simple, but effective, example of this heroic and superbly trained tank corps in action.

The mass of threatening, murderous tanks crawled towards our frontline troops

After the Syrian offensive had been beaten off in the southern and central sectors, their main effort was concentrated along the northern front. We faced a total of 500 tanks and 700 armoured troop carriers. The 7th Brigade was deployed to stop this thrust, and the battle fought between 'Booster' Hill and Tel Hermonit, in the area that later became known as the 'Valley of Tears', began.

On Monday morning (the 8th), after a devastating preliminary bombardment, a group of tanks and troop carriers, with the support of heavy covering fire from rockets and artillery, moved towards the tanks of the 7th Brigade. Our imperturbable artillerymen laid down a barrage on the enemy who were only 4000m away. But their valiant efforts were not enough to stop the mass of threatening, murderous tanks crawling towards our front-line troops. There were no reinforcements available to us, and we could not support the 7th Brigade. Every officer and man of that unit knew that they could expect no help. They would have to rely on their own strength and the superb fighting qualities of the Centurion tank.

Once the Syrians had forced a way through our minefields, their tanks and supporting infantry converged on the anti-tank ditch. They knew that we had turned all the crossing points into killing grounds, but they were highly-motivated and ready to accept very heavy casualties. Their MTU bridgelayers were the Centurions' first targets until, one after another, they were knocked out, together with dozens of their escorting T55 and T62 tanks. Despite massive losses, the Syrians came on, and such was their courage that infantrymen with entrenching tools succeeded where the bridgelayers had failed: they constructed causeways over the ditch in the face of heavy-machine gun fire.

Ignoring their losses and the obstacles in their path, the Syrians continued to advance in an almost suicidal fashion until their leading tanks were only a few metres from the defences. From the beginning of the battle, the entire area in which the brigade had been deployed, including areas deep behind the lines, had been heavily shelled. It was totally impossible to re-arm those tanks standing in the firing line, nor could they move to the rear, where the brigade's ammunition depot was located, because any withdrawal would have opened dangerously large gaps in our weakly-held front line.

Ammunition was running out and there were no reinforcements to replace our losses, although some isolated tanks did manage to move about 2000m to the rear and gather a few precious shells before returning to the battle. In some cases our tanks returned to their positions at the same time as the emplacements were overrun by the advancing Syrians. These enemy tanks were destroyed by our tanks still in position, swinging their 105mm guns through 180 degrees to fire at the enemy's thinner rear armour. At the same time, the Syrians were also being engaged by our re-armed comrades returning from the ammunition depot. At such close ranges our guns wrought untold damage on the Syrian hordes. When these intruders had been destroyed, our tanks turned their guns forward again, and, from a range of only a few metres, were able to destroy the next wave that the enemy threw at us.

This battle, in all its ferociousness and horror, ranged on into the night of 8/9 October, and became more intense after dark. Unlike the Syrians, our tanks and troops were not equipped with night-fighting equipment, and the enemy were able to press their attacks at close range. One battalion commander, Avigdor Kahalani, turned his tank's gun to the side and the barrel struck the turret of a passing Syrian tank.

By this stage of the battle I was finding it very difficult to keep in touch with my subordinates as it was very dangerous to move along the front line because of the heavy and incessant shelling. It was particularly difficult to fix up a meeting with my commanders in the midst of a battle, because to do so we needed to use our radios, and the Syrians always listened in. To make matters worse, our maps of the Golan Heights had fallen into their hands. Once they had discovered our meeting place they would take precise aim with their artillery and rockets, then shell the position.

'We are not moving, not one step, not even one centimetre; the fate of the State is in our hands'

The system that we used to avoid these difficulties was very simple; each of the commanders chose a nickname that the Syrians would not understand. The commander of the brigade took the nickname 'Spider', and I picked the name 'Nimbus'. Being the name of a storm and rain cloud, I thought it appropriate. After choosing our names we could contact each other and set up a meeting: 'Nimbus is sending a bottle of whisky to Spider' at such and such a place. Although we have all left the armed forces, we still use these names amongst ourselves to this day.

Everyone could see that the Battle of the Valley of Tears was going to be decisive; if the Syrians broke through the 7th Brigade, there was nothing to bar their path to the Jordan river. I took heart, however, when one of the officers of the brigade said: 'We are not moving, not one step, not even one centimetre; the fate of the State is in our hands.' Fortunately, a few reinforcements did trickle through. At the crack of dawn on Tuesday (9 October), a small tank force was organised in a rear camp. It was made up of tanks that had been damaged, and then repaired, with great

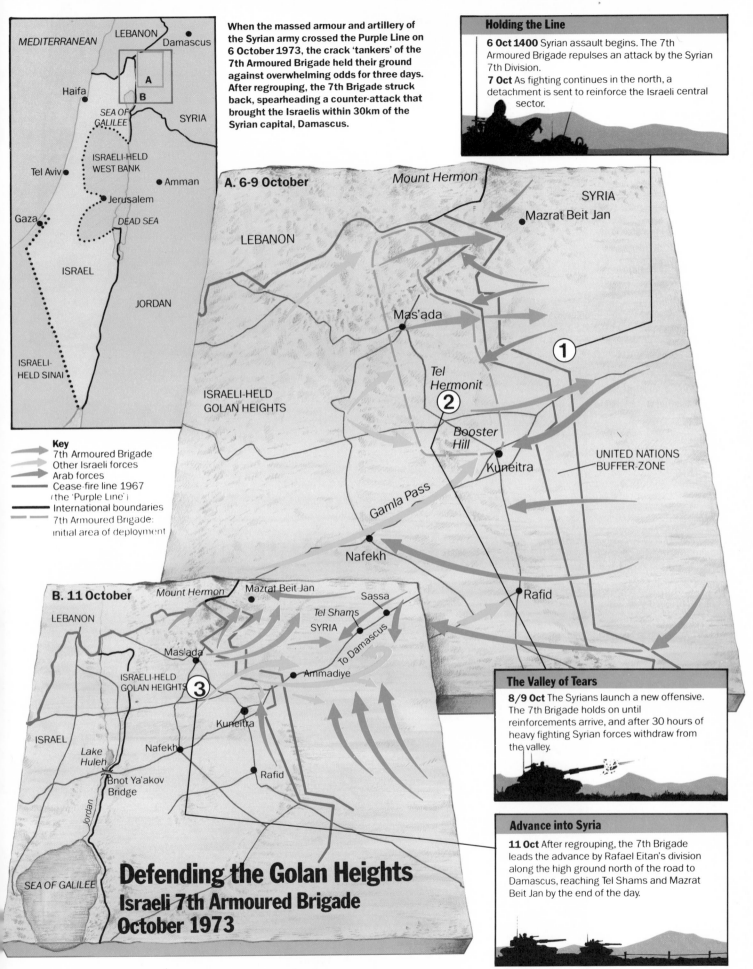

When the massed armour and artillery of the Syrian army crossed the Purple Line on 6 October 1973, the crack 'tankers' of the 7th Armoured Brigade held their ground against overwhelming odds for three days. After regrouping, the 7th Brigade struck back, spearheading a counter-attack that brought the Israelis within 30km of the Syrian capital, Damascus.

Holding the Line

6 Oct 1400 Syrian assault begins. The 7th Armoured Brigade repulses an attack by the Syrian 7th Division.

7 Oct As fighting continues in the north, a detachment is sent to reinforce the Israeli central sector.

A. 6–9 October

Mount Hermon

SYRIA
Mazrat Beit Jan

LEBANON

ISRAELI-HELD
GOLAN HEIGHTS

Mas'ada

Tel Hermonit

Booster Hill

Kuneitra

UNITED NATIONS
BUFFER-ZONE

Gamla Pass

Nafekh

Rafid

Key
- 7th Armoured Brigade
- Other Israeli forces
- Arab forces
- Cease-fire line 1967 (the 'Purple Line')
- International boundaries
- 7th Armoured Brigade: initial area of deployment

B. 11 October

Mount Hermon

Mazrat Beit Jan

Sassa

Tel Shams

SYRIA

LEBANON

Mas'ada

To Damascus

ISRAELI-HELD
GOLAN HEIGHTS

Ammadiye

ISRAEL

Kuneitra

Lake Huleh

Nafekh

Rafid

Bnot Ya'akov Bridge

Jordan

SEA OF GALILEE

Defending the Golan Heights
Israeli 7th Armoured Brigade
October 1973

The Valley of Tears

8/9 Oct The Syrians launch a new offensive. The 7th Brigade holds on until reinforcements arrive, and after 30 hours of heavy fighting Syrian forces withdraw from the valley.

Advance into Syria

11 Oct After regrouping, the 7th Brigade leads the advance by Rafael Eitan's division along the high ground north of the road to Damascus, reaching Tel Shams and Mazrat Beit Jan by the end of the day.

BURDEN OF COMMAND

The Israeli commanders responsible for the running of the Yom Kippur War were men who had made soldiering a career; most had fought as company or battalion officers during the War of Independence and had risen steadily in their chosen profession as the IDF won its famous victories in 1956 and 1967.

The Yom Kippur War brought out the best and worst sides of the senior Israeli Commanders. In particular, Major-General Gonen, the GOC Southern Command in Sinai, had an uneasy relationship with the commanders of his two reserve armoured brigades, Major-Generals Adan and Sharon. Both were technically superior to him, both were dynamic, offensively minded and opinionated, and neither had any great regard for his abilities.

The failure of a counter-attack on 8 October brought matters to a head, and the Israeli government felt compelled to send General Bar-Lev to mediate between the three men. Sharon, however, flew in the face of his authority and made an unauthorised attack against the Egyptians on 9 October. Sharon's assault failed and, although it found a weakness in the Egyptian lines that was exploited in the Israeli counter-offensive of 15-16 October, Bar-Lev requested that Sharon be relieved of his command. General Dayan, the Israeli Minister of Defence, refused to accept Bar-Lev's recommendations as Sharon was a prominent political figure and public knowledge of his dissent might weaken the morale of the armed forces.

When the Israelis launched their counter-offensive Sharon played a secondary role to Adan and the bickering continued, but with a renewal of the offensive spirit and a fair degree of accord on overall strategy the generals directed their aggression against the enemy rather than each other.

Left: The high-water mark of the Syrian advance – a T-55 knocked out just in front of the Israeli HQ at Nafekh. Below: Centurions of 7th Armoured roar forward. Bottom: Key commanders on Golan. From left, 'Yanush' Ben Gal, who commanded 7th Armoured, his battalion commanders Yoss El Das and Avigdor Kahalani (the gun of Kahalani's Centurion actually touched the turret of a Syrian tank during close-quarters fighting at night), then 'Raful' Eitan, overall commander of the Israeli forces on Golan, in discussion with, far right, a member of the staff of the Israeli C-in-C, David Elazar.

devotion, by our ordnance crews. They were manned by wounded tank crews drawn from hospitals or soldiers who had returned hastily from leave when the war broke out. This unit was led by Yossi Ben Hanan, an officer who had commanded an armoured force in the 7th Brigade in the past. I sent this force out as reinforcements at one of the most critical moments of the battle. Most of the tanks engaged in defensive actions had only three or four shells left, and I directed this new force, which numbered 20 tanks, towards the flank of the Syrian assault. They were in fine form, and began destroying Syrian tanks as soon as they reached their new positions.

During this hard-fought armoured battle the regular security troops on the Golan Heights, infantry of the Golani Brigade, held all but one of their positions despite being cut off by the Syrian advance. There is no fitting way to express the value of their actions or describe the heroism of those soldiers, and it was

one of these posts, located well to the rear of the main Syrian attacks, that reported: 'Far to the east we see Syrian vehicles turning back.' This was at noon on 9 October, 30 hours after the beginning of the attack in the Valley of Tears.

Below them, in a mess of twisted, burnt-out wrecks, lay the cream of the enemy's troops

It meant we had won: with their strength almost exhausted and down to their last few rounds, the men of the 7th Brigade had defeated the last Syrian attack. As the smoke of battle cleared they saw the full extent of their victory. Below them, in a mess of twisted, burnt-out wrecks, lay the cream of the enemy's troops. The men of the 7th Brigade had destroyed over 500 tanks, armoured personnel carriers and other fighting vehicles but, after 30 hours of

PREPARING FOR WAR

Faced by the overwhelming might of implacable enemies on all fronts, the Israelis have been forced to create a nation in arms.

After the 1948 War of Independence, it was recognised that the regular troops stationed along the state's borders could hope to do no more than delay an assault, and that only the rapid mobilisation of all Israelis eligible for military service could defeat the Arab armies.

Both men and women are eligible for military service at 18 years. Although the period of conscription is three years for men and two for women, recruits remain on the reservist list for up to 34 years. During this time, each reservist is required to attend a month-long refresher course each year. In times of war, mobilisation is extremely rapid; within 72 hours the armed forces' peace-time strength can be increased from 40,000 regulars and 120,000 conscripts to a total of around 500,000. Mobilisation orders are broadcast over the national radio network. When reservists hear their unit's code-name, they gather their equipment and assemble at pre-arranged rendezvous points. Units, however, need to have the flexibility to move between commands as the strategic situation demands.

The Israeli victory in the Yom Kippur War owed a great deal to the organisation and combat readiness of their armed forces. After the initial Egyptian and Syrian surprise attacks had been blunted, the rapid build-up of reservists at their assembly points enabled the military authorities to plan their counter-offensive in the knowledge that they had a sufficient number of units to go on to victory.

combat, they did not have the strength to climb out of the turrets of their tanks to cheer their famous victory.

By 1200 hours on Tuesday the noise of the artillery had ceased. We had held our positions and won the battle. The State of Israel was safe – although there were only 40 undamaged tanks in the brigade out of the 90 that had been ready for action on the 6th. Our next task was to organise a counter-attack aimed at breaking through to the east of the Golan Heights. The time was set for Thursday afternoon (11 October) – that meant we had 48 hours to prepare for action. The forces earmarked for the battle were the 7th Brigade, the Golani infantry brigade and a small paratrooper unit.

After four days of non-stop fighting in fierce, bloody battles we were determined to succeed in the forthcoming offensive, irrespective of the odds we might face. I called my officers together. Although tired, filthy and bearded, they listened intently to every word. I cut the talk short and said:

'Go to sleep now and make sure every soldier gets some rest and eats the best food the division management can supply. From tomorrow morning we will continue our preparations and have a final briefing before we go forward.'

On the eve of the operation, the 7th Brigade had been reinforced to 100 battle-ready tanks, with fresh crews, and a soaring fighting spirit. The breakthrough was carried out quite easily. We sustained very few losses, morale was high and, later that day, our forces, led by the 7th Brigade, halted 30km from the Syrian capital, Damascus.

One day, after the counter-attack and the capture of the Syrian part of the Golan Heights, I went out to visit a forward position in the north of the sector, at the foot of Mount Hermon. It was a small post that suffered greatly from constant shelling. The Syrians apparently had a lookout on the approach roads to the post, and as soon as we drove to within a few metres of the post, there was a heavy rain of mortar

Above far left: Joyous Israeli soldiers after the retaking of Mount Hermon. Above left: Centurions of 7th Armoured – after the first 30 hours of fighting, only 40 of the original 90 tanks were undamaged. Above right: Removing a dead tankman from his vehicle. The retrieval of battle casualties was considered of paramount importance in the Israeli Army. Above far right: Eitan (seated centre) briefs men of his command during the fighting. Below: From defence to attack – Israeli armoured forces push on towards Damascus.

shells, followed by a precise and heavy blast. We officers ran to take cover in a Syrian T34 tank; its motor had been removed, leaving the hull to be used as a kind of armoured shelter for the men. We sat there crouching, all stuffed in the 'shelter', with shells exploding all around, making a horrendous din on the roof and sides of the tank. We were becoming almost totally deaf from the tremendous noise, while we waited for that blessed shell which would put an end to everything, but it never came. There was a lull in the shelling, we got out of the T34 and entered the post. We shared our experiences of the shelling with the soldiers, before returning to our headquarters in the rear.

Later, near Tel Shams, I again found myself the target of very accurate artillery fire from the Syrian positions, although we could not identify the precise location of the enemy fire. I went to a post held by our forces at Tel Shams, and found myself a quiet corner. Using my binoculars, I began to survey the area

under Syrian control opposite our position. It did not take long to find the guilty party: a Syrian SU100 self-propelled gun, hidden by basalt rock. I called to the commander of the tank crew at the post – they belonged to the 7th Brigade. I identified the target for him and asked, 'Can you destroy it?' He estimated the distance, surveyed the approach road to the firing position and said, 'Yes.' After three shots, at a distance of 3500m, he destroyed the SU100.

By the winter of 1973/4, we were firmly in possession of the Golan Heights, and had recaptured Mount Hermon. The war had ended successfully for Israel; but at one stage, only the courage and professional excellence of the 7th Armoured Brigade had saved the young nation from catastrophic defeat.

THE AUTHOR Major-General Rafael Eitan was in charge of the Israeli forces on the Syrian border during the Yom Kippur War and is now a member of his country's parliament, the Knessett.

SCORPION
AND
SCIMITAR

THE BLUES AND ROYALS

The Blues and Royals were formed as a regiment in 1969 through the amalgamation of two of the oldest and most famous cavalry regiments of the British Army, the Royal Horse Guards (the Blues) and the Royal Dragoons (1st Dragoons). The Blues trace their origins to a Regiment of Horse raised in 1650, which was named the Royal Regiment after the restoration of King Charles II. The Royal Dragoons were created in 1661 by Charles II as a troop of horse to garrison Tangier, and were originally known as the Tangier Horse.

The two regiments fought in almost all the British Army's major campaigns, distinguishing themselves particularly in the Seven Years War and the Peninsular Campaign. At Waterloo, the Blues formed part of the Heavy Cavalry Brigade, while the Royals were part of the Union Brigade, and both brigades made decisive charges during the battle.

In World War II, both regiments were re-equipped with armoured cars, the Blues combining with the Life Guards in the 1st and 2nd Household Cavalry Regiments (HCRs). The 1st HCR and the Royals fought in the Western Desert, and at El Alamein the Royals penetrated the enemy lines at night and spent two days behind the front causing chaos before leading the southern flank of the subsequent rapid advance. The regiments later participated in the Normandy invasion and the liberation of Belgium and Denmark.

Today, with the Life Guards, the Blues and Royals form the Household Cavalry.

The armoured vehicles of the Blues and Royals proved an invaluable asset to the British Army during the Falklands campaign

IT WAS A bright moonlit night, with a deep frost, as Captain Roger Field of the Blues and Royals took his Scimitar light tank into the battle for Wireless Ridge. The atmosphere was quite eerie, with the intermittent chatter of distant machine guns and the sudden flashes of bursting illuminants. The only movement came from the little groups of stretcher-bearers, dark figures against the white carpet of frost, carrying their sad loads. Exhausted, they put down their stretchers to exchange a brief word and gain what comfort they could as they passed. The harsh conditions, the constant whine of artillery shells, the small groups of men huddled together for warmth, and other groups moving gently forward for the next attack suggested to Captain Field that he had strayed into a World War I battlefield, rather than the Falklands campaign of the technological 1980s.

As part of 3 Troop, the Blues and Royals, Captain Field and his Scimitar were providing vital fire support for 2 Para's assault on Wireless Ridge. In the final phase of the operation a gunnery technique known as 'zapping' was employed. The tank crews would engage suspected enemy positions with a burst of machine-gun fire to provoke a response, which they would then silence with the main gun. The Scimitar's 30mm Rarden cannon, with its high velocity and great accuracy, was especially suited to this job, and few Argentinian positions were able to reply after being 'zapped'. The commander of 3 Troop, Lieutenant Lord Robin Innes-Ker, was astonished at the number of Argentinians who signed their own death-warrants by using torches or lighting cigarettes. Three Troop was engaged in its turn by 0.5in machine guns firing armour-piercing rounds and by 20mm air-defence guns firing in the ground role, but the standard of Argentinian gunnery left much to be desired, and no hits were recorded. By first light 2 Para had secured Wireless Ridge, and their CO, Lieutenant-Colonel David Chaundler, reported that the suppressive fire of the Blues and Royals in the final phase had been accurate and devastatingly effective.

This acknowledgement of the effectiveness of armour in the Falklands was very welcome to the Blues and Royals, for it had been some time in coming. When hostilities had begun back in early April 1982, the CO of the regiment, Colonel James Hamilton-Russell, had received the order to provide two 14-man reconnaissance troops for deployment with the Task Force. In the 36 hours before embarkation, preparation was confined to essential mobilisation procedures, thorough cleaning of vehicles and equipment, preparation for sub-arctic conditions, and intelligence briefings. How the two troops were to be used was at this stage pure guesswork, and the main emphasis was on speed of deployment.

Thus it was that 3 and 4 Troops of B Squadron, the Blues and Royals, each with two Scorpions and two Scimitars, with one Samson recovery vehicle in support, embarked their vehicles on the MV *Elk* and their crews on the SS *Canberra*. They were now under operational command of Headquarters 3 Commando Brigade and formed the sole armoured element of the Task Force. When they finally sailed on 9 April, few of those on board had any conception of what they faced.

During the long voyage to the South Atlantic, the Blues and Royals' Combat Vehicles, Reconnaissance Tracked (CVRTs) were maintained aboard MV *Elk* by a three-man team led by Sergeant Reid, REME. On board SS *Canberra* the crews attached themselves to 3 Para and joined in the rigorous routine of fitness, first-aid, personal weapons and specialised training. During a short stop at Ascension Island, men and vehicles were reunited for a few hours of valuable gunnery practice. Vehicles were prepared for wading, and crews were rehearsed in a newly improvised skill, that of firing the main armament from the bows of a Landing Craft Utility (LCU) pitching about in a rough sea. Although somewhat hazardous, it proved effective, and when the landings eventually took place, each LCU had two CVRTs in the bow to counter opposition on the beaches.

The pause at Ascension Island was also used to redistribute men, vehicles, weapons and stores into a more logical configuration for what was to come. The two troops then transferred to the assault ship, HMS *Fearless*, for the second part of the voyage, and left Ascension Island on 10 May in company with the amphibious force. As they headed south, the weather worsened and by 15 May everyone understood

Page 159: Three-man crews of the Blues and Royals, armed with 9mm Sterling L2A3 sub-machine guns, on parade before their armoured vehicles. In the centre is the four-wheeled FV721 Fox reconnaissance vehicle which, in common with the tracked Scimitar, carries a 30mm Rarden L21 gun. Below: Scorpion light tanks are taken ashore in a Landing Craft Utility (LCU). Below left: The Blues and Royals seized a chance to sharpen up their co-ordination and marksmanship during the brief wait on Ascension Island.

how aptly named were the 'Roaring Forties'. By the time the force approached the Total Exclusion Zone (TEZ) the Argentinian cruiser *General Belgrano* had been sunk, orders for the landing given and all doubts as to future intentions removed. The plan proposed a landing in the area of San Carlos Settlement by 40 Commando and 2 Para, followed by 45 Commando at Ajax Bay and 3 Para at Port San Carlos.

D-Day was to be 21 May and soon after first light on D-1 the force crossed into the TEZ amid much apprehension over air and sub-surface attack. However, the appalling weather, with fog and high seas, prevented enemy action, and, with some eight hours of darkness still left, HMS *Fearless* slipped into Falkland Sound. The Royal Marines of 40 Commando, with 3 Troop attached, landed unopposed at San Carlos Settlement but the CVRTs had some difficulty in disembarking due to overhanging rocks. Four Troop were supporting 3 Para for their landing at Port San Carlos, just around the headland to the north, and there was a delay which led to a daylight landing, fortunately, also unopposed.

Initially, the tasks in the beach-head for the Blues and Royals were to provide fire support for the battalions clearing the area and then to occupy defensive observation positions on the surrounding hills. Moving into these positions in the dark, the troops had their first taste of the rough going they were to experience on the Falklands, and there was a recurrent problem of wire fences getting wrapped around the vehicles' sprocket-wheels. Cover was non-existent and vehicles were dug-in by combat engineer tractor or, where possible, concealed in

The prevailing view was that the light tanks would have little part to play in the infantry battle

barns. Positions were adjusted periodically during the build-up in the beach-head, but most of the action took place in the air, and there were frequent alerts. The Blues and Royals spent a frustrating time in the beach-head before the troop leaders were able to demonstrate that the vehicles could handle the atrocious terrain. During this time the assault by 2 Para on Goose Green took place, for which Lieutenant-Colonel 'H' Jones had requested CVRT support. Unfortunately, this was not granted. The most cursory assessment of the terrain in the islands will show that the going for vehicles is tough and, in many places, impossible. With the exception of the vicinity of Port Stanley, there are no roads as such, only tracks joining the widely dispersed settlements, and these frequently become impassable in winter. The appearance of bare and open moorland is deceptive because extensive areas are bog and waterlogged ground. As the ground rises to the central mountainous area, steep outcrops of rock, interspersed with small ravines filled with boulders (known as stone-runs), impede movement. Small wonder then that the prevailing view was that CVRT mobility would be severely restricted and that the light tanks would have little part to play in the infantry battle.

Eventually the break-out from the beach-head began, and 4 Troop, commanded by Lieutenant Mark Coreth, was ordered to support 3 Para on their march to Teal Inlet in the north. There now arose a problem which was to recur throughout the campaign: the re-supply of fuel and ammunition when the only means of moving it was by all-too-scarce helicopter. On this occasion a shortage, caused by the LSL *Sir Lancelot* ditching her complete load of fuel

when it was found that she had an unexploded bomb on board, prevented the troop moving. The troop leader, however, used his initiative, and some devious means, to hijack fuel from elsewhere, and managed to set off after the battalion the next day, a fine example of the regiment's irrepressible spirit during the campaign. Picking up some 3 Para casualties from the line of march, 4 Troop drove through the night, crossing the San Carlos River 'with paddles out and snorkles up' only to be bombed, fortunately ineffectively, by a passing aircraft at first light. They arrived triumphantly at Teal Inlet on the morning of 29 May.

Next day 3 Troop, commanded by Lieutenant Innes-Ker, was tasked to escort the 25 BV202 (tracked, articulated oversnow) vehicles of Brigade Headquarters the 30km to Teal Inlet. This turned into something of a nightmare as many of the vehicles got bogged or broke down in the darkness, and the kinetic-energy tow ropes carried by the CVRTs were put to good use. The trip took 17½ hours and was described by the troop leader as resembling 'the M4 westbound on a Friday evening'. The column was delivered safely, however, and 3 Troop went on to join 4 Troop at Estancia House, meeting thick fog and a number of close shaves with groups of friendly

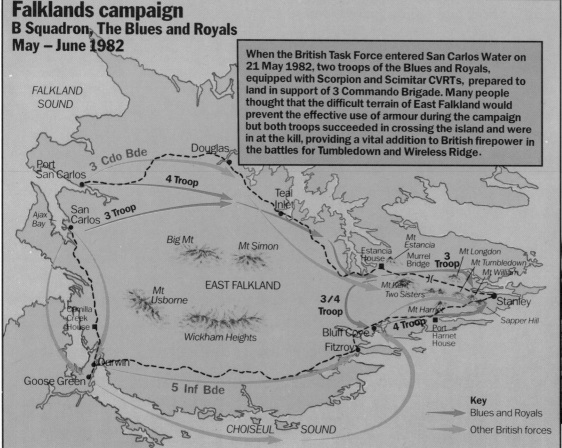

Falklands campaign
B Squadron, The Blues and Royals
May – June 1982

When the British Task Force entered San Carlos Water on 21 May 1982, two troops of the Blues and Royals, equipped with Scorpion and Scimitar CVRTs, prepared to land in support of 3 Commando Brigade. Many people thought that the difficult terrain of East Falkland would prevent the effective use of armour during the campaign but both troops succeeded in crossing the island and were in at the kill, providing a vital addition to British firepower in the battles for Tumbledown and Wireless Ridge.

FALKLAND SOUND

Port San Carlos
3 Cdo Bde
Douglas
4 Troop
Teal Inlet
Ajax Bay
San Carlos
3 Troop
Big Mt
Mt Simon
Estancia House
Mt Estancia
Murrel Bridge
3 Troop
Mt Longdon
Mt Tumbledown
Mt William
Mt Usborne
EAST FALKLAND
Mt Kent
Two Sisters
Stanley
Camilla Creek House
Wickham Heights
3/4 Troop
Mt Harrier
4 Troop
Port Harriet House
Sapper Hill
Bluff Cove
Fitzroy
Darwin
Goose Green
5 Inf Bde
CHOISEUL SOUND

Key
Blues and Royals
Other British forces

infantry. Three Para planned to assault Mount Longdon, with both troops in support, but in the course of recce and preparation they came under heavy artillery and mortar fire directed from strongly-held enemy positions on Mount Longdon and Two Sisters. In view of this strong opposition, the brigade commander ordered the postponement of the assault. Both troops then ran a taxi service to get 3 Para back to Estancia House. Here Lance-Corporal of Horse Meiklejohn and his vehicle, recovered and repaired after turning over in a peat hole, rejoined 4 Troop.

By this time 5 Infantry Brigade had landed at San Carlos and was pushing forward quickly in the south. Both troops were ordered to cross the central range of hills to join 5 Brigade at Bluff Cove. This journey was an unknown quantity; the 'going' map said it was impassable and for the first time there was the possibility of minefields. The best estimate of timing for the trip was two days; in fact it took just six hours. Lieutenant Coreth enlisted the services of a guide who, when they reached the first bog, said 'no'. The Blues and Royals said 'yes' and when they came out

Top left: Only two miles from Stanley, a mud-bespattered but indefatigable Scorpion advances towards Moody Brook. Top right: As the paras' long tab across East Falkland to Stanley neared completion, a spell aboard a Blues and Royals' CRVT was bliss indeed. Left: Lieutenant Mark Coreth, whose Scorpion was damaged by a mine on Mount Tumbledown, enjoys the novelty of a confiscated Argentinian Panhard armoured car. General Menendez, though liberally supplied with Panhards equipped with 90mm guns, made no use of them in defence of Stanley. Bottom left: The proud colours of the Blues and Royals are borne to victory aboard a Scimitar.

the other side the guide, in amazement, could only comment, 'My God, what a f.....g vehicle'. They pressed on through swamps, stone-runs and past rocky outcrops, exchanging fire with some unidentified infantry, encountering thick fog and ice-cold wind. As they arrived at Bluff Cove, the commander of 5 Brigade, faced with the urgent task of consolidating his position against possible counter-attack, described the occasion:

'I never expected them to make it so quickly . . . I looked up and saw them winding down the side of the mountains towards us, their leading vehicles mud-spattered and rain-soaked and their commanders half-frozen in their turrets. It was one of those moments I am not likely to forget.'

While at Bluff Cove, the Blues and Royals were to witness the attack on the logistic ships *Sir Galahad* and *Sir Tristram* at Fitzroy. Their vehicles were put to use ferrying some of the more seriously wounded survivors from the beach to the medical aid post.

In the next few days the two troops carried out a variety of tasks in support of the Scots and Welsh Guards. On the evening of 7 June, 4 Troop provided support for the recce platoon of the Scots Guards who

were to go east along the coast to establish a covert patrol base in the area of Port Harriet House. Having escorted them into position, the troop remained in support, withdrawing again before dawn. Two nights later, the patrol was forced by very accurate mortar fire to abandon its position, sustaining a number of serious casualties. Three Troop went forward by night to gather in the 20 or so guardsmen who were extricating themselves under fire. There were minefields to think about, but nobody knew where; after a difficult and dangerous night, the recce platoon was returned by the troop to its battalion at Bluff Cove.

From now on the two troops split and operated independently. By 11 June, the British land force was ready for the final battle for Port Stanley, and Major-General Jeremy Moore planned a three-phase attack. In Phase One, the Commando Brigade was to capture Mount Longdon, Two Sisters and Mount Harriet. In Phase Two, 5 Brigade and 2 Para, now back under command of 3 Commando Brigade, were to capture Wireless Ridge, Mount Tumbledown and Mount William. Finally, in Phase Three, the Welsh Guards were to take Sapper Hill. The Blues and Royals were not involved in Phase One, but 4 Troop was to support the Scots Guards' attack on Mount Tumbledown and 3 Troop was grouped with 2 Para for their attack on Wireless Ridge in Phase Two. By first light on the morning of 12 June all the Commando Brigade objectives were taken, frequently against fierce opposition, and the attack was a complete success.

Lieutenant Coreth's Scorpion struck an anti-tank mine which lifted it about a metre into the air

The Scots Guards' attack on Mount Tumbledown on the night of 13/14 June was preceded by a diversionary action against an enemy position, to the south of the battalion objective, that overlooked the main track from Fitzroy to Port Stanley. A strong patrol was carried forward after dark to a debussing point by 4 Troop who then advanced along the track, drawing the enemy fire and providing fire support to the infantry. While negotiating a previously undetected crater in the track, Lieutenant Coreth's Scorpion struck an anti-tank mine which lifted it about a metre into the air and completely immobilised it. Blinded by the flash and temporarily concussed, the three-man crew was, however, unhurt; 'shaken but not stirred' as they commented later! The troop leader quickly moved to Corporal of Horse Stretton's neighbouring Scorpion and continued to direct fire support from there amid a hail of artillery and mortar fire. The ensuing fight, lasting some two hours, ended with the destruction of the enemy position and by this time the main assault was well under way. The Scots Guards patrol then extricated themselves, still under heavy fire, through a minefield, and sustained further casualties – in all two dead and eight wounded. The troop successfully assisted the return of the survivors to safety and then resumed direct fire support for the main attack, which finally succeeded by daybreak. The Argentine commander subsequently admitted that he had been entirely deceived by the diversionary attack into thinking it was the main assault on his position.

Meanwhile 3 Troop, stowed with over double their normal load of ammunition, recrossed the mountain range – this time by day, but not without incident – and joined 2 Para to the east of Estancia House. They had to leave Lance-Corporal of Horse Dunkley and his Scimitar at Fitzroy, waiting for a replacement gearbox – the only major assembly to fail in either troop throughout the campaign. While stuck there, Dunkley claimed a kill with his 30mm cannon on a Skyhawk attacking Fitzroy. When mobile again, his Scimitar rejoined the troop for the assault on Wireless Ridge.

Two Para, having learned from their costly victory at Goose Green, were determined to obtain maximum fire support from all sources including CVRTs. They therefore planned their assault in four phases, three of which were to be supported by 3 Troop. Moving forward on foot, Lieutenant Innes-Ker recced fire positions within 300m of the enemy, from where he could provide the intimate support necessary after the indirect fire had lifted. The passive night sights of the CVRTs acted as the eyes of the battalion, and were superb at locating enemy positions. The barrage of fire laid down by 3 Troop, and particularly the use of the 'zapping' technique against Argentinian defensive positions, ensured the success of the operation.

By first light 2 Para were in possession of Wireless Ridge, and when 3 Troop joined D Company at the eastern end of the ridge they were greeted with the amazing sight of infantry targets everywhere. The troop engaged furiously with machine guns and main armament, but when the troop leader had landed a few 76mm rounds among the enemy he realised that something was wrong; they had not dived for cover or run away but had just ignored it and carried on towards Port Stanley. They were looking at a dejected and beaten army. Confirming this with a couple more rounds, a sense of humanity prevailed and he called a halt to the firing. The immediate reaction of the crews was one of disappointment; their tails were up and they relished the possibility of a really good chase. This emotion was followed moments later by a surge of relief.

3 Troop, carrying men of 2 Para, were the first British forces to re-enter Port Stanley

Soon afterwards the brigade commander authorised the advance on Port Stanley and 3 Troop, carrying men of 2 Para and with the flag of the Blues and Royals proudly flying from the lead vehicle, were the first British forces to re-enter the town at mid-day on 14 June. There they found thousands of weapons abandoned, helicopters burnt out, vehicles turned over and a complete absence of any resistance from the broken Argentinian army. By 1600 hours a ceasefire was agreed and the final surrender followed.

THE AUTHOR Colonel James Hamilton-Russell, MBE, was commander of the Blues and Royals during the Falklands campaign.

Right: On 12 October 1982 a parade of 1200 men and women who participated in the Falklands campaign was held in the City of London. Officially described as a 'gesture of thanks to the Task Force', many compared the event with the London victory parades held after the two world wars. The Blues and Royals, represented here by two Scorpions and two Scimitars, are seen saluting the Lord Mayor of London and the Prime Minister. Below: A Scorpion crew has a break from the relentless drive to Stanley. Seen to the right of the 75mm gun are the vehicle's smoke dispensers.

THE CVRT

The broken, boggy terrain of the Falklands is so unlike the 'tank country' of conventional thinking that many doubted whether the Blues and Royals could make a useful contribution to the campaign. It was a fine opportunity for the regiment to prove the agility of their extraordinary CVRT, the Combat Vehicle Reconnaissance (Tracked). The CVRT has a crew of three (commander, driver and gunner/radio operator). Designed to be light enough to enable a pair to be carried by a C-130 aircraft, it weighs some eight tons, and yet its wide tracks reduce its nominal ground pressure to less than that of a fully laden soldier on his feet.

The Samson recovery vehicle and the Scorpion and Scimitar light tanks are all variants based on the same Alvis CVRT chassis. The British Army has further variants, though none saw action in the Falklands. Differing mainly in their armament, Scorpions and Scimitars are normally deployed in pairs.

The Scorpion carries a 76mm L23A1 anti-tank gun, firing either High Explosive (HE) or High Explosive Squash Head (HESH) rounds. The HESH round impacts against the target tank and then detonates, showering the crew inside with lethal steel shards. A 7.62mm L431 machine gun is also mounted. The Scimitar is armed with a 30mm Rarden cannon, whose Armoured Piercing Special Effects round and other shells can stop light armour. Its machine gun is the 7.62mm L37A1.

The Scorpion/Scimitar team was extremely valuable in the infantry support role and is likely to play a major role in any similar future conflict.

Scorpion crewman, the Blues and Royals, Falklands 1982

Dressed in standard DPM combat jacket and trousers, and a woollen scarf and high leg boots to protect against the bitterly cold Falklands winds, this crewman is equipped with a plastic helmet fitted with a boom microphone. Normally the helmet would be worn only in the CVRT. The crewman has a pair of Avimo general purpose prismatic binoculars and is armed with a British 9mm Sterling L2A3 sub-machine gun. It is common practice to provide tank crews with a means of self-defence should they have to operate outside their vehicle.

CHARIOTS
OF FIRE

In June 1982, during Operation Peace for Galilee, the Israeli Merkava tanks were blooded on the battlefield of the Lebanon

THE MERKAVAS THRUST across the Israeli border at 1100 hours on 6 June 1982. Throwing up a cloud of dust in their wake, the tanks swept through the town of Rosh Hanikra, perched on a headland above the azure waters of the Mediterranean. It was almost 15 years to the day that the Israelis had launched their air force and armoured columns in an attack that clinched victory in the Six-Day War of 1967 almost before it began. For the 80,000 Israelis pushing northwards into Lebanon along a 63km front, that was a good omen.

Sergeant Boaz, a 21-year-old *kibbutznik* riding into battle for the first time, was a gunner aboard one of the lead Merkava main battle tanks. Rumbling northwards along the coastal road towards his unit's first tactical objective, Boaz took stock. As part of Colonel Eli Geva's 211th Armoured Brigade, Boaz was heading for the ancient Phoenician port city of Tyre, now a stronghold of the Palestine Liberation Organisation (PLO). 'I was trembling with excite-

ment,' he later recounted. 'I knew this was my testing time. Not just for me, but for the Merkava as well. was the first time in action for both of us.'

Behind the three-brigade spearhead, under Brigadier-General Yitzhak Mordechai, were more than 400 Merkavas, Centurions and American M-60 battle tanks. Jammed south of Rosh Hanikra, and waiting to move, they constituted an impressive display of Israeli military power. Together with hundreds of M-113 armoured personnel carriers and M-109A self-propelled guns, this heavy armour made up Division 91. The division had been tasked to ram through the PLO strongholds along Lebanon's coastal highway to Damour, south of Beirut, and destroy the 1500-strong guerrilla force that had kept the settlements of northern Galilee under the gun for the past decade.

To the east, a central task force of 18,000 men and 220 tanks launched a two-pronged assault with the intention of encircling Beaufort Castle, a strategic PLO bastion. From here, its mission was to push north through the scrub-covered mountains towards the PLO's 'Iron Triangle' around the market town of Nabatiyeh. Having secured the area, the force would then attempt to occupy Jezzine to the northwest. At this juncture, the central task force would split into two groups. The first, commanded by Brigadier-General Avigdor Kahalani, would link up with Mordechai's force along the coastal highway and move on Damour. The second group, commanded by Brigadier-General Danni Vardi, was tasked to advance north through the treacherous Barouk Range to Lake Qaraoun. By advancing to the west of the Syrian

Previous page: While a Merkava crew keep a close eye on PLO positions, belts of 7.62mm ammunition are fed into one of the tank's machine guns. Below, far right: Using the boom microphone attached to his 'bone dome' helmet, an Israeli tank commander directs operations during the coastal push towards Beirut. Having swept aside PLO guerrillas as it passed through Tyre and Sidon, a Merkava column (right) halts briefly south of Damour.

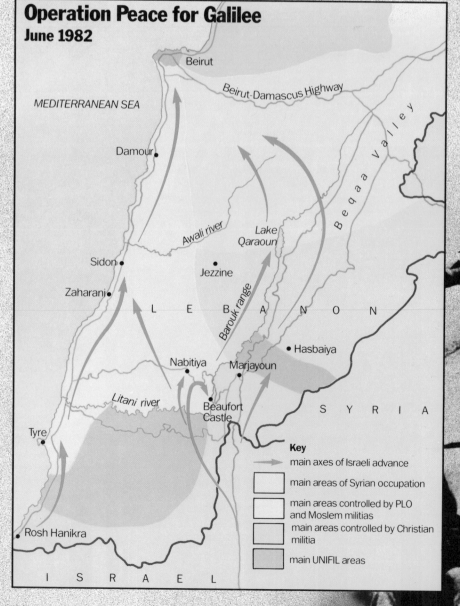

Operation Peace for Galilee
June 1982

MEDITERRANEAN SEA

Beirut

Beirut-Damascus Highway

Beqaa Valley

Damour

Awali river

Lake Qaraoun

Sidon

Jezzine

Zaharani

Barouk range

L E B A N O N

Hasbaiya

Nabitiya

Marjayoun

Litani river

Beaufort Castle

S Y R I A

Tyre

Key

main axes of Israeli advance

main areas of Syrian occupation

main areas controlled by PLO and Moslem militias

main areas controlled by Christian militia

main UNIFIL areas

Rosh Hanikra

I S R A E L

1st Armoured Division in the Beqaa Valley, this force would be able to cut the Beirut-Damascus highway – thereby severing the Syrians' lifeline to Damascus.

Finally, an eastern task force comprising 38,000 men and 800 tanks, including Merkava units, was to push along the eastern ridge of the Beqaa Valley – outflanking the Syrians between two Israeli battle groups. The eastern task force was led by Major-General Avigdor Ben-Gal, a veteran of the 1967 and 1973 wars and one of the most able commanders of the Israeli Defence Force (IDF). Known as Operation Peace for Galilee, the original Israeli objective was to smash the PLO in southern Lebanon.

On the coast, the 211th Armoured Brigade, with Boaz riding his low-hulled Merkava, swept past startled Dutch and Fijian troopers from the United Nations peace-keeping force. Speed was vital as the brigade advanced through the citrus groves south of Tyre, but the column was confined to a narrow road that quickly became jammed. The tanks and M-113 Zelda armoured personnel carriers came under intense fire from the PLO ambush groups entrenched in positions along the road. In response, Israeli fighter-bombers and artillery laid down a barrage on PLO strongpoints. A-4 Skyhawks and Kfir fighter-bombers streaked overhead through a curtain of shoulder-fired SAM-7s, ejecting hot-air balloons – some white, some scarlet – to deflect heat-seeking missiles.

The action swiftly engulfed Boaz and his comrades in their Israeli-built Merkavas – the pride of the armoured corps. Boaz fired round after round from his 105mm M64-L7 main armament as the PLO fighters, dressed in their lizard-pattern camouflage fatigues, flitted through the dappled, sweet-smelling groves. Rocket-propelled grenades and Sagger anti-tank missiles were fired at point-blank range as the Israeli column slowed to a halt. Boaz later recounted:

'We were fighting at distances of only a few feet sometimes, literally swinging from one target to another. We took several hits and some partially penetrated our armour. But none did any real damage. We seemed to run into one ambush after another. The APCs were particularly vulnerable and some were knocked out.'

The PLO missiles turned the Zeldas into death traps, easily penetrating the steel-aluminium alloy skins. As a result, many of the infantrymen refused to ride in them and reverted to the age-old mode of advance – their feet. The Israelis pushed on to the Rashadiyeh refugee camp south of Tyre, a sprawling PLO bastion

MADE IN ISRAEL

During the 1950s, Israel purchased most of her armoured vehicles from either France or Great Britain. British Centurions, upgraded to include a 105mm main gun and V-12 engine, comprised the backbone of the Israeli Armoured Corps. A number of Sherman, M48 and M60 tanks were also acquired from the United States. In 1966, two British Chieftain tanks arrived in Israel to undergo a series of secret trials. However, the outbreak of the Six-Day War in June 1967 resulted in Britain cancelling all export orders. Israel was now forced to rely on the American exports of the M48-60 series. Concerned that Arab pressure might curtail their one remaining source of main battle tanks, Israeli defence planners realised the necessity of developing a 'home-grown' tank industry.

The Merkava (which means 'Chariot' in Hebrew) project was born in 1970. Under the close supervision of General Israel Tal (above), two teams were set up. While the first started work on the development of the tank itself, the second began to mobilise the military industrial infrastructure that was necessary if the project was to be self-sustaining. General Tal worked closely with the design team, and as head of the project his credentials were impressive. A veteran of the 1948 war, the 1956 Sinai campaign and the Six-Day War, Tal was recognised as one of the world's leading exponents of armoured warfare.

The first production models of the Merkava main battle tank entered service in 1979. Over 200 enterprises had been involved in the production of some 30,000 components – a remarkable achievement within such a relatively short period of time.

MERKAVA MAIN BATTLE TANK

Crew: 4
Dimensions: Length (gun included) 8.63m; width 3.7m; height 2.64m
Weight: Combat loaded 56,000kg
Engine: Teledyne Continental AVDS-1790-5A V-12 diesel developing 900hp at 2400 rpm

Performance: Maximum road speed 46km/h; range (road) 500km; vertical obstacle 1m; trench 3m; gradient 60 per cent; fording 1m

Armour: Conventional cast and spaced
Armament: One 105mm M64-L7 gun; one 7.62mm machine gun co-axial with main armament; one or two 7.62mm machine guns mounted on commander's and loader's hatches; one 60mm roof-mounted mortar; smoke dischargers

Above: In a radical departure from conventional tank design, the Merkava is equipped with a heavily armoured rear hatch that allows access and exit by a route other than the exposed turret. This adds to the survivability of the crew in a pitched battle, and allows them to re-arm their tank while being sheltered from enemy fire. Above right: Israeli infantrymen open supplies at the head of a Merkava column. Far right: The pride of the Israeli Armoured Corps.

of bunkers and strongpoints. The guerrilla garrison had a strength of 1500, together with a score of Soviet-built T-34 tanks. The Israelis could also expect to encounter fixed artillery in the form of a few hull-down T-54s and T-55s.

By dusk, the coastal column had encircled Tyre and cut off the ramshackle shantytown of Rashadiyeh. One of Mordechai's lead battalions was assigned to bypass Tyre and set up a road block to the north. However, it ran straight into a PLO ambush and was attacked from the rear as it attempted to withdraw. As this battalion fought for its life, the brigade that included Boaz's Merkava battalion thrust north, leaving the second echelon to mop up Tyre. This task took five days of savage house-to-house fighting, and the Palestinians put up a stiff and bloody resistance before the sheer firepower of the Israelis overwhelmed them. A young PLO fighter echoed his comrades' thoughts as the Israeli tanks rumbled past through a cloud of choking grey dust: 'I never knew there were so many tanks, how can we fight them?' He had been blooded, just as Boaz had been. The latter recalled:

'By nightfall we'd reached the Litani River north of Tyre. The fighting eased, but we knew we'd have to do it all over again when we reached Sidon. I felt as though I'd been through the wringer. But I'd survived. I don't even know how many we killed. But they kept popping up all over the place – in the groves, behind walls, on the rooftops. Young kids, 15 or 16, but they all seemed to have RPGs. I couldn't believe it. We shot them down. We even had the 7.62mm going. Everywhere you looked, they were there.'

When dawn arrived on 7 June, Boaz and his tankies broke up their night-time laager. Accompanied by an endless chain of air strikes and a seaborne landing at the Awali River, north of Sidon, they moved off towards Lebanon's provincial capital. The guns thundered all day as Brigadier-General Kahalani's central force linked up with the coastal spearhead at the Zahrani oil refinery.

The 56-tonne Merkavas, the long-barrelled self-propelled guns and mobile artillery hammered PLO strongpoints in Sidon. Buildings were literally shredded, and Vulcan gatling guns fired thousands of rounds per minute – slicing in half apartment blocks where PLO ambush groups lay in wait. Huge palls of billowing smoke hung over the seaside city like a shroud. Helicopters clattered low through the smoke, leapfrogging the armoured assault units to take PLO strongpoints.

Elements of Kahalani's force encircled the sprawling Ein el-Hilweh refugee camp in the hills to the east of Sidon. The Israelis, ordered to keep civilian casualties to a minimum, began inching into the shantytown. It would take them six days to clear the area of the 300 guerrillas who were dug in around the alleyways and cement-block houses. The PLO fought to the last man.

Einan filled his tank up at a petrol station and ordered the owner to send the bill to Tel Aviv!

With Kahalani's advance stalled, unable to force a route through Sidon for the push on Damour, the Israeli fighter-bombers swooped out of the skies and hammered PLO strongpoints. Eventually, Geva's spearhead brigade, reinforced by another brigade, bulldozed a way through the city's debris-strewn streets, past burnt-out cars and the crumpled bodies of guerrillas.

Meanwhile, to the east, Brigadier-General Vardi's force inched towards Jezzine and Major-General Ben-Gal's column moved to within range of the Syrian units. Vardi attacked Jezzine on day three, 8 June, and ran into a PLO-Syrian force augmented by a T-62 tank battalion and commandos. Eight Israeli M-60s were lost in the battle that ensued, but a score of Syrian tanks were destroyed. Further east, Brigadier-General Menachem Einan's Division 162 pushed into the Chouf Mountains. When petrol ran low, Einan filled his tanks up at a petrol station and ordered the owner to send the bill to Tel Aviv! Soon after, the Syrians sent in Mi-24 Hind and Gazelle attack helicopters armed with anti-tank missiles. Several Israeli tanks were picked off, and just before dawn on the following day a Syrian brigade ambushed Einan's vanguard, knocking off several more tanks. At the urging of their Defence Minister, Ariel Sharon, the Israelis decided to take on the

THE MERKAVA MAIN BATTLE TANK

Work began in earnest on the Merkava in 1970. Experience gained by the Israelis during the Six-Day War had proved that battlefield mobility was no substitute for armour protection, and the Yom Kippur War underlined this fact. With limited resources at their disposal, the Israelis required a tank design that stressed survivability – both for the tank itself and for the crew. The order of priorities for the new tank was therefore protection, firepower and mobility. The hull of the Merkava is constructed of cast and welded steel, with a broad and well-sloped glacis plate at the front. The armour construction comprises two layers, separated by diesel fuel, and this gives protection against the shaped-charge warhead used in anti-tank missiles.

The provision of air conditioning is seen as an important factor during prolonged engagements, and a rear escape door eliminates the hazards of a turret bail-out under fire. Combat experience in the desert had highlighted the need for a tank design that offered a low target profile. The Merkava is thus able to remain virtually hidden while using its gun in a hull-down position.

The Merkava's main armament is a 105mm M64-L7 rifled tank gun, firing HEAT, APDS, APFSDS and phosphorus rounds. The Merkava can carry more ammunition than most other main battle tanks, and the main-gun rounds are stored in heat-resistant containers in the stowage area at the rear of the hull. The fire-control system features an American Cadillac Gage stabilising mechanism, a modified M13 ballistic computer and a laser rangefinder.

An improved Mark II Merkava, with advanced hydraulic suspension, is currently under development. There are also plans for a Mark III. This will have a 1200 horsepower engine and a 120mm main gun.

171

Syrians. They had no real choice – the alternative was to leave their eastern flank exposed to Syrian firepower. Operation Peace for Galilee had developed into a drive for Beirut, with the objective of completely smashing the PLO in the Lebanon.

The Israeli forces on the coastal highway thrust towards Damour, where guerrillas from both the Popular Front for the Liberation of Palestine and the Democratic Front for the Liberation of Palestine were firmly entrenched. Using caves and abandoned buildings as shelter, the guerrillas fought a ferocious battle for survival. The Israelis were forced to resort to close-quarters combat to winkle them out one by one.

The battles in the eastern sector soon became the focus of attention. Einan was experiencing difficulty in extricating his units from the Syrian assault and required the assistance of the Israeli Air Force. First, however, the Syrian surface-to-air missile (SAM) batteries deployed around the Beqaa Valley had to be knocked out. The assault was carried out with devastating effect. The Israelis began jamming the SAM systems with electronic counter-measures, and 'spoofed' them using remote-control drones designed to simulate the radar signatures of attack aircraft. Once the Syrians' radars locked on to the pilotless drones, they had lost the contest.

Armed with laser-guided bombs, F-15 Eagles and F-16 Falcons circled their targets like hungry hawks. Guided by E2C Hawkeye planes, the fighter-bombers peeled off and swooped in on the SAM batteries. The Syrians scrambled their MiGs, but it was too late. Seventeen of the 19 batteries in the Beqaa Valley were taken out, and the remaining two damaged. In addition, 41 MiG-21s and MiG-23s were shot down without loss to the Israeli Air Force. By 12 June, the victory tally had risen to 91 enemy fighters – one quarter of the Syrian Air Force. It had been one of the most one-sided air battles in history.

Meanwhile, on 9 June the Israeli armoured spearheads captured vantage positions overlooking the Beqaa Valley and the Beirut-Damascus road. Their aim was to launch a three-prong attack to secure the road, but they came up against heavy Syrian opposition – supported by anti-tank guided weapons and artillery. As the Merkava units battled forward, special tank-killer paratroop units were airlifted by Chinook helicopters into the mountains. The Syrians pulled back slowly, bitterly contesting every inch of ground. Israeli gunships swept in to take a heavy toll of enemy T-62s, often flying along the deep wadis or ravines in an attempt to curve in behind the Syrian positions. On 11 June, the Israelis finally broke through on hills that dominated the highway, but ran into Syrian armoured reinforcements and swarms of commandos from 10 special forces battalions. Again, the Israeli Air Force came to the rescue.

The Merkavas of the coastal highway force now swung northeast through the hills that overlook

Israeli Merkava tank officer, Lebanon, 1982

The Israeli Defence Force places a high priority on survivability, and this first-lieutenant wears the new Israeli-made Type 602 Kevkar helmet, designed to protect the head against shrapnel. The green Nomex flame-resistant overalls would, in battle, be supplemented by a fragmentation jacket and heavy-duty flameproof gloves. At his side is a Galil 5.56mm short assault rifle with folding stock.

Above, far left: Armed with an RPG-7 rocket launcher, a PLO guerrilla sets an ambush for Israeli armour. Although several Merkavas fell prey to these weapons (below left), the PLO proved unable to stem the Israeli advance towards Beirut (above left). Above: Colonel Eli Geva, the commander of the 211th Armoured Brigade. Below: The eastern task force commander during Operation Peace for Galilee, Major-General Avigdor Ben-Gal.

Beirut, and headed for the highway. Here, shortly after noon on the 11th, the combined Israeli forces came face to face with the T-72 tanks of the Syrian 82nd Armoured Brigade. The two most powerful tanks in the opposing armies – the Merkava and the T-72 – were about to meet on the battlefield. It was the Syrians' last throw, and they were relying on the T-72's 125mm main armament to win the contest. The fighting was fierce as Israeli fighter-bombers screamed overhead to blast the 82nd's column on the Beirut-Damascus road. Scores of T-72s, still on their transporters, were destroyed.

In the tank battle that ensued, the Merkavas sliced through the T-72 formations, knocking out a dozen enemy tanks in quick succession. These were the first T-72s to be destroyed in combat, and, although several Merkavas were damaged, none was permanently disabled.

Sergeant Eli, one of the Merkava commanders, later described the battle at Ein Zahlata, just south of the highway:

'We were hit when we entered the village, and the lead tank took several hits in a Syrian tank ambush. Two of our crew were killed and two wounded. A further three infantrymen were killed when they attempted an evacuation.

'We decided to gain control of the village by moving our tanks to better positions on the slopes. From there we had a better view, and our leader spotted enemy tanks hidden in bushes about 30m away. I spotted another at point-blank range, only 10m from us, and fired almost automatically. It was a reflex action. We both hit our targets. I spotted five more T-72s in the village and again opened fire. We hit all five.'

'The T-72s were torching in front of us, one after the other. Then, suddenly, it was all over'

By this time, Boaz was a battle-hardened veteran. He had seen his tank commander sliced in two by an RPG as he stood in the turret of his combat-scarred Merkava. He later described the climax of the close-quarters battle: 'There was no time to think, just load and fire, load and fire. The T-72s were torching in front of us, one after the other. Then, suddenly, it was all over.'

Lieutenant-General Rafael Eitan, the Israeli Chief of Staff and mastermind of Operation Peace for Galilee, paid the following tribute to the Merkava units:

'This was the first combat experience for the Merkava and it performed well. It fought T-55s, T-62s and T-72s and showed itself more than a match for them. We lost no Merkava crewmen in action against tanks because of the tank's safety factors, even though several were hit. The Merkava demonstrated itself to be safer than any other tank we know.'

A negotiated ceasefire between Israel and Syria had broken down by the afternoon of 12 June. Fighting continued until 25 June, when a new ceasefire was arranged and the Syrians began to withdraw eastwards towards the Beqaa Valley. The major operations of the Israeli-Syrian conflict had now passed, and the IDF was at last able to concentrate its attention on the Palestinians in West Beirut.

THE AUTHOR Ed Blanche is a journalist of the Associated Press. He covered Operation Peace for Galilee and the subsequent siege of Beirut.

ZONES OF FIRE

'Ready, take aim, fire!' This rather simplified notion of the three stages involved in using an infantry weapon is more applicable to the firing range than the modern battlefield. There may, of course, be occasions when, lacking sufficient time to plan out your defence in detail, you will have to follow this simple maxim. When a firefight suddenly breaks out during a reconnaissance patrol, for example, there is precious little time for anything other than levelling your rifle and delivering rapid bursts of automatic fire.

However, if you have the advantage of being able to prepare defensive positions, you must ensure that maximum use is made of every weapon at your disposal. The techniques of building fighting positions will be of help in this respect, but the skills of digging in against the enemy should be supplemented by accurate plotting of the fields of fire available to you. To do this, you must draw what is known as a 'range card' for every emplaced weapon, from the automatic machine guns to anti-armour systems such as the TOW and Milan.

A range card is basically a rudimentary sketch of the surrounding terrain. On it are delineated your primary sectors of fire, the main geographical fea-

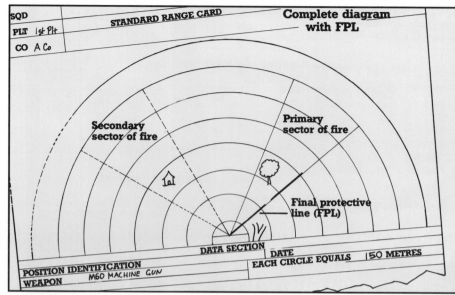

Below: A US Marine of the 2nd Reconnaissance Battalion mans an M60 GPMG position in Beirut in 1982. When mounted on a tripod, the M60 has a maximum effective range of 1800 metres.

tures and the ranges at which your defensive weapons will be at their most effective.

To begin with, allot to each of your weapons a primary and secondary sector of fire – the latter should be fired into only as a last resort, and when there are no targets in your primary sector. Wherever the terrain allows you should assign a final

protective line (FPL), along which suppressive fire can be laid down to greatest effect. In battle, this will become the primary sector limit closest to your position. When not firing at specific targets, your men should lay their guns along the FPL.

While plotting your FPL, however, you may find that large areas of 'dead space', where direct fire cannot penetrate (behind houses or hills, for example), offer the enemy refuge from your fire. If this is the case, you must plot what is known as a principal direction of fire (PDF). It should point towards a gully or ditch that leads into your position, enabling platoon members to fire directly down the approach.

It also may be necessary to designate locations within your sector of fire where targets are most

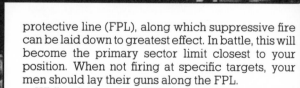

likely to appear. Mark these carefully on the range card, along with any natural or man-made target reference points that can be used to locate approaching targets. These reference points are an invaluable asset when siting anti-armour weapons for direct fire.

The final element to be marked on the range card is the maximum engagement line, beyond which you cannot engage a target. This is applicable to anti-armour weapons only, and is determined by assessing the maximum range of each weapon and setting this against the lie of the land.

Range cards should be drawn up as soon as your platoon takes up position. In the case of a General Purpose Machine Gun (GPMG) the procedure is as follows. After plotting the primary and secondary sectors of fire and sketching in any prominent features of the terrain that could be potential targets, use a compass to determine magnetic north and work out the location of your gun in relation to the prominent features of the terrain.

Also using the compass, determine the azimuth from the terrain feature to the gun position. Estimate the distance from the gun to this feature, and write this information on the range card. Then write down the eight-digit map co-ordinates of your position. This is essential for, if the going gets too hot, it may be necessary to call down an air strike on enemy positions. By connecting the sketch of each feature with the gun position by means of a straight line through the azimuth, you will have succeeded in plotting the basic element of the range card – your primary sector of fire. It only remains to sketch in the final protective line and principal direction of fire (the latter should be drawn with a broken line), while also labelling potential targets in order of priority.

You must now prepare the data section of the range card. Centre the traversing handwheel of the gun and lay the sights for direction. Having been assigned an FPL, lock the traversing slide on the extreme left or right of the bar and align the barrel on the FPL by moving the tripod legs. Now traverse the slide to the other side and move the tripod to align the barrel on the limit of your primary sector of fire. Align on the PDF by traversing the slide until your gun is aimed at the centre of the target.

Each time this procedure is carried out, read off the direction and elevation from the elevating handwheel and the traversing slide and mark these, along with a description of the target and the range, on the data section of your range card. The reading on the left-hand edge of the traversing slide will tell you how the gun has been laid for direction, while combining the number above the first visible line on the elevating handwheel with that on the traversing handwheel will give you your elevation data.

By analysing range card data, you will be able to ascertain how far the gun needs to be depressed for rounds to strike the ground along the FPL, and how far you will need to traverse the weapon for it to be laid on the left or right of each target. No data need be added for your secondary sector of fire, since your gun will be mounted on the tripod when firing along this line.

The range card for an anti-armour weapon performs the same function as that for the machine gun, enabling you to determine, quickly and accurately, the information you need to engage targets in your sector. Once you have determined your primary and secondary fields of fire, plot in the prominent features of the terrain and the dead space of your sector. Then draw in the range to expected target locations

and mark marginal data such as your weapon on the card. Make a copy of the finished range card and send this to the unit leader so that he knows exactly where his anti-armour weapons are sited. He will then be able to plug any weak points in the overall defensive position.

Top: Men of the 101st Airborne Division set up a 0.5in Browning MG in a position commanding the approach to Hagenau in January 1945. The muzzle is kept covered until ready to fire to keep snow out of the barrel. Above: An empty tin can serves as a makeshift feeder for the ammunition belt of this M60 machine gun.

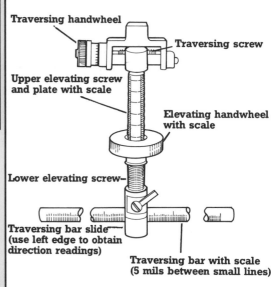

Traversing and elevating mechanism of an M60 machine gun

Traversing handwheel

Traversing screw

Upper elevating screw and plate with scale

Elevating handwheel with scale

Lower elevating screw

Traversing bar slide (use left edge to obtain direction readings)

Traversing bar with scale (5 mils between small lines)